Antiheroines of Contemporary Media

Antiheroines of Contemporary Media

Saints, Sinners, and Survivors

**Edited by Melanie Haas, N. A. Pierce,
and Gretchen Busl**

LEXINGTON BOOKS
Lanham • Boulder • New York • London

Published by Lexington Books
An imprint of The Rowman & Littlefield Publishing Group, Inc.
4501 Forbes Boulevard, Suite 200, Lanham, Maryland 20706
www.rowman.com

6 Tinworth Street, London SE11 5AL, United Kingdom

British Library Cataloguing in Publication Information Available
ISBN: 9781793624567 (cloth) | ISBN: 9781793624581 (pbk)

Library of Congress Control Number: 2020944227

Contents

Acknowledgments

We would like to thank all of our families and friends for bearing with us through the process of putting this work together. No project of this magnitude is created in a vacuum, and it takes an incredible amount of time and energy to see something like this to completion. Without the support network of our families and friends, this project may have never come to fruition.

We would also like to express our gratitude to Judith Lakamper, Shelby Russell, and Becca Beurer for picking up our call-for-papers flyer and seeing the value in this project, and then patiently and competently guiding us through the publication process.

This work builds on the work of so many previous scholars that it would be impossible to name them all, but we owe each of them a debt of gratitude for their work. Additionally, we would like to express our thanks to all of our scholarly mentors and colleagues who've challenged us to further academic inquiry in the fields of popular culture, media studies, narrative, and feminism.

Ultimately, none of this discussion would be possible if the characters discussed and analyzed in these chapters did not exist. Therefore, we would like to thank all of those responsible for creating these characters and thereby engaging audiences in these complex discourses.

Finally, this project is a work which we hope will help to empower women. The content was always intended to be discussions of powerful women, and that has been accomplished. Through a series of happy coincidences, the book is written entirely by women and is edited by women, a feat which would not have been possible in the not too distant past. Therefore, we would like to acknowledge our debt to all of the women who have fought to get us to a point where a project like this is possible, and thank all of the women who will continue to fight.

Introduction

The narratives we employ, enjoy, and (re)produce are fundamental to our understanding of the world, our roles in it (both chosen and prescribed), and the ways we navigate intersections between ourselves, our identities, and our perceptions of others. New narrative models encourage us to question, challenge, and change long-held suppositions of dominant discourses; fictional narratives that employ feminist epistemologies, in particular, encourage audiences to interrogate gender and sexuality in mainstream arenas. Until recently, the role of women in dominant Western discourses has predominantly focused on women as mothers and caretakers within the domestic sphere, or alternately as sexualized objects. Both categories of the virgin/whore or saint/sinner dichotomy place emphasis on women as beings without agency or purpose, except as defined by men, and limited to inhabiting accepted social roles. The ascent of the antiheroine in contemporary culture challenges the boundaries that limit women to idealized motherhood and domestic partnership, allowing space for narratives that diverge from social prescriptions and characters who embody visions of womanhood that affirm choice, agency, and alterity.

While antiheroes have been a staple of Western literary narratives since the classical era, since the turn of the twenty-first century there has been a notable increase in the number of narratives centered on anti*heroines*. This rise is particularly remarkable in television series, where, as Margaret Tally explains, antiheroines have become a typical feature.[1] In her influential monograph, *The Rise of the Anti-Heroine in TV's Third Golden Age*, Tally discusses many of these pioneering antiheroines, some of whom are also examined in this book, such as *Scandal*'s Olivia Pope, *How to Get Away with Murder*'s Annalise Keating, *Homeland*'s Carrie Mathison, and *The American*'s Elizabeth Jennings. Tally argues that "The anti-heroine's emergence coincided with the end of a number of series centered on male anti-heroes" and that these antiheroes served "as a kind of flawed hero [who] makes moral compromises, often in an effort to reach a desired end or to help the protagonist secure a fair conclusion."[2] Tally contrasts the role of the antiheroine with that of the antihero, contending that "although the female anti-heroine can also be considered a standard character on a range of television shows today, . . . an easy definition eludes her. If you look at any number of dictionary entries, they will usually define her as a female anti-hero, but this obscures as much as it reveals what she is."[3] Working from the notion that, like her male equivalent, she is a flawed heroine who makes moral compromises is far too simplistic, if we acknowledge that such compromises can only be judged within the patriarchal system that informs them.

This rise of the antiheroine that Tally examines could easily be a result of the ongoing fight for increased women's visibility and gender equality in the United States. As women have gained a measure of power in politics, society, and entertainment, thus beginning to exercise increasing control over the production of cultural artifacts, they have started to demand narratives that feature diverse representations of characters who reflect the complexities of women's real lived experiences. The women portrayed in contemporary media are more complex than their predecessors, evidencing the reality of inter-secting issues of class, race, gender, and sexuality in the lives of women beyond the page or screen, and reflecting those complexities for audiences. Also, as audiences in general have grown more savvy, the general public's need for more varied plotlines and edgier characters has heralded a new era of multi-dimensional, complex characters, resulting in the depiction of self-determining, independent, and sometimes villainous women whose goals lie beyond the social prescriptions of heteronormativity, docility, domesticity, submission, and other traits stereotypically attributed to women. These characters are flawed individuals, struggling with both internal and external conflicts. These women are not fairy-tale perfect princesses; they are more human, more relatable, sometimes even a bit wicked, and they often take unconventional routes to achieve their aims. Through these narratives, we cheer their deviousness, pettiness, malevolence, and artifice. We admire their cunning and determination. And we recognize that they're not looking for a prince on a white steed to come and save them; they're perfectly willing and able to do the work of saving themselves (or seizing their own crowns). These are women who do not hesitate to go their own way: it's their way or no way.

Antiheroines are not entirely new to contemporary literary narratives; after all, some of the most enduring and popular women characters are anti-heroines, including figures like Medea, Lady Macbeth, Scarlett O'Hara, Thelma and Louise, and Beatrix Kiddo. Along with their twenty-first-century counterparts, like Lisbeth Salander, Amy Dunne, Cersei Lannister, Claire Underwood, Olivia Pope, Annalise Keating, and Nancy Botwin, they are primarily established in popular imagination as selfish, scheming, devious, or manipulative. Depending on their specific circumstances, these women might lie, cheat, steal, manipulate, and even kill to achieve their goals. However, the argument can be made (as it is by many of our contributing authors) that such women are merely using the tools available to them to protect themselves and their own interests, pushing back against oppressive systems to define their own lives. Self-determination and self-interest are foundational to their actions, displacing the notion that women should be self-sacrificing in relation to the men and children in their lives by privileging the goals, priorities, and perspectives of others over their own desires, hopes, and achievements. These antiheroines are those characters we love to hate, but who we also respect and may even wish to emulate, even as they work outside of the bounds of traditional morality in order to achieve their own ends.

This book expands the scholarly discussion on antiheroines by offering new examinations of such fictional narratives, asking how the lives of women can be reimagined and re-inscribed through the use of the antiheroine in the popular imagination. This collection examines how antiheroine characters allow us to interrogate the ways in which "normalcy" is defined, focusing particularly on how notions of "normal" function as a means for patriarchal institutions to define, delimit, and discount women. The narratives discussed in this book engage the antiheroine trope in ways that allow for the representation of a competent, cogent feminine subjectivity.

SAINTS, SINNERS, AND SURVIVORS

Antiheroines of Contemporary Media: Saints, Sinners, and Survivors is divided into three sections, beginning with "Making a Mess of Motherhood," which focuses on the complexity of antiheroines who are also mothers. The first chapter, "From 'Basic Bitch' to 'Boss Bitch': Morality and Motherhood in NBC's *Good Girls*" by Henriette Seeliger and Tiara Sukhan, examines how Beth, Annie, and Ruby reject traditional notions of motherhood by embracing a life of crime. While the mothers' need to provide for their children is the initial catalyst, over the course of two seasons their criminal actions are increasingly driven by their desire for personal fulfillment. Seeliger and Suhkan argue that the antiheroines of *Good Girls*, principally Beth, function to critique neoliberal, postfeminist pressures for mothers to "lean in" and "have it all." Next, Brenda Boudreau's "Challenging Cultural Attitudes to Maternal Ambivalence through Antiheroines in *The Americans* and *Homeland*" investigates how *Homeland*'s Carrie Mathison and *The Americans*' Elizabeth Jennings struggle with being spies while also being mothers, often engaging motherhood with substantive resentment and uncertainty. However, Mathison and Jennings refuse to be defined by societal expectations of motherhood, which Boudreau argues allows both characters to remain beloved antiheroines, not in spite of their maternal ambivalence, but because of it. Both Seeliger and Sukhan and Boudreau's chapters demonstrate that mothers are too often judged on a "good" or "bad," "saintly" or "demonic" binary, dependent on whether they are willing to put their own personal goals before the perceived needs of their family. Lucinda Rasmussen's "Tracking the Relationships between Post-feminism, Representations of Ageing Women, and the Rise of Popular Misogyny as Portrayed in FX's *Sons of Anarchy* (2008–2014)" continues the exploration of motherhood, offering a unique discussion of how middle ageism intersects with misogyny. Her analysis focuses on Gemma Teller Morrow, arguing her characterization as an antiheroine functions as a plea to return to a nostalgia-laden, conservative era where young white males are positioned as the head of the social order. The final chapter in this section is "'As Bad as Him': Reframing Skyler White as *Breaking Bad*'s Overlooked Antiheroine" by Melanie Piper. Piper revisits *Breaking Bad*'s Skyler White to examine how she regains her agency in the shadow of victimhood to eventually become her husband's primary criminal co-conspirator. Piper conducts an analysis of key moments in Skyler's arc, revealing White as neither victim nor villain, but as a deeply flawed woman who actively works to control her circumstances. By focusing on the persistent characterization of Skyler as a mother who occupies a feminine domestic space, Piper exposes the deeply gendered differences in the way we understand male and female antiheroes. These final two chapters in the first section both remind us how narratives centered on antiheroine characters work to critique society's double standards for men and women.

The second section, "Women to Watch (Out For)," also focuses on television, beginning with Melanie Haas's examination of *Scandal*'s Olivia Pope and *How to Get Away with Murder*'s Annalise Keating and their importance as Black antiheroines. Haas demonstrates that antiheroines like Pope and Keating work to move beyond stereotypical narratives and provide complex, multi-faceted representations of powerful Black women. She applies an intersectional lens to argue that Pope and Keating challenge negative constructs of both race and gender, especially the ideals of beauty and femininity ascribed to Black women. In demonstrating the audience's desire to root for these powerful women—whose actions are motivated by notions of justice that do not always correspond to definitions of "good" or "bad"—Haas shows that these antiheroines encourage us to challenge oppressive social systems. In the next chapter, "Where the Streets Have No Shame: Queen Cersei Lannister's Journey to Alternative Patriarchy," Louise Coopey examines the character arc of *Game of Thrones*' Cersei Lannister, following her development from subjugated wife and mother to ruthless queen. Coopey argues that Cersei uses the lessons of the patriarchy, learned from her father, to directly challenge its validity by claiming a form of masculine hegemony before subverting it to seize power. Cersei's rejection of expectations proscribed upon her as a wife, mother, and daughter demonstrates how fictional—even fantastical—antiheroines highlight the hypocrisy of modern gender roles. The final chapter of this section is Kathleen Waites's "*Killing Eve* and the Necessity of the Female Villain du Jour." Waites compares the TV series to its source material, Luke Jenning's novel *Codename Villanelle*, to question whether the struggle between Villanelle and Eve is a sexier postmodern version of the classic "divide and conquer" trope—pitting one woman against another to keep the dominant androcentric hegemony in control. Waites argues that the female-authored show explores an alternative scenario between the lines of either/or, one that finds a space for a female identity that straddles the line between the wild female West and Lacan's Symbolic Order. Each of these chapters examines powerful women who directly defy expectations of women as the "weaker sex." By cheering on these antiheroines, audiences are encouraged to question the virtues so often assigned to the ideal woman, as well as the patriarchal systems that impose them.

Antiheroines of Contempory Media: Saints, Sinners, and Survivors' concluding section, "Crazy is a Sexist Word," focuses on antiheroines and portrayals of mental health. We begin with Liz Evans's assessment of domestic noir fiction, "Rewriting the Psycho-Bitch: Exploring the Psychological Complexity of the Antiheroine in Contemporary Domestic Noir Fiction," which examines the potential for contemporary domestic noir fiction to effectively frame the complex shadow side of the female psyche without collapsing into psychopathology. Focusing on several contemporary novels, Evans examines the archetypal bad girl through the lens of feminist, psychoanalytic, and post-Jungian archetypal theory. By comparing the protagonists of *Gone Girl* and *Girl on A Train* with those of *Her* and *Alys Always*, she demonstrates that associating the wrath of such problematic antiheroines with discourses of madness limits their potential to represent modes of female resistance. Evans's study is followed by another deconstruction of the irrational woman, "'Maybe She's Not Such a Heinous Bitch After All': Representations of the Antiheroine in *Crazy Ex-Girlfriend*." Analyzing four key milestones in her journey, Salerno argues that CW's *Crazy Ex-Girlfriend*'s Rebecca Bunch assumes the role of "killjoy" in order to embrace self-love, community, and integrity amid a disingenuous, toxic culture. Championing parody and positive representation, *Crazy Ex-Girlfriend* crafts a narrative that works tirelessly to undo the stigma of mental illness, while putting a flawed, emotionally raw, and socially conscious antiheroine at the center of it all. Anja Meyer continues the discussion of antiheroines and mental health in "The Antiheroine and the Representation of PTSD: The Case of *Jessica Jones*," arguing that Jones exemplifies the antiheroine trope not because she is a superhero "behaving badly," but because she is a vulnerable woman suffering from post-traumatic stress disorder, having survived a rape perpetrated by the series' main antagonist. Meyer highlights the controversial notion of "heroism," emphasizing Jones's self-conflicted relationship with her physical powers and the psychological toll of "trying and failing" to be a hero. By focusing on the show's narrative structure, in particular the use of flashbacks, Meyer argues the show offers one of television's most successful depictions of a woman living with trauma. The section, and the book, concludes with Siobhan Lyons's "'Small-Breasted Psycho': Debunking the Female Psychopath in *Killing Eve*." Lyons explores the lengths Villanelle goes to in order to survive in a patriarchal world, and the characterizations of "psychopaths" that the series challenges. While Villanelle's foil, Eve, is characterized as "normal," her behavior mirrors Villanelle's more unstable behavior, illustrating that normality is relative and the term "psychotic" is erroneously used to describe complex women. Lyons argues that narratively constructing both women as antiheroines problematizes oversimplified notions of "good" and "bad" women. This final section reveals how antiheroine narratives highlight a need to reexamine the deeply gendered definitions we ascribe to psychological disorders and to destigmatize mental illness.

Overall, the arguments contained in this book all explain that, ultimately, antiheroinism is a more realistic depiction of women, as women are far more complex and require a far more sophisticated representation than other standard tropes allow. All of the characters discussed in these pages are far from perfect. Their actions often wreak havoc, creating hardship, pain, and sometimes death for those around them. And yet these characters are not villainous masterminds. Though they may commit heinous acts at times, they are also dedicated professionals, loving mothers, loyal friends, ardent lovers, devoted wives, and staunch patriots; in these roles, they face many of the same struggles that real women do. They encounter and resist discrimination. They worry about whether to have children, and, if they do have children, they strive to do what is best for them. They cope with infidelity and betrayal. They support their friends and families through all kinds of difficulties, from the loss of a parent to a violent attack. They face the social stigma of their aging. They struggle with mental health issues from PTSD to bipolar disorder to OCD. All of these are things that real women face in their own lives, often feeling like they are failing to meet all of the challenges they face. These antiheroines are clearly not role models, as the actions they take against those who wrong them or those under their protection are usually far more extreme than most women would take—although some women might certainly contemplate those options. What these antiheroines do is provide representation on the screen of women who are not perfect and who do not meet, and often actively oppose, the outdated but still ever-present impossible standards for women. And yet, these flawed women generally still enjoy some level of success. Women watch these characters make much bigger mistakes than most would and still thrive. Thus, these antiheroine characters have the power to give real women an understanding that they do not have to be perfect and hope that they can be successful even though they make mistakes.

Finally, and perhaps most importantly, these discussions demonstrate that the antiheroine provides a means of creating solidarity among women, a way for women to reach out to other women to combat isolation, objectification, and subjugation. The antiheroine actively rejects silence and suffering. She chooses to act, and whether it is her speech or her actions that do the talking, she is invested in a powerful narrative of self-recognition. She realizes her own strength, and the strength and ability of others. Unlike so many women represented in literature and popular media, the antiheroine, and those who look to her for representation, do not have to go it alone. Unlike the antihero, the solo counterpart to the Western model of a hero fighting injustice alone, there is room in the narrative of the antiheroine for collective action. In making her own rules and choosing her own path forward, the antiheroine opens a space to address the power of solidarity and shared experience. This makes the antiheroine an incredibly important and timely character type, one that deserves this kind of in-depth investigation. While this collection focuses almost exclusively on television antiheroines, we hope to see in coming years such analysis expanding the discussion of how antiheroines are presented in other media, particularly how such narratives challenge our expectations of women's experience in Western cultures.

NOTES

1. Margaret Tally, *The Rise of the Anti-Heroine in TV's Third Golden Age*. Cambridge, 2016, 1.
2. Tally, 5.
3. Tally, 6.

Part I

Making a Mess of Motherhood

Chapter One

From "Basic Bitch" to "Boss Bitch"

Morality and Motherhood in NBC's Good Girls

Henriette-Juliane Seeliger and Tiara Sukhan

"Girls today can be anything. CEO, Olympic gold medalist, even a Supreme Court Justice. We've finally broken that glass ceiling, and, wow, sure looks good from the top." This singular moment of extra-diegetic narration, in a youthful female voice, opens the pilot episode of NBC's *Good Girls* (2018–), a network television program about three mothers who turn to armed robbery, money laundering, and drug dealing to meet the financial needs of their families. *Good Girls* has been described as a "gentler," more feminine version of *Breaking Bad*,[1] suggesting that a network television show about women in crime needs to be less gritty than a cable program about male criminals in order to be both legible and palatable to viewers.[2] The title itself is potentially problematic, a cheeky throwback to alliterative gender-essentializing characterizations ("good girls" and "bad boys"), but this initial provocation is arguably just one indication of the subversive challenge to dominant gender narratives to come. We argue here that *Good Girls* does much more than provide a more feminine twist to the crime drama and an alternative, possibly less violent, television narrative for female viewers. Despite assertions that its plot "may not be entirely believable,"[3] the show raises complicated questions about what it means to be both a woman and mother in the United States in the twenty-first century. *Good Girls* ultimately challenges the dominant narrative that women "can be anything" they want, as the current social and economic realities make it incredibly difficult, if not impossible, for most women to achieve the kinds of success in both their work and home lives that "Lean In" style messaging tells them to demand.

The positions in life that are typically regarded as markers of achievement in a work environment whose rules were shaped by men range from a well-paid job in a respected field, to reaching a leadership position that comes with a certain degree of responsibility, or becoming financially independent—ideally while also having a happy family life. The markers of contemporary feminist success at work (a well-paying job that is both fulfilling and time-flexible) and home (high-achieving, well-adjusted children and an attentive and sexually satisfied partner) are too often inaccessible to women whose intersectional identities are marked by financial insecurity and a lack of education, and these are factors which disproportionately impact women of color. Women in the United States are still underrepresented in leadership positions,[4] work in low-paid jobs more often than men,[5] and juggle the majority of the housework in relationships,[6] even when they work full time. Motherhood presents additional, often unanticipated challenges to women, and *Good Girls* examines these "costs of motherhood."[7] The series exposes the discrepancies between a neoliberal vision that suggests that anyone can achieve anything if only they work hard enough, and the real everyday lives of women who encounter pervasive structural barriers to this promised success, through the lack of initiatives "such as paid maternity leave, affordable, quality childcare, and family-friendly policies in the workplace."[8]

Beth Boland, played by Christina Hendricks of *Mad Men* fame, is the central protagonist of the series. While Hendricks shares the spotlight with Mae Whitman's Annie (Beth's sister) and Retta's Ruby (Beth's childhood friend), it is Beth who ultimately undergoes the biggest transformation from "basic" middle-class suburban homemaker to aspiring criminal "boss bitch."[9] Beth is also presented as the epitome of a certain kind of constructed television femininity, bound by perceptions of both delicacy and submission. When we first meet her, she is a throwback to Donna Reed and June Cleaver—running her home with seemingly effortless efficiency, existing to serve her husband and children with nary a thought for her own needs and desires. Her husband does not trouble her with problems like how to pay the mortgage or even how to work the television remote control, and it doesn't occur to her to trouble herself, at first blissfully content with the gendered division of labor that characterizes her household. Beth's journey through the series forces her to confront many of her adult life choices and to find them wanting, whereas her sister and friend join her in criminal activity primarily to address their own financial problems. As she undergoes the most significant (and, as suggested, sometimes ambivalent) development, we will be using Beth Boland as our primary example, but we will continue to refer to Annie and Ruby more briefly.[10]

When we first meet Beth, we see that she has committed to a life as a homemaker in order to raise her four children while her husband Dean runs a car dealership. When she discovers that he has been cheating on her with his secretary this unravels a whole web of deception, including the news that his financial mismanagement is threatening to cost the Bolands their home in a quiet middle-class neighborhood. Beth's friend Ruby Hill and her husband, Stan, represent a stereotypical African American working-class family—both partners work long hours at low-paying jobs and try to pick up extra shifts as often as possible. Their daughter has health problems which cannot be adequately addressed with the medical insurance they can afford—a telling reminder that access to medical treatment cannot be taken for granted in the United States where socialized medicine is a utopian fantasy. Annie Marks is Beth's younger sister; she impulsively married young and then quickly divorced. With no formal education, she works part-time as a cashier at a local supermarket. She has a teenager, Sadie, struggling with gender identity; and while Annie loves her child, she barely earns enough money to afford necessities—extra expenses like a new laptop for school are out of the question. When her ex-husband suggests that he and his new wife are seeking custody of Sadie because they can afford to provide more opportunities, Annie's financial troubles are compounded by the need to seek legal representation to fight the suit. These three struggling mothers frame the program's premise, as the pilot episode illustrates how they ultimately conclude that crime is the only way out of their respective financial predicaments. A series of complications with the money they steal then forces them to participate in further criminal activities, which proves especially thrilling for Beth, who hides her boredom and fragile sense of self behind a façade of cheery domestic efficiency. While the financial demands of motherhood provide the initial motivation for this foray into crime, the program eventually begins to explicitly address the moral dilemma these women face in having to reconcile their identities as good people with their ongoing illegal activities, particularly once such activities are no longer required to meet pressing financial needs.

ON-SCREEN MOTHERS

The figure of the mother is present in stories throughout varied histories and cultures. She is at different turns loved, worshipped, praised, and blamed—carrying all of the burden of responsibility, but seldom afforded any significant credit for how her offspring turn out. Jacqueline Rose asserts that "motherhood is, in Western discourse, the place in our culture where we lodge, or rather bury, the reality of our own conflicts, or what it means to be fully human."[11] Because mothers bear such a substantial burden for the physical and emotional well-being of their children, they have historically been expected to embrace caregiving and homemaking as their primary vocation. As the financial burden of living in the United States has increased for families, so has the need for mothers to work outside the home, sometimes at multiple jobs. Despite this fact,[12] the idealized popular image of motherhood is slow to reflect reality: 70 percent of Americans still believe a father should be working full-time, but only 12 percent believe this also holds true for mothers.[13] This can partly be attributed to the often conservative representation of motherhood in the media, which keeps repeating the same stock characterizations and moral lessons.[14] In film and television, motherhood has historically been represented as "the most important" and "fulfilling" job in society, despite the fact that, in real life, the labor of mothering is often considered "dreary, uninspiring and mentally unchallenging."[15] These representations perpetuate an unattainable ideal of motherhood. Mothers are not only held responsible for the most basic physical and emotional needs of their children, but they also carry the burden of all their future success and achievement. "Good mothers" are "altruistic beings who devote themselves entirely to their children" and "put [their] children first, rather than [themselves]," organizing social lives, sports activities, and extracurriculars of all kinds in order to provide every possible advantage over the competition (that is other mothers' children).[16] This phenomenon has been alternatively named "intensive mothering,"[17] "intensive parenting,"[18] "new momism,"[19] or the "mommy mystique."[20] This ideal of motherhood, very narrow both in racial and socioeconomic terms, is often reinforced in popular media, which presents us with stories that "are not so much a reflection of the real world, as a value-laden repackaging of it that perpetuates gender myths."[21] In addition to this, the difficulties mothers and families often face are blamed, under neoliberalism, on an individual lack of perseverance rather than structural barriers and inequality.[22]

Traditional television narratives "often cast motherhood in moral terms, juxtaposing the 'good mother' with the 'bad mother,' who frequently is a working mom, a lower-income mom, or someone who does not conform to traditional gender roles of behavior, ambition, or sexual orientation."[23] For the medium's first few decades, television mothers were primarily featured in the situation comedy genre, reinforcing rigid gender roles within the nuclear family in programs such as *The Donna Reed Show* (ABC, 1958–1966) and *Leave it to Beaver* (CBS, 1957–1963). Until the 1970s, it was rare to see a sitcom mother work outside of the home, and while working mothers are more commonplace in the 1980s and beyond, they were still expected to rationalize their choice to work, and to prioritize the needs of their children whether fathers were present or not. Roseanne Barr's "unruly"[24] portrayal of Roseanne Connor's working-class family in *Roseanne* (ABC, 1988–1997) is a rare example of a television program that seriously engages with the impact of economic precarity, as class critique is not a feature of most US television programs.

The Good Wife (CBS, 2009–2016) is probably the most recently broadcast program to engage with the moral discourse which characterizes wives and mothers as "good" or "bad." The series begins as the titular character, Alicia Florrick, joins her husband at the podium for a press conference where he announces his resignation from public office in the wake of a sex and corruption scandal. He is facing criminal charges and she is forced back in the workplace after having suspended a promising legal career thirteen years earlier to raise her two children. Like *Good Girls'* Beth Boland, she has been the perfect suburban housewife, choosing to make meeting the needs of her husband and children her whole world. And like Beth Boland, the moment of rupture in her marriage is predicated on her husband's adultery. While for Beth this news actually pales in comparison to the financial jeopardy his bad business decisions have put the family in, for Alicia it goes to the heart of everything she thought she was working for. She was the "good wife" and what did it get her? She is humiliated and forced to sell her home and downsize into an apartment while her husband serves a short prison sentence, but she has the education and connections to quickly find employment at a law firm where she begins to do very well. That the firm is co-run by a former law school classmate and potential love interest is a large part of why she gets this opportunity. Like Beth, her confidence grows as she throws herself into something outside the home that she is also good at. Even when it appears that she might be reconciling with her husband, she is quick to tell him that she wants to keep working. Her mother-in-law disapproves, tele-graphing a historical perception of mothers, who choose to work when they do not need to, as selfish.

As a contemporary television program, *Good Girls* defies simplistic distinctions between "good" and "bad" mothers, providing counterexamples to dominant narratives of motherhood and raising complex questions about the relationship between motherhood and morality in the process: How far can the boundaries of morality be extended in the name of family and mother-hood? How far can and should a mother go for her family? How much self-sacrifice is inherent to motherhood? None of the three mothers neatly fits into the category of "good" or "bad," but they are forced to choose between what is necessary for their families and what is legal. To Beth Boland, being a "good person" is entirely separate from breaking arbitrary laws that do not hurt anyone. As long as she has her family's best interest in mind, the meas-ures she will have to take to ensure their well-being do not necessarily turn her into a bad person even if they challenge conventional morality. *Good Girls* challenges viewers to consider what they themselves might be willing to do for their children as "[a]ny audience sympathy or empathy is 'intricate-ly bound up with moral judgments of value.'"[25] Thus, while Beth, Annie, and Ruby continually walk the line between the domestic and the criminal worlds, between hero and villain, we cannot help but enjoy the ways in which their actions turn traditional conceptions of morality and motherhood upside down, providing symbolic relief for all the big and small injustices mothers still face. Through the juxtaposition of the competing demands motherhood places on each of the three main characters, *Good Girls* shows how undervalued, yet simultaneously idealized and idolized the role of the mother still is, yet it resists providing a simple and final answer to the question of what makes these "girls" good.

"GOOD PEOPLE NEVER GET ANYTHING GOOD": CHOOSING CRIME WHEN THE SOCIAL CONTRACT IS BROKEN

Many television programs perpetuate the idea of easy motherhood by ignoring issues such as the need for flexible work hours, affordable childcare, or the lack of personal time for oneself. Instead, we are presented with a happy, ever-smiling, slim and well-dressed mother who juggles all her different jobs successfully: the "myth of the supermom" has become the new standard.[26] According to Katherine Kinnick, "the good mother, the noble mother-saint, makes her family her highest priority, continually sacrifices her own interests for the good of her family, and conforms to expected gender roles of femininity."[27] Beth Boland is initially presented to viewers as the epitome of the "good mother," doing exactly that. The pilot opens with a shot of Beth in her kitchen, skillfully juggling every aspect of her busy family's life. She keeps track of four noisy children whose schedules she knows by heart, prepares their school lunches, while simultaneously cleaning up the kitchen. Rather than helping, her husband Dean is running late, stopping only to drink coffee and queue for his lunch bag just like his kids.[28] Beth is a perfectionist, the kind of woman who puts beverages on a coaster so that she does not get water stains on the wooden furniture, and whose sole occupation is to cater to her family's every need.

Superficially, Beth has nothing to complain about; she has a husband and a family, lives in a nice house, and does not need to go to work—her life represents the mommy ideal. However, from the beginning, this seeming ideal is represented as stifling and depressing. As her sister Annie observes, watching Beth cutting chicken fingers into little stars, "You're like the Stepford mom—without a pulse."[29] Although she does not explicitly say so, it is obvious that Beth is not happy with her life as it is either. Despite all her efforts, she is constantly under-appreciated because she is, after all, *just* a homemaker. Her husband Dean takes for granted that she will manage the household and the kids successfully without complaint. He humors her attempt to solve the family's financial problems by opening new bank accounts, noting her lack of credit profile as she hasn't had a job since high school when she "worked at the DQ,"[30] while her sister Annie pities her for the life she has chosen.

Ironically, the transition from "basic bitch" to "boss bitch" is made possible for Beth precisely because she is consistently undervalued and underestimated by other people—particularly men. When her husband Dean learns that she has smuggled counterfeit money across the Canadian border for the gang leader who employs them, for example, he immediately assumes that "dangerous people took advantage of [her]" (S1, E6, minute 39).[31] Similarly, both the *Good Girls'* crime boss, gangster Rio, and Annie's "civilian" boss at the supermarket, Boomer, think of her as a soft-hearted, "idiot housewife" who lacks both the brains and the strength to succeed in the criminal world (S1, E2, minute 14).[32] Even the FBI agent on their case is initially fooled by Beth's innocent façade and finds it easier to believe her lies than to assume a suburban homemaker and mother might have been chosen to work for a ruthless drug dealer. As a result, Beth skillfully exploits the image of the "dumb house-wife" to cover up the true extent of her criminal success. In fact, her invisibil-ity in the mass of underappreciated suburban homemakers is what qualifies her for the job in the first place: when Rio wants to kill her for having (inadvertently) stolen from him, she points out quick-wittedly that "when bad things happen to good people," it attracts attention.[33] By making the skills she has acquired as a housewife and mother the perfect starting point for her criminal activities, *Good Girls* emphasizes how underappreciated and under-valued housewives and mothers are. Being a good mom does not pay off for Beth, either financially, emotionally, or personally, and her initial financial motivations are from the beginning interwoven with her personal desire to prove to herself that she can do much more.

The series further complicates the question of female "goodness" by contrasting the women's moral framework and actions with those of the various men in their lives. Dean cheats on Beth, re-mortgages their family home without telling her to cover up his own mistakes, and then later pre-tends to have cancer to force her to stay with him. Annie's boss Boomer, upon recognizing her during the supermarket robbery, first tries to extort her for sex in exchange for his silence, then tries to rape her when she refuses, and finally attempts to set her up for drug possession. Minor characters Greg and Brian both cheat on their wives with Annie, and two male FBI agents are shown ignoring their own families in order to bring down Beth, Annie, and Ruby. While these men may not all be involved in criminal activities, their behavior is often equally problematic when compared with the women, who are judged far more harshly. In terms of the disapprobation they receive from the men in their lives, the actual criminal activities these women are involved in seem to pale in comparison to the "crimes" of thinking for themselves and taking initiative to do what is necessary for their families once it becomes clear that following the rules and being "good girls" doesn't pay the bills.

Crucially, then, it is not only the fact that they can make a lot of money very quickly, or the ease with which they are able to rob their first target, but it is the fact that legal means fail to address the problems their families face, which drives Beth, Annie, and Ruby into crime. Beth's initial motivation is the need to make up for her husband's failure and to provide for her family, ensuring her children's well-being at any cost, just as would be expected of a "good" mother. She has to ensure both the stability of her kids' lives, as well as plan ahead for their future, and because she cannot do so within the confines of traditional morality, she has to resort to illegal measures. As a result, the first season of *Good Girls* frames Beth's criminal activities largely in domestic terms (the jobs Rio gives them are "like driving for Uber"; she signs her friends up for criminal activity as if it were a "bake sale"). When Rio asks Beth playfully, "What you wanna be then, huh? A fireman? Astronaut?" she replies, "I don't know. A good person."[34] Rio's ironic reply, "No, you're way more interesting than that" again emphasizes the often incompatible tension between being a good person by moral standards and leading a good life by economic and social standards.

Thus, the series takes a very basic moral question as its starting point: What if being a "good person" is not rewarded? Earning "legit" money means "working like dogs and barely scraping by."[35] Beth would struggle to get a well-paying job because she has no formal qualifications, post-secondary education, or work experience. Ruby and Stan are unable to adequately support a family on two regular incomes, while Annie works long hours at minimum wage. When additional expenses compound already precarious financial situations, crime quickly becomes a viable option for desperate people to make quick money. Faced with the possibility of losing the family home, Beth is determined to find a way to pay the mortgage, Ruby needs to find money for their daughter's treatment because she does not have health insurance, and Annie cannot afford a custody lawyer to fight for her daughter without some extra cash. But even when these problems have been solved, the mothers are all too aware that their children will always need something else, be it braces, hormone blockers, or college tuition fees. The basic financial demands put on families that cannot rely on universal health care or affordable education make it necessary for the women to resort to illegal measures to earn extra money. The fact that they do so for their children rather than out of selfish greed serves as a moral justification, exposing the structural flaws in the public institutions that most American citizens rely on. Annie's child is bullied at school when they begin questioning their gender identity and altering their gender expression from hegemonic femininity to a presentation more aligned with male dress codes. The school does nothing to protect the child, sending the message that this kind of intolerance is acceptable, and Annie is forced to figure out how to keep Sadie safe on her own. When Ruby and Stan are threatened with jail time if they do not tell the FBI what they know about Beth's criminal activities, it serves as a reminder of the disproportionate number of African Americans currently incarcerated in the United States. This threat is effective, because it is real—just as they cannot afford specialist medical treatment for their daughter, they would not be able to afford the kind of legal counsel that might protect them. When

Ruby is desperate for money to pay her daughter's medical bills, she is forced to get a predatory "payday" loan, her circumstances making her ineligible for a regular bank loan with more manageable interest rates. These social and economic realities, the implications of which are often disproportionately borne by women and people of color, defy the neoliberal narrative of inevitable success, if only one is willing to work hard enough. It is their disillusionment about the fact that being "good" women does not pay off in a world where wealthy white men make the rules that drives the "Good Girls" into crime. Beth sums it up:

> All those fairy tales they told us when we were little girls? The morals were always, if you're good and if you follow the rules, if you don't lie and you don't cheat, if you're good, you'll get good things. And if you're a dick, you get punished. But what if the people who made up those stories are the dicks? . . . What if the bad people made all that up so the good people never get anything good?[36]

Once disappointment gives way to cynicism, Beth is released from her compunction to believe in socially constructed myths about upward mobility and the rewards promised to those who work hard and follow the rules. But as Beth is also somewhat less financially precarious than her sister and friend, she must also reconcile herself to the fact that she isn't turning to criminality just out of necessity—she enjoys the way it makes her feel powerful and confident. This allows her to see her life in a new light—to reevaluate her choices and discover that, in the context of motherhood, self-fulfillment is just as important as sacrifice.

FROM BASIC BITCH TO BOSS BITCH: RECONCILING MOTHERHOOD AND SELF-FULFILLMENT

Since Beth is driven into crime in order to protect her children and save her family home, she is initially only able to rationalize her criminal activities in these terms. Her primary identity is that of mother, thus crime is at first only a means of empowering her to be a supermom who will do anything for her kids, and she is able to keep it separate from her family life. However, as she gets deeper into the criminal world, her activities cease to be framed only in domestic terms, and rather begin to blur the clear division that Beth has sought to keep between her outside job and her domestic façade. In season 2, we find her meeting Rio at the playground, at school recitals or swim training, and when she cannot find childcare, she even has to bring her kids along on a drug delivery, losing her youngest child's precious blanket in the process. She comes close to being killed or imprisoned on multiple occasions, and when she agrees to put up an injured gangster on the run he recuperates in her daughter's bed (while her daughter sleeps elsewhere). This increasing overlap between her two separate identities makes it impossible for her to continue to rationalize her criminal behavior. As the series evolves, Beth is forced to confront her own cognitive dissonance. She has gone onto crime to save her family, but now what was supposed to be the solution to her problems has become a new problem itself, putting her children into even greater danger. Yet she continues to be drawn to criminal activity, by both the thrill of the forbidden and the sense of personal accomplishment her success brings her.

Beth begins to shed the role of demure, feminine, domestic housewife and enters the masculine world of crime and cars: she assumes management of the car dealership from her incompetent husband Dean, challenges Rio who has been using the dealership as a secret distributing system for drugs, and eventually takes over the combined business. Beth is not plagued by a guilty conscience anymore, fearing what will happen if she has to go to prison, but instead now openly challenges the FBI agent Jimmy, finding it "almost fun"[37] when the FBI come to raid the dealership. "Good" mothers embrace domesticity, conform to traditional gender roles by taking care of their family's every need, cooking, cleaning and keeping the house in order. "Bad mothers," by contrast, are "self-centered, neglectful, preoccupied with career, or lacking in traditional femininity,"[38] in that they resist hegemonic norms of both comportment and wholesome beauty. It seems, then, that Beth is gradually transitioning from supermom to "bad" mother, preoccupied by the thrill of transgression, and unable to give it up. As she struggles to keep her two identities apart, her criminal activities increasingly begin to have a negative effect on her family: Dean gets shot,[39] her son Kenny develops psychological problems, and her daughter appears to go missing, later anticlimactically found to be hiding in the closet because mommy has so little time for her these days.[40]

Beth is ultimately punished for being a "bad," career-focused mother when Dean, having given her an ultimatum to stop what she is doing or lose her family, finally takes the kids and leaves her, a moment she later describes as hitting "rock-bottom."[41] Kinnick describes how popular media often frames a woman's decision to leave even high-ranking jobs in order to be with her children through a "rhetoric of personal choice." According to this rhetoric, women are not thwarted in their career ambitions by structural issues such as sexism in the workplace, the "glass ceiling," or inflexible work hours, but only by their personal and seemingly "natural" desire to be with their offspring.[42] Beth is shown to regret having missed so much family time, leaving post-it notes with loving messages by her children's beds before she leaves early in the morning.[43] When Dean finally leaves her, it appears that she has been properly chastised, and she makes the seemingly voluntary decision to return to a more domestic role. Beth attends self-help meetings and describes herself as an "addict."[44] Because she "cannot lose [her] kids again," Beth seems determined to reinvent herself and be "normal." She goes to the playground with other moms instead of meeting Rio there, organizes school benefits with the same meticulous planning that she has brought toward the robberies, and channels all her surplus energy into baking. Yet, Beth soon comes to realize what we have known from the start: that she can never go back to her old domestic life, even if this will have a negative impact on her family. As she tries to reunite with her old friends, who are "elevating domesticity to a competitive art form,"[45] Beth is quickly bored by the banality of their lives and the amount of effort they put into catering to their children's ill-mannered wishes. At the store, she nicks a Chapstick just for the thrill of it, and when all her carefully crafted Halloween cakes are returned to her because *one* child does not like peanuts she gives up on the performance of "supermomism" perhaps for the last time.[46]

Through the representations of such complex motivations and considerations, *Good Girls* rejects the simple stereotyping of working mothers and instead points to the impossibly high demands put on women and the almost unachievable task of having to reconcile your work and your family, of having to decide between yourself and your children. Beth is deeply divided between her job and her family. She rejects the idea that her children's problems may have anything to do with her being away from them, instead banning phones from the dinner table in an attempt to create "normal" family problems. However, she is also constantly confronted from all sides with external expectations of perfection that deny the possibility of being *both* a mother and a fulfilled working woman. Her argument to avoid certain kinds of tasks that challenge her moral sensibilities or put her at personal risk ("I have a family. I have children"),[47] does not work with Rio anymore. Eventually, Rio gets annoyed by what he terms the "bitch-ass drama," that is Beth's insistence on being a mother, too. When she insists, "I'm a mother," Rio replies, "You're a drug dealer,"[48] making it clear that in his world she cannot be both things at once. Beth struggles to reconcile the different roles she wants to play, and as a result, she fails to live up to any of them. Eventually, Rio refuses to meet her at school recitals and swim training anymore because he gets the impression that she values her family life over the business. He is a father himself, but just as he states that he never works "while on vacation," Rio insists that Beth needs to put her private life aside and prioritize her work life. The two roles of mother and drug dealer are mutually exclusive, it seems, and the series thereby brings attention to the many competing demands put on mothers.

Good Girls breaks down the simple dichotomy of "bad" working mother and "good" stay-at-home mom: in Beth it gives us a woman who enjoys both working and being with her family and struggles to reconcile the competing demands these two roles place on her. She is torn between what she wants for herself—a "real job" that provides personal satisfaction and even fun—and the demands of traditional motherhood and femininity placed on her by her husband. While she really tries to live up to the ideal of the good mother, Beth's dilemma shows us that while there may be women who find domesticity blissful, it is unsatisfying for many. Too often, mothers who work are socially shamed for enjoying professional fulfillment, as if loving your job and loving your children are mutually exclusive. *Good Girls* also explores the role of fatherhood in healthy child development. Contrary to Beth's smug assumption that her husband would not be able to take care of the kids by himself when she takes over the dealership, Dean grows into the role of stay-at-home dad with considerable ease. Beth thought that Dean would "need a village"[49] to raise their kids if she was gone and he initially has to rely on a chaotic arrangement of organizational tools to keep track of all the information Beth just keeps in her head. However, by the end of season 2 he juggles the daily household chores just as easily as she did; he makes French toast, smooths tangled hair into ballerina buns, and keeps his kids under control. *Good Girls* suggests that masculinity does not depend on earning a paycheck—a good father can thrive taking care of his offspring. Yet a mother who insists on her individual subjectivity aside from her family must still be wary of doing so at the cost of her inherent "goodness." The series refuses to provide an easy solution to this dilemma, confronting us with the harsh, "unattainable standards of perfection" so many mothers face: "Mothers can never quite be *good enough.*"[50]

CONCLUSION: WHAT MAKES A MOTHER "GOOD"?

Good Girls raises complex moral issues, not only about what makes a good mother, but also what makes a good person, in general, and whether it is possible at all to live up to outdated standards of morality in a globalized, capitalist world, where everyone is out for themselves. As various scholars have pointed out, cautionary tales of women who lose all hope of finding personal happiness through love and eventually children, as the result of their focus on themselves and their career, are a common theme in motherhood representations on US television.[51] Intelligence in women is represented as dangerous, openly ambitious women are represented as "ice queens" or "dragon ladies," and only those women who repent of their selfish ambitions and choose to give up their career in favor of a more domestic, family-oriented role, are rewarded.[52] Through the character of Beth Boland, seemingly the quintessential "good mother," *Good Girls* challenges the stereotypical ideals and narrow definitions of what makes a good mother. Beth starts out as a supermom, but from the very beginning, it is clear that this role does not make her happy. Even when she has the chance to apply her skillset to something more profitable and personally rewarding, Beth still rationalizes her choices in the context of her need to care for and protect her family. *Good Girls* exposes the fact that the standards women are held to in the context of feminine domesticity and motherhood can no longer be attained conventionally by simply being "good." *Good Girls* shows that the pop cultural message "that women [can] do it all without accommodations from the workplace, government-sponsored social supports, or even maid services or fast food"[53] is a myth if these women are also supposed to be the morally unquestionable, Madonna-like "good moms." Women trying to juggle all of this on their own will inevitably find themselves faced with failure or they will have to resort to questionable methods that may even endanger their families.

Admittedly, in some ways, *Good Girls* seems to fall into the same traps that so many other representations of women and mothers on television have fallen. Kinnick bemoans the lack of relatable, authentic moms and the prevalence of "outlandish plots" that "ignore . . . the real dramas linking politics and motherhood, like family-work-life balance, the glass ceiling, and latch-key children."[54] While *Good Girls* may present us with something of an "outlandish plot," the politics of motherhood in our contemporary historical moment is one thing the program definitely embraces rather than ignores. Perhaps, whatever absurd plotting there is can also be useful as a metaphorical commentary on the absurdly impossible task that mothers have in trying to adequately balance the range of obligations they encounter when trying to provide for their families in an increasingly neoliberal society. By claiming that women have broken the glass ceiling and then showing women who struggle with low-income, low-prestige jobs, *Good Girls* serves to effectively challenge the myth of meritocracy embedded in the so-called American Dream. In this world, *Good Girls* suggests, the feminine ideal of being "good" does not pay off and as Beth comes to realize this she is left profoundly disappointed and deeply unsatisfied.

Other more problematic issues can be taken up within the program. Although it is essentially structural, social, and political shortcomings that drive the three women into crime, the gradual shift toward personal profit and enjoyment threatens to reduce the importance of structural inequality. This focus on the role and responsibility of the individual in addressing economic precarity without the suggestion of policy solutions, mirrors traditional representations of motherhood which "frame problems facing mothers as 'personal problems' rather than problems needing systemic, public policy solutions."[55] We are also left wondering why there is a need to present the moral justification of motherhood for these women to be "allowed" to turn to crime, while no such rationalizations are offered for Rio as a criminal father.

Despite these shortcomings, *Good Girls* raises complex questions and complicates traditional discourses and media representations of the cultural associations between motherhood and morality, without over-simplifying the question of what makes a "good" mother. It does so both on the narrative and on the meta-fictional level, which are tightly interwoven. Within the narrative, Beth, Ruby, and Annie need to find moral justifications for their criminal actions, which they find in the ideal of the good mother who would do literally anything for her kids. Simultaneously, however, the series questions the rightfulness and authenticity of this ideal. While frequently "the media idealize and glamorize motherhood as the one path to fulfillment for women, painting a rosy, Hallmark-card picture that ignores or minimizes the very real challenges that come along with parenthood," *Good Girls* takes the economic and domestic struggles of mothers as its very starting point.[56] All three women come up short of the ideal: Beth may look like a supermom, but she is deeply unhappy with her life as it is, Annie and Ruby are concerned less with personal fulfillment, but their personal circumstances make it impossible for them to meet the financial needs of their families without turning to crime. Although her kids' well-being was her initial motivation, Beth quickly finds that a life of crime is more fun, more profitable, and overall more appealing to her than a life as housewife and mother. She does not want to quit because "it feels good to be really good at something."[57] Learning from Rio and cultivating her skills, she is finally turned into a "boss bitch." The aphorism on her favorite mug, "I'd rather be crafting," is a highly ironic emphasis of this—she really would not.

Although Beth consciously sheds the ideal of motherhood described by Kinnick, we do not get a sense that she is judged narratively. While the male characters within the show may judge and punish her harshly (Dean takes her kids away and files for a divorce, the FBI agent seems to hate her more because she is a mother involved in criminal activity, and Rio tries to control and manipulate her), her actions are sanctioned both for the sake of her family and by the fact that she is fighting to be taken seriously by men who constantly look down on her. Although Beth may be transgressing the boundaries of conventional morality in the process, we cheer for her. Our point of view is aligned with hers as we are able to find a point of identification and through viewing psychoanalytically occupy the position of undervalued homemakers ourselves. *Good Girls* presents us with the difficulties women face in reconciling and balancing their own needs and the demands made on them by society. Beth Boland's struggles demonstrate that motherhood is not necessarily "the sole raison d'être for female existence,"[58] but neither is she just a career woman. Beth is a good mother because she will do almost anything for her kids, but no longer at the expense of her own desires. Beth insists, against the resistance of both Dean and Rio, on refusing the mutual exclusivity of a singular way of being a woman and mother. She does not acquiesce to demands or presumptions that she will or can be only one thing or the other—mother or worker. She will not choose between her children and herself, reinforcing a postfeminisst insistence on intersectional subjectivity. In doing so, *Good Girls* rejects a dominant narrative of our time: that by becoming mother, all other aspects of a woman's life will become secondary to this new, all-encompassing role. The series thus complicates traditional notions of the ideal mother, juxtaposing the competing demands put on women by the various roles they play in life and which often contradict and overshadow their own wishes and desires. Through its representation of a range of "complicated antiheroes,"[59] *Good Girls* shows that all women mother differently and as long as they love their children, there is no such thing as a single form of ideal motherhood. By resisting an answer to the question of maternal "goodness" the program embraces an ambivalent and imperfect messiness that women are seldom afforded on television, and it is to be commended for it.

NOTES

1. Both programs begin with slightly comic scenes of chaotic criminal activity before reverting to a period "three weeks earlier" in order to provide context for the predicament our protagonists now find themselves in. However, while *Breaking Bad*'s comic absurdity quickly gives way to stark and disturbing violence as Walter White quickly realizes that his own survival depends on eliminating his enemies, the women in *Good Girls* initially remain hapless and generally incompetent criminals. This suggests that female criminality is better played for laughs than as an authentic reflection of the implications of increasing wealth inequality.

2. Kristen Baldwin, *"Good Girls* Is a Gentler, Girlier *Breaking Bad*: EW Review," *Entertainment Weekly*, February 9, 2018, https://ew.com/tv/2018/02/09/good-girls-nbc-review/; Eliana Dockterman, *"Good Girls* Is the Perfect Show for this Moment," *Time*, February 26, 2018, https://time.com/5163688/good-girls-nbc-review/; Shirley Li, "Why Good Girls Is Such a Rewarding Show," *The Atlantic*, May 24, 2019, https://www.theatlantic.com/entertainment/archive/2019/05/good-girls-nbc-season-2-christinahendricks/590173/.

3. Rotten Tomatoes, "Good Girls: Season 1," accessed October 15, 2019, https://www.rottentomatoes.com/tv/good_girls/s01.

4. Judith Warner, Nora Ellmann, and Diana Boesch, "The Women's Leadership Gap," *Center for American Progress*, November 20, 2018, https://www.americanprogress.org/issues/women/reports/2018/11/20/461273/womens-leadership-gap-2/.

5. Bureau of labor Statistics, "Highlights of Women's Earnings in 2017," August 2018, https://www.bls.gov/opub/reports/womens-earnings/2017/home.htm.

6. Bureau of labor Statistics, "American Time Use Survey—2018 results," June 19, 2019, https://www.bls.gov/news.release/pdf/atus.pdf.

7. Claire Cain Miller, "The Costs of Motherhood Are Rising, and Catching Women Off Guard," *New York Times*, August 17, 2018, https://www.nytimes.com/2018/08/17/upshot/motherhood-rising-costs-surprise.html; Ann Crittenden, *The Price of Motherhood: Why the Most Important Job in the World Is Still the Least Valued* (New York: Henry Holt, 2001).

8. Katherine N. Kinnick, "Media Morality Tales and the Politics of Motherhood," in *Mommy Angst: Motherhood in American Popular Culture*, ed. Ann C. Hall and Mardia J. Bishop (Santa Barbara, Denver, and Oxford: Praeger, 2009), 2.

9. Both of these titles are given to Beth by gangster boss Rio, and this evolution in the way he characterizes her helps to chart her development from demure suburban homemaker in the beginning of the series to a bold and confident criminal operator. His assessment of her as a "basic bitch" in the 2nd season in one episode, "Mo Money Mo Problems," simultaneously trivializes her "ordinary" life while also acknowledging her value as criminal who can avoid law enforcement profiling. This characterization follows a scene where Beth makes a point of

drawing attention to the status of all three women as "regular people" in a desperate attempt to make him think twice about killing them all after discovering that they were unable to return all of the money they had inadvertently stolen from him. She wants to demonstrate that if something bad happens to them, people will care because it will mean it could happen to anyone and that will bring attention on him that he does not want. She resists the term "basic bitch" but is still grateful that the opportunity provided by her "basic" identity ultimately saves her life. The shift in Rio's assessment of Beth, to "boss bitch" comes in the second season and functions as an indicator of her increasing independence and the shedding of her ideals of domestic femininity. Although it is evidently a marker of his appreciation, the use of the term *bitch* in the show must be viewed critically. As the term "basic bitch" is often used as yet another way to denigrate traditional femininity, the program must take some responsibility for the messaging implied by its unreflective usage. There is a suggestion that being all the things that the term "basic bitch" denigrates (in the series it is the life of the suburban homemaker) is a bad thing, while being a "boss bitch" is a good thing—even if it requires one to become a criminal.

10. Unfortunately, due to the limited scope of this paper, both Nancy, Annie's ex's new wife, and Mary Pat, a welfare mom from the neighborhood, could not be discussed. The parallels between Beth's and Mary Pat's storylines, especially in moral terms, might bear fruitful results in further studies, however.

11. Jacqueline Rose, *Mothers: An Essay on Love and Cruelty* (London: Faber & Faber, 2018), 1.

12. Sarah Jane Glynn, "Breadwinning Mothers Continue to Be the U.S. Norm," *Center for American Progress*, May 10, 2019, https://www.americanprogress.org/issues/women/reports/2019/05/10/469739/breadwinning-mothers-continue-u-s-norm/.

13. Kim Parker, "Women More Than Men Adjust Their Careers for Family Life," *Pew Research Center*, October 1, 2015, https://www.pewresearch.org/fact-tank/2015/10/01/women-more-than-men-adjust-their-careers-for-family-life/.

14. Kinnick, "Media Morality Tales," 3, 23.

15. Katie Milestone and Anneke Meyer, *Gender and Popular Culture* (Cambridge: Polity Press, 2012), 105.

16. Stephanie Lawler, *Mothering the Self: Mothers, Daughters, Subjects* (London and New York: Routledge, 2000), 153; Milestone and Meyer, *Gender and Popular Culture*, 106.

17. Sharon Hays, *The Cultural Contradictions of Motherhood* (New Haven: Yale University Press, 1996), 4.

18. Frank Furedi, *Paranoid Parenting: Why Ignoring the Experts May Be Best for Your Child* (Chicago: Chicago Review Press, 2002).

19. Susan J. Douglas and Meredith W. Michaels, *The Mommy Myth: The Idealization of Motherhood and How It Has Undermined All Women* (New York: Free Press, 2005), 4.

20. Judith Warner, *Perfect Madness: Motherhood in the Age of Anxiety* (London: Vermillion 2006), 33.

21. Ann C. Hall and Mardia J. Bishop, "Introduction," in *Mommy Angst: Motherhood in American Popular Culture*, ed. Ann C. Hall and Mardia J. Bishop (Santa Barbara, Denver, and Oxford: Praeger, 2009), x; E. Ann Kaplan, *Motherhood and Representation: The Mother in Popular Culture and Melodrama* (London: Routledge, 1992); Kinnick, "Media Morality Tales," 8.

22. Hall and Bishop, "Introduction"; Kinnick, "Media Morality Tales," 3–4.

23. Kinnick, "Media Morality Tales," 3, 10.

24. Kathleen K. Rowe, "*Roseanne*: Unruly Woman as Domestic Goddess," *Screen* 31, no. 4 (Winter, 1990).

25. Beverley Skeggs, Nancy Thumim, and Helen Wood, "It's Just Sad: Affect, Judgement and Emotional labor in Reality TV Viewing," in *Domesticity, Feminism and Popular Culture*, eds. Joanne Hollows and Stacy Gillis (London: Routledge, 2008), 145, quoted in Rebecca Feasey, *From Happy Homemaker to Desperate Housewives: Motherhood and Popular Television* (London and New York: Anthem Press, 2012), 180.

26. Hall and Bishop, "Introduction," ix; Kinnick, "Media Morality Tales," 4–6.

27. Kinnick, "Media Morality Tales," 9.

28. *Good Girls*, season 1, episode 1, "Pilot," directed by Dean Parisot, aired February 28, 2018, on NBC, https://www.netflix.com.
29. *Good Girls*, season 1, episode 1, "Pilot," directed by Dean Parisot, aired February 28, 2018, on NBC, https://www.netflix.com.
30. *Good Girls*, season 1, episode 3, "Borderline," directed by Kenneth Fink, aired March 12, 2018, on NBC, https://www.netflix.com.
31. *Good Girls*, season 1, episode 6, "A View from the Top," directed by So Yong Kim, aired April 2, 2018, on NBC, https://www.netflix.com.
32. *Good Girls*, season 1, episode 2, "Mo Money, Mo Problems," directed by Alberto Del Rey, aired March 5, 2018, on NBC, https://www.netflix.com.
33. *Good Girls*, season 1, episode 2, "Mo Money, Mo Problems," directed by Alberto Del Rey, aired March 5, 2018, on NBC, https://www.netflix.com.
34. *Good Girls*, season 2, episode 4, "Pick Your Poison," directed by Phil Traill, aired March 24, 2019, on NBC, https://www.netflix.com.
35. *Good Girls*, season 1, episode 8, "Shutdown," directed by Nzingha Stewart, aired April 16, 2018, on NBC, https://www.netflix.com.
36. *Good Girls*, season 1, episode 9, "Summer of the Shark," directed by Michael Weaver, aired April 23, 2018, on NBC, https://www.netflix.com.
37. *Good Girls*, season 2, episode 10, "This Land Is Your Land," directed by Lee Friedlander, aired May 5, 2019, on NBC, https://www.netflix.com.
38. Kinnick, "Media Morality Tales," 9.
39. *Good Girls*, season 2, episode 1, "I'd Rather Be Crafting," directed by Michael Weaver, aired March 3, 2019, on NBC, https://www.netflix.com.
40. *Good Girls*, season 2, episode 7, "The Dubby," directed by So Yong Kim, aired April 14, 2019, on NBC, https://www.netflix.com.
41. *Good Girls* (S2, E10), "This Land Is Your Land."
42. Kinnick, "Media Morality Tales," 13.
43. *Good Girls* (S2, E7), "The Dubby."
44. *Good Girls* (S2, E10), "This Land Is Your Land."
45. *Good Girls* (S2, E10), "This Land Is Your Land."
46. *Good Girls* (S2, E10), "This Land Is Your Land."
47. *Good Girls* (S2, E7), "The Dubby."
48. *Good Girls* (S2, E7), "The Dubby."
49. *Good Girls* (S2, E9), "Summer of the Shark."
50. Milestone and Meyer, *Gender and Popular Culture*, 106–7.
51. Susan Faludi, *Backlash: The Undeclared War against American Women* (New York: Crown, 1991), 82, 97; Kinnick, "Media Morality Tales," 6–11.
52. Kinnick, "Media Morality Tales," 8, 11, 13.
53. Kinnick, "Media Morality Tales," 6.
54. Kinnick, "Media Morality Tales," 4.
55. Kinnick, "Media Morality Tales," 3–4.
56. Kinnick, "Media Morality Tales," 3.
57. *Good Girls*, season 2, episode 11, "Hunting Season," directed by Jenna Lamia, aired May 12, 2019, on NBC, https://www.netflix.com.
58. Hall and Bishop, "Introduction," xiv.
59. Li, "*Good Girls* Is a Rewarding Show."

BIBLIOGRAPHY

Baldwin, Kristen. "*Good Girls* Is a Gentler, Girlier *Breaking Bad:* EW Review." *Entertainment Weekly*, February 9, 2018. https://ew.com/tv/2018/02/09/good-girls-nbc-review/.
Bureau of labor Statistics. "American Time Use Survey—2018 results." Accessed June 19, 2019. https://www.bls.gov/news.release/pdf/atus.pdf.
———. "Highlights of women's earnings in 2017." Accessed November 1, 2019. https://www.bls.gov/opub/reports/womens-earnings/2017/home.htm.

Cain Miller, Claire. "The Costs of Motherhood Are Rising, and Catching Women Off Guard." *New York Times*, August 17, 2018. https://www.nytimes.com/2018/08/17/upshot/motherhood-rising-costs-surprise.html.

Crittenden, Ann. *The Price of Motherhood: Why the Most Important Job in the World Is Still the Least Valued*. New York: Henry Holt, 2001.

Desperate Housewives. Season 1, episode 8, "Guilty." Directed by Fred Gerber. Aired on November 28, 2004, on ABC. https://www.primevideo.com.

Dockterman, Eliana. "*Good Girls* Is the Perfect Show for this Moment." *Time*, February 26, 2018. https://time.com/5163688/good-girls-nbc-review/.

Douglas, Susan J. and Meredith W. Michaels. *The Mommy Myth: The Idealization of Motherhood and How It Has Undermined All Women*. New York: Free Press, 2005.

Faludi, Susan. *Backlash: The Undeclared War against American Women*. New York: Crown, 1991.

Feasey, Rebecca. *From Happy Homemaker to Desperate Housewives: Motherhood and Popular Television*. London & New York: Anthem Press, 2012.

Furedi, Frank. *Paranoid Parenting: Why Ignoring the Experts May Be Best for Your Child*. Chicago: Chicago Review Press, 2002.

Glynn, Sarah Jane. "Breadwinning Mothers Continue to Be the U.S. Norm." *Center for American Progress*, May 10, 2019. https://www.americanprogress.org/issues/women/reports/2019/05/10/469739/breadwinning-mothers-continue-u-s-norm/.

Good Girls. Season 1 and 2. Created by Jenna Bans. Aired 2018–2019, on ABC. https://www.netflix.com.

Hall, Ann C. and Mardia J. Bishop. "Introduction." In *Mommy Angst: Motherhood in American Popular Culture*, edited by Ann C. Hall and Mardia J. Bishop, ix–xvii. Santa Barbara, Denver, and Oxford: Praeger, 2009.

Hays, Sharon. *The Cultural Contradictions of Motherhood*. New Haven: Yale University Press, 1996.

Kinnick, Katherine N. "Media Morality Tales and the Politics of Motherhood." In *Mommy Angst: Motherhood in American Popular Culture*, edited by Ann C. Hall and Mardia J. Bishop, 1–28. Santa Barbara, Denver, and Oxford: Praeger, 2009.

Lawler, Stephanie. *Mothering the Self: Mothers, Daughters, Subjects*. London and New York: Routledge, 2000.

Li, Shirley. "Why *Good Girls* Is Such a Rewarding Show." *The Atlantic*, May 24, 2019. https://www.theatlantic.com/entertainment/archive/2019/05/good-girls-nbc-season-2-christina-hendricks/590173/.

Milestone, Katie, and Anneke Meyer. *Gender and Popular Culture*, Polity Press, 2012.

Parker, Kim. "Women More Than Men Adjust Their Careers for Family Life." *Pew Research Center*, October 1, 2015. https://www.pewresearch.org/fact-tank/2015/10/01/women-more-than-men-adjust-their-careers-for-family-life/.

Rose, Jacqueline. *Mothers: An Essay on Love and Cruelty*. London: Faber & Faber, 2018.

Rotten Tomatoes. "Good Girls: Season 1." Accessed October 15, 2019. https://www.rottentomatoes.com/tv/good_girls/s01.

Rowe, Kathleen K. "*Roseanne*: Unruly Woman as Domestic Goddess." *Screen* 31, no. 4 (Winter 1990): 408–19.

Skeggs, Beverley, Nancy Thumim, and Helen Wood. "It's Just Sad: Affect, Judgement and Emotional labor in Reality TV Viewing." In *Domesticity, Feminism and Popular Culture*, edited by Joanne Hollows and Stacy Gillis, 135–50. London: Routledge, 2008.

Warner, Judith. *Perfect Madness: Motherhood in the Age of Anxiety*. London: Vermillion, 2006.

Warner, Judith, Nora Ellmann, and Diana Boesch. "The Women's Leadership Gap." *Center for American Progress*, November 20, 2018. https://www.americanprogress.org/issues/women/reports/2018/11/20/461273/womens-leadership-gap-2/.

Chapter Two

Challenging Cultural Attitudes to Maternal Ambivalence through Antiheroines in *The Americans* and *Homeland*

Brenda Boudreau

As books such as *Mediated Moms: Contemporary Challenges to the Mother-hood Myth* and *The Mommy Myth: The Idealization of Motherhood and How It Has Undermined All Women* make clear, the intensive mothering ideology that tells mothers that they must put their children's needs before their own and suggest that mothers cannot be fully satisfied or fulfilled without lavish-ing excessive time and energy on their children has left many mothers feeling inadequate and incompetent.[1] Thus, as Susan Douglas and Meredith Mi-chaels note, "new momism" is "the insistence that no woman is truly com-plete or fulfilled unless she has kids" and "to be a remotely decent mother, a woman has to devote her entire physical, psychological, emotional and intel-lectual being, 24/7 to her children."[2] Cable television, in particular, has tried to challenge this romanticized view by giving us heroines who are "flawed yet authentic professionals struggling with family commitments and occupa-tional demands."[3] Thus, shows like *Nurse Jackie*, *Weeds*, and *The Killing* explore female characters that some critics called antiheroines, given their willingness to break laws and social norms to get what they want. These characters were judged much more harshly than their male antihero counter-parts such as Anthony Soprano and Walter White, largely because, for many of these women, their antiheroism stemmed, at least in part, from their failure to be good mothers.

I would like to suggest that two recent cable series give us antiheroines who more explicitly challenge our cultural anxieties about motherhood in the twenty-first century because they foreground maternal ambivalence and give us characters who are the antithesis of idealized mothers. Both Carrie Mathison in *Homeland* (Claire Danes) and Elizabeth Jennings (Keri Russell) in *The Americans* have been judged by many viewers for their lack of intensive mothering, and both frequently made the "Worst Mothers on Television" lists (even as they showed up on the "Most Badass" lists).[4] Elizabeth and Carrie also, however, continue a recent trend in television and film that give us complicated characters who exemplify the "aberrant mother " defined by Suzanna Danuta Walters and Laura Harrison: "Neither monster nor angel, this aberrant mom is not quite a twenty-first-century feminist heroine but she does upend more traditional depictions of maternal identity. Unabashedly sexual, idiosyncratic to a fault, and seriously deleterious in her caretaking skills, she seems to live largely in the high end of popular culture."[5] Throughout their respective series, Carrie and Elizabeth struggle with being women spies while also being mothers, often doing the latter with a large amount of resentment and incompetence. Ultimately both characters decide that children are secondary to their roles as spies. I would argue that both characters remain beloved antiheroines not only *in spite of* their maternal ambivalence but *because* of it.

Both of these women feel like they have a patriotic destiny to help protect their countries (Russia for Elizabeth and the United States for Carrie), and a firm (and justified) belief that they can do so more effectively than many of the others around them. Their hyper-confidence is both a blessing and a curse for the two women, but overall, the narrative arcs of both series suggest that Carrie and Elizabeth are uniquely qualified to protect their countries. They are intelligent, intuitive, fearless, and fully capable of physically protecting themselves and others around them; more importantly, they are willing to sacrifice their own psychological well-being or even physical safety for a mission's success. Their relationship with their children, however, is far more complicated. Neither one actively sought out motherhood based on some internal desire or need, and their children are often seen as obstacles to their work. When push comes to shove, it is motherhood that is relegated to the back burner when Carrie and Elizabeth believe they must act in the best interest of their government and their country.

Carrie and Elizabeth, then, become antiheroines at least in part because of their maternal ambivalence. As Margaret Tally notes, "The antiheroine that has arisen on popular television shows is a deeply flawed, yet at the same time, sympathetic character. She is one who is neither uniformly good nor evil, but has qualities that mark her as being capable of doing bad things for good reasons."[6] This strikes me as particularly true, as both series grapple with the ambivalent motherhood of two professional women who ultimately choose to privilege their jobs, despite the negative judgment they receive for how these choices affect their children. Given the roles they play for their countries, however, they are "justified in their depravity."[7] I argue that these characters give a normalizing voice to the idea of maternal ambivalence and the conflicted, and even irreconcilable, feelings mothers sometimes have for their children. These series reflect what Milly Buonanno has said about the appeal of liminality in antiheroines whom we root for, despite their moral failings: "[L]iminal spaces and figures resist traditionally held dichotomies; in doing so, they cooperate to problematize and call into question dichotomous thinking and binary assumptions, thus displaying a potential for change."[8] By closely examining Carrie and Elizabeth's maternal ambivalence, we can see what Margarthe Bruun Vaage calls the "potential of the antiheroine to question the gendered order of things and undermine more normative representations of womanhood in popular culture."[9]

THE AMERICANS

In the pilot of *The Americans*, we are introduced to Elizabeth and Philip Jennings, undercover Russian spies living in a Washington, DC, suburb in a large, beautiful house and raising two pre-teen children while working as travel agents. At night, however, Philip and Elizabeth become spies who will cheat, lie, steal, and even kill in an effort to gain intelligence for their country. *The Americans* is based on the real-life arrest of Russian sleeper agents in 2011, when the CIA uncovered several spies who had been sent to the United States to live as Americans while simultaneously collecting information on government agencies and academic institutions. Joe Weisberg, the creator of the show, decided to set the series in the 1980s at a time when the Cold War and anti-Russian sentiment was much more pronounced.[10] Philip and Elizabeth are involved in extremely dangerous (and often violent) operations assigned to them by The Center, a shadowy network of KGB "handlers" who give them assignments that they must perform without question or hesitation.

We find out in the very first episode that Elizabeth was recruited by the KGB to be a Russian agent when she was sixteen years old and went through extensive combat training. We also find out in a flashback that Elizabeth was raped by her commanding officer Timoshev while training. Showing Elizabeth as psychologically damaged colors how the audience responds to her in subsequent seasons because she is often cold and distant with both her husband and children. Elizabeth left Russia for the United States with her mother's blessing at the age of twenty-two, knowing she would likely never see her mother again. Elizabeth comes to the United States in 1965 with Philip Jennings (Matthew Rhys), though they know virtually nothing about each other. Their KGB officers invent complicated lives for each of them, and they are not allowed to speak of their Russian pasts or real lives, even with each other. In order to be successful spies, they have to assimilate and live a "normal" American life as "real" Americans. Elizabeth's entire life is built on a façade of a conventional family, and she and Philip end up with one daughter, born in 1967 and one son, born in 1970, and together the couple own and operate their own business, a travel agency. The travel agency is the perfect screen for their frequent quick departures and extended absences. During the first five seasons, both Philip and Elizabeth are involved in extremely risky undercover missions, most of which happen at night. They take turns staying with the children in the house, although it is not long before they are both absent overnight, leaving their daughter Paige to assume supervision of her brother and the household.

Throughout the series, Elizabeth is given extremely dangerous missions which could lead to her arrest and even death, but she is fearless. We see her engage in hand to hand combat on several occasions, and she is unflinching when she needs to kill someone, male or female, often having to do so spontaneously when something goes awry with a mission. She is also willing to suffer any pain necessary to protect the mission. At the end of season 1, for example, she takes a bullet in the side without her children ever suspecting that something is wrong (Philip and Elizabeth explain her absence from home by telling the kids that she has to care for a sickly aunt).[11] In a later episode in season 3, Elizabeth injures a tooth when she gets into a physical fight with two FBI agents. Knowing that the FBI is looking for someone matching her description and with her injuries, Elizabeth submits to Philip pulling out a tooth with pliers, with only a shot of whiskey to deaden the pain.[12] Elizabeth is almost machine-like in her ability to continue to move through their "normal" days without complaint or divulging how she is feeling physically or emotionally, even to Philip. Initially, she is unquestioning in the assignments she is given by The Center and trusts that contributing to the greater good of her country will negate any morally questionable actions she is asked to take.

It is not only her loyalty to Russia (which presumably comes at the expense of the United States) that makes Elizabeth an antiheroine, however, but the way she treats her role as a mother. Elizabeth is not cruel or unkind to her children when the series first opens, but she is decidedly emotionally distant. Being a wife and mother is central to the identity that Elizabeth has adopted as part of her cover, and part of her "performance" is what that means in the United States, specifically. For Elizabeth, parenting is influenced by her own austere and difficult childhood in Russia, and she sees her own children as spoiled Americans who have no idea how difficult life can be outside of their comfortable middle-class lives. When Paige talks back to her one night, Elizabeth snaps; "Do you know what my mother would have done if I had talked to her like that? You get to dress how you want, use the phone, watch TV. You do NOT get to speak to me like that."[13] Elizabeth's parenting is centered almost entirely in the kitchen, with her preparing breakfast, lunch, and dinner, and often rushing to get the children off to school or dinner wrapped up so she can disappear for the evening on a spy mission. If she and Philip cannot be home because of "work," she leaves a casserole of some sort for Paige and Henry to reheat, and the family scenes are almost all set at the kitchen table, eating either breakfast or dinner. Elizabeth provides for her children, but clearly has a hard time opening up to them or expressing emotion, and there is rarely a demonstration of physical touching or affection of the kind Philip shares with his children. Indeed, she often seems surprised by the fact that Paige and Henry are maturing and changing as they get older, and seems shocked, for example, when she finds a bra that Paige has bought for herself at the mall.[14] Elizabeth's way of connecting with Paige, then, is to offer to pierce Paige's ears with a needle, the same way hers had been done by her mother. This is one of many scenes in which Elizabeth connects to her lost mother through her daughter, which might explain why so much of Elizabeth's attention focuses on Paige.

It is no surprise that it is Philip, not Elizabeth, who starts to question what their assignments from The Center ask them to do and the effect they may have on their children. As their jobs become increasingly dangerous, Philip and Elizabeth are forced to more directly confront what might happen to their children if they are killed or arrested. Elizabeth certainly worries about what will happen to Paige and Henry if she and Philip are arrested or killed, but unlike Philip, she is unwilling to let that fear ever get in the way of her job. Elizabeth's hierarchy is Russia, Philip, and then her children, and she repeatedly says that she will not betray her country under any circumstances, even for her children. When Philip suggests in the first season that they turn themselves over to the Americans and disappear, Elizabeth is adamantly opposed and incredulous that Philip would even consider turning his back on what she sees as a moral obligation to serve their country.[15] This is not to say that Elizabeth does not love her children, but she seems very matter-of-fact in acknowledging that Philip is the better parent. At the end of season 1, when Philip and Elizabeth are convinced that their cover is going to be blown, they arrange an escape plan, and Elizabeth insists that Philip has to be the one to take the children to Canada if things go badly in their mission. He tries to argue that the children need their mother, but Elizabeth doesn't back down: "I know what you're trying to do, but listen to me. If one of us is going down, and one us is staying with the kids, Philip, after everything—it should be you. . . . I want it to be you. You're the one they want—the one they understand."[16] This kind of scene will repeat itself throughout the series, but I think it shows Elizabeth's pragmatism. Philip is more comfortable with the lives they are living in the United States, and he does seem better equipped to be an American parent, given Elizabeth's understanding of what that means.

Paige is the child who seems to struggle most with her parents' absences. She is self-motivated to do her homework and driven to get good grades and accepts responsibility for her brother when she is asked to do so. She also seems like a lonely teenager, and one who is trying to figure out who she is without the help of involved parents. This is, of course, part of the reason she is so drawn to Pastor Tim and his wife Alice when she starts going to church and helping out with other church members in the homeless shelter. They spend time asking Paige questions about herself in ways that her parents never do and see a uniqueness in her personality that her parents seem oblivious to. Paige is sensitive and interested in helping others in need, but she is also searching for parental figures. As she becomes older, Paige starts to seriously question her parents' secretive behaviors and strange overnight trips, speculating that they might both be having an affair and convinced that they are lying to her. She finds her mother in the basement doing laundry in the middle of the night or finds her parents' bed unmade in the morning, anomalies that make no sense to her. Henry, on the other hand, seems completely unconcerned by his parents' strange, unscheduled absences and accepts how little they are involved in his life.

Henry is often at the periphery of the action during the series, since he is clueless about his parents' roles as spies and ignorant to the lie they are living. When he does try to get their attention to show them his computer games, both Philip and Elizabeth are dismissive. Clearly there is an emotional void, however, given how he develops a surrogate friend/father relationship with Stan Beeman, the FBI agent who lives across the street. By the fifth season, Henry is hardly ever in the house, and there is very little concern expressed by Philip or Elizabeth about where he might be or who the new people he is hanging out with are.

When Elizabeth and Philip finally decide to tell Paige in season 3 the watered-down truth about being Russian spies, Henry is marginalized even more. When a teacher calls to report that Henry is doing extremely well in math and asks permission to move him into an advanced algebra class, both Philip and Elizabeth are genuinely shocked. Later in the car, an incredulous Elizabeth says, "I thought he spent all his time playing video games." When Philip and Elizabeth confront him, Henry is clearly insulted.[17] The fact that they are so out of touch with their son and what he is doing reinforces for Henry how little his parents actually pay attention to him. This contributes, no doubt, to his desire to go away to boarding school with some of his friends, which Philip and Elizabeth eventually allow him to do. Henry is very matter of fact about his mother's lack of emotional attachment to him and assumes that emotional distance is just part of who his mother is.

When the Center decides they want to start grooming the sixteen-year-old Paige to be a second-generation spy in season 3, Philip is vehemently opposed, while Elizabeth is quick to latch onto the idea. From Elizabeth's perspective, Paige is the by-product of the long-range mission she and Philip have been engaged in and bringing in an American-born child makes logical sense to her. She holds onto this rationalization even when Philip tries to guilt her into imagining Paige doing the morally reprehensible things he and Elizabeth are often asked to do by The Center. For Elizabeth, however, the sacrifices Paige will be asked to make seem far less than what she herself made when she left Russia and never saw her mother again; bringing Paige into their spying is a way for Elizabeth to challenge the spoiling of her children that she has felt compelled to do as an "American" parent in terms of consumer goods and the lack of demands they have put on Paige and Henry. If Elizabeth believes in the nobility of her mission in the United States as much as she professes to do throughout the series, it makes sense that she would want to bring her daughter into the cause. She introduces Paige to their KGB handler, Claudia, and starts introducing Paige to Russian television, food, and culture.[18] She justifies her actions to Philip by saying that Paige will now have something concrete to believe in and a tangible way to react to injustice that goes beyond a protest march, but in truth, Elizabeth wants to be loyal to her own mother who had unhesitatingly told the sixteen-year-old Elizabeth that she had a duty to serve her country.

Elizabeth sees the world as a vicious place that is often unfair, and she seems to genuinely believe that by exposing Paige to this truth she is helping Paige to grow up and become more resilient. One night when she and Paige are accosted in a parking lot by two men, one of whom has a knife, Elizabeth goes into badass mode, and ends up killing one of them with his own knife.[19] Paige is terrified for weeks after, at least in part by the fact that her mother shows no remorse or sign of traumatization from the event, so much so that she starts having nightmares and sleeping in the closet. Elizabeth begins to teach Paige self-defense moves, but she tells Philip privately, "I'm sick of treating her like a goddamn kid."[20] She wants Paige to be strong and more like Elizabeth herself, who will not allow herself to be destroyed by adversity.

Elizabeth also seems unsympathetic to what becoming a spy will mean for Paige in terms of her personal relationships; but again, for Elizabeth, the cause always trumps any discomfort or pain it might cause an agent, even if it's her own daughter. When Paige starts dating Matthew Beeman, the FBI agent Stan's son, Philip and Elizabeth are most worried that she will eventually have sex with him, something that Elizabeth says, "muddies the water" and might make Paige slip up and reveal something about her family. They decide to teach Paige some techniques for keeping her emotions in check in order to remain in control of a situation. When Paige protests by asking, "For the rest of my life I have to be fake with my boyfriends?" Elizabeth answers, "It's not fake. You hold back what you need to. Everybody does."[21] For Elizabeth, lying and manipulating are part of her skill set, and she imagines that she is helping Paige navigate the world.

One of Elizabeth's espionage techniques over the six seasons is her ability to make people trust her, often manipulating them to do her bidding with the promise of friendship, romance, or sex. She begins working the psychological angle with Paige in such a way that Paige wants to join her parents, even though she doesn't fully understand what it is that they do. Being jumped has made Paige want to be able to defend herself physically in the same way her mother did. In truth, if Elizabeth had not had the hidden abilities she had when she and Paige were accosted in the dark lot, they would have, no doubt, been robbed and probably been physically or sexually assaulted. Elizabeth later confesses to Paige that she was raped when she was eighteen during her training, and the way that she dealt with the trauma was to train herself well enough to know that nobody could ever hurt her again. [22] This might make Elizabeth seem manipulative, but learning self-defense does empower Paige.

It becomes harder and harder as the series progresses to know whether Elizabeth is being sincere with her daughter or if she is still actively "training" her for possible co-option into becoming a Russian spy herself. For example, she starts volunteering at the soup kitchen with Paige to try and demonstrate her own interest in social justice, and she takes Paige to what Paige calls a "bad neighborhood" and tells her that she and Philip were involved in a Civil Rights movement, knowing that this will inspire her daughter. [23] Elizabeth seems sincere in her desire to give her daughter to believe in something, to feel that she can make a difference in the world, but Paige does not have a loyalty to another country and she does not have the intrinsic motivation that her parents would have to work for Russia, so her commitment to training seems more motivated by wanting validation from her mother.

Elizabeth never waivers in her sense of responsibility to the cause, although her family clearly is beginning to come to the forefront of her consideration. Surprisingly in season 4, when she thinks she may have been exposed to a toxic poison, her first thought is of Paige and Henry and she tells Philip to bring them up in the United States as Americans, presumably releasing Paige from her training. [24] When Philip decides he can't be involved with The Center anymore in season 5, he is allowed to pull out, but it leaves Elizabeth more vulnerable, both literally and emotionally. He expands the travel agency business while Elizabeth gets more and more involved in dangerous missions that begin taking a psychological toll on her. She is clearly resentful that Philip does not have the responsibilities she does and is not suffering from the weight of what she is being asked to do. Elizabeth's missions in the final two seasons become increasingly dangerous and violent, and she kills several people on her own. She loses weight, stops sleeping, and starts smoking constantly, becoming more and more emotionally distant from Philip.

When Elizabeth receives orders from The Center to rescue a Russian operative in Chicago, she decides to leave immediately, despite how it might look to Stan Beeman, who has invited them for Thanksgiving dinner. When Philip tries to tell her that he thinks they need to talk about what's going on between them—not to let "bad feelings fester," Elizabeth lashes back at him: "You can take your foreign bullshit and shove it up your ass. One of us is in trouble in Chicago. I'm going there to help him. One of us who's still doing his job. One of us who still gives a shit."[25] It's unclear whether Elizabeth feels resentful or betrayed that Philip has abandoned their spying partnership, but she does call him from Chicago and essentially asks him to come and help her when things start to go wrong with the mission, which he does. When he has to cut the hands and head off a dead Russian operative to mask her identity, Elizabeth sees the terrible toll that being a spy has taken on Philip and she vows to make sure he stays out.[26] At this point, her loyalty is 100 percent to her country, though, and she goes to see Paige to tell her she needs to decide if this is a commitment she is ready to make, knowing she may not have friends and relationships: "Your father—he made a mistake when he committed to this life. He was young. If you do this, it has to be forever. That's the kind of work it is. It's okay if this isn't what you want."[27] Paige says yes, although, clearly, it is her mother's approval she is seeking. There is an irony in Elizabeth's persistence in bringing Paige into the espionage given what she has seen it do to Philip over the years—and, for that matter, to herself.

Paige starts to ask more questions as she takes on more responsibility working with various assignments from The Center and as she tries to imagine her life as a Russian spy. Paige's moral compass is far more pronounced than her mother's, and she wonders if sex will be a tool she will be expected to utilize in her spying efforts. In fact, when she finally realizes that her mother does, in fact, use sex to manipulate potential collaborators or dupes, Paige is horrified and calls her mother a whore: "How many times? How many men? Were you doing this when I was a baby? You're a whore. Does Dad know he married a whore?"[28] Elizabeth is unapologetic, however: "I wasn't brought up like you were. I had to fight . . . for everything. We were proud to do whatever we could. Sex. What was sex? Nobody cared. Including your father."[29] Philip is fully aware that she has sex with other men (as does he with female agents), and he is often listening in on these encounters. For Paige, Elizabeth has betrayed her role as Paige's mother by having sex with strangers, and it is this realization that is somehow worse than anything she has realized about her mother's job up to that point. Ironically, Paige never once questions if her father did the same thing. If anything, Paige's accusations are so rooted in normative definitions of femininity that she comes across as naive and judgmental and ill-suited to follow in her mother's footsteps.

In the last two seasons, Elizabeth starts to more explicitly question The Center's orders and to rebel against them. She feels remorse for the false friendships she creates in efforts to get information, and for the betrayals she has to effect to get the information she needs. Indeed, she even kills another KGB officer who has been assigned to assassinate a delegate to the United States—Gorbachev summit when she realizes that The Center does not want Gorbachev to negotiate a nuclear deal with the Americans.[30] Elizabeth suddenly realizes that The Center does not necessarily represent her country and her countrymen, and it's a devastating loss for her, but one she is willing to throw away in order to do what she believes is right. It also, however, reinforces the reasons audiences have rooted for her over the years, even though she was an enemy spy inside foreign territory fighting against the United States: we have respected, on some level, the moral imperative that pushed her to sacrifice both herself and her children to a higher cause.

By the end of the final season when Stan Beeman and the FBI starts closing in, it seems telling that Elizabeth's first response is to pick up Paige and Henry and head for the Canadian border. Philip, however, is the one who insists that they have to leave Henry behind. Paige comes with them as far as the Canadian border and then gets off the train before they can stop her, presumably cutting ties to her parents forever.[31] Elizabeth's expression is the rawest and devastated we have seen throughout the six seasons. She really has lost everything at this point—her children and her connection to The Center. She is returning to Russia without a sense of purpose; although Philip is by her side, she has irrevocably lost Paige and Henry, and it's a loss that seems deep and genuine as she asks Philip if he thinks their children will remember them.

HOMELAND

Like Elizabeth, Carrie Mathison is also a deeply patriotic female operative, although her role in the CIA is no secret and she appears initially as a heroine fighting for the safety of the United States. After receiving an Arabic language degree from Princeton, she is recruited into the CIA in 1999 at the young age of twenty and quickly becomes a key agent in the organization. Post 9/11, Carrie fought with Homeland Security to prevent another attack on American soil, a role that makes her heroic. However, like Elizabeth, Carrie also carries secrets—although hers are much more connected to the bipolar disorder she has been secretly treating for years under the care of her sister and doctor, Maggie. Convinced that this kind of mental illness will seriously jeopardize her career as a CIA agent, Maggie monitors Carrie's medications and prescribes the drugs that Carrie needs in order to function. Carrie is intelligent, driven, brave, and capable of defending herself, but unlike Elizabeth, she is also hyper-emotional and prone to reacting without thinking based on these emotions.

Carrie's illness is ironically what allows her to be particularly good at her job; the series suggests that in her manic phases she is able to put together puzzle pieces in cases and make connections that she might not otherwise be able to do, although there is a fine line between manic and psychotic as Carrie knows well during the course of the series. During the seven seasons of the series she has had several psychotic breaks that required her to be hospitalized and she has received electroshock therapy twice. There have been many critics who have written on the problematic alignment between Carrie's mental acuity and expertise in her job and her mental illness.[32]

Despite any obstacles her illness presents, however, Carrie's obsessive focus on her missions make her an excellent agent. Even in the first two seasons, Carrie thinks about her body as a tool to be used to complete her missions, much like Elizabeth does. When Carrie suspects that Nicholas Brody, a returned prisoner of war held by al-Qaeda terrorists for eight years, might have been turned against his country while in captivity, she begins an aggressive surveillance of him and his family. When that investigation is shut down, she doesn't hesitate to manipulate the situation to begin an affair with him. Carrie starts developing feelings for Brody, even as she seriously questions whether he could potentially be planning a terrorist act against the United States.[33]

When Carrie finally admits halfway through in season 3 that she is pregnant with Brody's child, Carrie's ambivalence starts showing itself immediately. She has known she was pregnant given the dozens of pregnancy tests she used, but she was also clearly in denial, continuing to drink excessively. By this point, Brody has been exonerated, and he has joined the CIA for a covert operation in Iran. When he is captured and executed in front of her in Iran, Carrie decides to have the baby, partly, perhaps because of her grief, and also as a way to honor Brody.[34] She goes to see a gynecologist who tells her she has a clear image of the baby, although throughout the appointment, Carrie seems apathetic and a little freaked out. When she confesses that she had been drinking heavily in the last few months, the doctor is clearly disgusted: "Even though you knew?"[35] When Carrie says she hasn't exactly been "painting a nursery" the doctor jumps to conclusions: "Are you telling me you want to terminate?" When Carrie says no, the doctor tells Carrie that her iron is low and her blood pressure is high, and that Carrie is going to have to change the way she's living—"You're not on your own anymore."[36] The doctor is judgmental and completely dismissive of the idea that Carrie might feel ambivalent about having a baby.

Carrie is shamed repeatedly and more frequently than Elizabeth ever was in *The Americans*, perhaps because her life is far less secretive. Herein is the rub, however. There is an assumption by literally everyone around her that being pregnant brings with it some kind of natural maternal inclination, which Carrie absolutely refuses. She doesn't want to see the ultrasound, she doesn't want to prepare a nursery, and she most definitely does not want to imagine a different life for herself, something her family and colleagues find incomprehensible. She is not in denial, since she has decided to have the baby, but she is also certain that she does not want to keep it. She admits to her partner, Peter Quinn, when she is offered a high-ranking position in Istanbul that she firmly believes that she cannot be a mother with her job and her mental illness. When Quinn tries to express his reservations, Carrie answers, "I'll be a great station chief. I'm fearless, obsessed, ruthless if I have to be, all reasons I can't. . . ." Again, Carrie is cut off by Quinn who tells her that the baby is a gift and he doesn't want to see her "fuck it up."[37] Carrie, however, is motivated by her own ambition and belief that she can affect real change within the CIA.

Carrie then makes a decision that she is going to give the baby up for adoption, finally realizing that a baby will dramatically impact her career in the CIA. When she announces this decision to her father and sister, however, they are adamant that she can't do so. Her father somewhat mockingly says, "Two tours in Bagdad, and now a baby brings you to your knees?"[38] When he says that he will take the baby himself, Carries asks very seriously, "You would do that?" At this point Maggie jumps in and tells her to wait and see how she feels after the baby is born, assuming that Carrie will feel radically different. Maggie, of course, believes that a maternal instinct is natural and is convinced that Carrie will feel differently after the baby is born: "I think she's going to ground you. Keep you focused . . . be healthy. I think you'll be astonished by all the love you have for her."[39] Maggie doesn't even consider Carrie's honest response that she only feels sad and scared, partly because to do so would make Carrie seem monstrous in Maggie's eyes.

This scene begins a tug of war that will continue over the next four seasons, with Carrie stepping away from her responsibilities and then presumably being pressured to return to them, particularly by her sister. We never actually see Carrie give birth, but instead see her daughter Frannie when Carrie loses her command of the Istanbul station and is sent back to the United States. When Carrie goes to her sister's house upon her return, she clearly hesitates both in the car and at the door. Maggie is passive aggressive throughout this entire exchange when she tries to hand Frannie over to Carrie who is obviously uncomfortable and tells her, "It's no surprise that Dad isn't pitching in as much as he said he would."[40] Maggie's resentment comes to the foreground: "I have my own career. Patients who rely on me. My kids. My husband . . . who I barely talk to by the way. This is not what we agreed. You were going to take her to Istanbul. We were backup. You bring a life into this world, you take responsibility."[41] The irony, of course, is that Carrie *did* try to take responsibility by putting Frannie up for adoption, but it was not a choice she was allowed to make, not in her father's or sister's eyes.

Carrie spends the day with Frannie at Maggie's insistence, but she has no real connection to her daughter, and even tells Frannie that now that her father Brody is gone, she no longer can remember why she had her. After briefly letting Frannie slip beneath the water while giving her a bath, Carrie is shaken but even more convinced that she is not cut out to take care of a child. This episode caused a huge outcry from viewers, some of whom read Carrie's actions as unforgiveable and criticized the show's writers for crossing such a taboo boundary, even wondering if this might finally turn off viewers for good.[42] Other critics, however, applauded the show's willingness to grapple with Carrie's very real postpartum depression: "Despite all of the ambient awareness about maternal mental illness and post-partum, and the horrific headlines that come along with it—the culture of motherhood can be all-consuming."[43] Carrie is given no space to deal with her conflicted feelings toward her daughter. As Orna Dornath notes, there continues to be hostility directed toward mothers who express regret or indifference toward the maternal experience: "Public airing of abhorrent maternal experiences may still be regarded as obscene"; women can be seen as pathological if they try to do so.[44]

When her sister tries to suggest that Carrie is being unfair to her daughter by returning to her job, Carrie very matter-of-factly tells Maggie, "That is where you are wrong. She's better off with you."[45] Maggie is clearly disgusted by Carrie's inability to bond with her daughter: "There's not even a diagnosis for what's wrong with you."[46] Once again, Carrie is painted as monstrous in her refusal to prioritize her daughter's needs over her own.

Throughout the next three seasons, Carrie's career becomes the pendulum on which her relationship with her daughter swings. When something goes awry with her career, she returns to Frannie and tries to fill her maternal role, but it doesn't take much to pull Carrie back into her espionage. When season 5 opens, two years have passed and Carrie is in Germany, living with her daughter and new boyfriend Jonas, and working as security for a German philanthropic company. There is a real sense in the series, I would argue, that Carrie's talents are not being used when she settles into a maternal role, something her old boss Saul articulates: "You needed to leave the CIA, fine, but to go over to the other side. You? What are you atoning for? Keeping America safe? Turning your back on your entire life. You're being naive and stupid, something you never were before."[47] When Carrie realizes that someone is trying to kill her, she sends Frannie back to her sister and gets her boyfriend Jonas to help monitor her while she is off her meds so she doesn't have a psychotic break: "There's this window when you have all this crazy energy but you're still lucid. That's when I did my best work. Took down a major insurgent network in Iraq, I stopped an attack on the state department in DC."[48] Again, it is Carrie's unique personality and illness that will help her save the day, even though it ultimately drives Jonas away. She proceeds to save the city of Berlin from a lethal sarin gas attack, although in the process she has a hand in nearly killing her beloved partner Peter Quinn when she insists doctors bring him out of a coma to find out what he knows, fully aware that it might lead to a cerebral hemorrhage. Like Elizabeth, Carrie puts her country first, over her daughter, her friends and her lovers, which also contributes to her antihero status.

In season 6, Carrie is back in the United States working for a non-profit company and again has Frannie with her, living in a house; although, like the previous season, the idyllic life doesn't last long and again Carrie makes unfortunate choices that threaten her daughter's safety. When she takes the brain damaged Quinn to her apartment to live with her when he refuses to stay in the hospital, she decides to leave Frannie with him until the babysitter gets there.[49] His paranoia snaps and ends with a standoff with the police as they surround the house. Carrie manages to get in and take Quinn down, but shortly thereafter child social service shows up to remove Frannie from the house and Carrie is caught between trying to hold onto her custody of Frannie at the same time as pursuing her CIA role.

In season 7, things finally come to a head between Carrie and her sister. Carrie moves in with Maggie after losing her job in the White House when an unhinged, paranoid president puts several key CIA agents in prison and has some of them killed. While Frannie is in school, Carrie continues to pursue her espionage and does so with increasing paranoia of her own. Maggie is convinced Carrie is sliding back into a psychological breakdown, particularly when she finds receipts that show Carrie is over $38,000 in debt and is carrying cards with different names and aliases.[50] A psychiatrist has made it clear that Carrie has developed a tolerance to her medication and needs to try some other drug, but the only way to do this is by hospitalizing her. Carrie, already in the middle of another case, is not willing to take the time to do this, however, despite her sister's threats to take Frannie away from her, and she makes a contact to start buying drugs on the street.

Carrie once again inadvertently puts her daughter directly in harm's way when she goes to Dante Allen's apartment with Frannie in tow. He is an FBI contact who she strongly suspects of espionage. Carrie decides to have sex with him to gain his trust and get information. Minutes later Saul and the CIA bust down the door to arrest him and an agent picks up a screaming Frannie in the other room.[51] Frannie is clearly traumatized by the incident and Maggie finally decides that she has an obligation as a doctor to protect Frannie from Carrie's abuse. By this point, it's hard not to agree with Maggie that Carrie is not going to be able to stay away from the CIA, and that settling down into an easy domesticity is not in the cards for her—and nor should it be, even though they begin a nasty custody battle. In the courtroom, Maggie takes the stand and says to Carrie: "I am not extraordinary like you, Carrie. I don't go around heading CIA stations. My job doesn't require me to risk my life. As it turns out, safe has its advantages too. A family, a stable home life. This is the thing I can offer Frannie. Things that you can't. A chance to be normal."[52] At first Carrie tries to argue that this is also what she wants, but ultimately, Carrie realizes that she can't walk away from the CIA and her dedication to serving her country. Carrie decides to let Maggie assume custody and goes to see Frannie one more time before she leaves for Germany with Saul. Maggie tells her, "Go—do what you were born to do."[53] To be ambivalent about this decision does not mean that Carrie doesn't love Frannie, but she has the courage to walk away.

CONCLUSION

Carrie and Elizabeth show us that motherhood is not always a good choice for some women, and intensive mothering is an unrealistic goal to impose on some—if not all—women. We love these antiheroines because they show the real challenges motherhood can create for some women and we applaud the series for giving us strong female characters who inspire our respect even though they cannot begin to live up to idealized motherhood. As Walters and Harrison put it, "But in an era of renewed anti-feminism and female power marketed as Palinesque 'mama grizzly' political porn, we are in dire need of some tough, messy, non-normative renegades to blast a few more holes in the maternal shrouds we've been wearing for far too long. The bad mother as anti-hero might be just what we need."[54] We may not like the choices we have seen Elizabeth and Carrie make, and we can be critical of the parenting choices, but I wonder if we might also see them as embodying what Elizabeth Fish Hatfield calls a "new form of feminism and motherhood that puts personal goals before motherhood as a service to the greater good, one possibly more valued than motherhood—national safety."[55]

Both Carrie and Elizabeth both know on some level that they are "behaving immorally which also helps define the antiheroine as one who transgresses but does so in the name of a higher good."[56] Carrie and Elizabeth cannot be heroic if they must also be responsible for a child, and given the series' arcs, they cannot simultaneously do their "jobs" as spies and agents and fulfill the cultural expectations of "good mothers." Forcing their audiences to grapple with this kind of cognitive dissonance is at least part of the genius of these series—we don't want the children to suffer unnecessarily, but we also don't want their mothers to settle into their maternal roles because they feel pressured to do so. These women are emotionally distant mothers but given the noble causes that each one is dedicated to pursue, they probably should have never been mothers in the first place, something I think both series ultimately conclude. Both Carrie and Elizabeth accept that they will have to sacrifice their children, just as they will have to sacrifice meaningful friendships and relationships if they are going to remain true to what motivated them in the first place. I would like to see these series as being hopeful, following Walters and Harrison: "We see this moment as strangely hopeful. For so long, mothers have been framed by and framed in through the binary oppositions of sacrificial saints and demonic destroyers of hearth and home."[57]

NOTES

1. Susan Douglas and Meredith Michaels, *The Mommy Myth: The Idealization of Motherhood and How It Has Undermined All Women* (New York: Free Press), and Heather Hudley and Sara Hayden, *Mediated Moms: Contemporary Challenges to the Motherhood Myth* (New York: Peter Lang, 2015).

2. Douglas and Michaels, *The Mommy Myth*, 4.

3. Amanda Lotz. *Redesigning Women: Television after the Network Era* (Urbana: University of Illinois Press, 2006), 3.

4. See, for example, "10 Worst and Best TV Moms," https://mom.com/entertainment/24415-10-best-and-worst-tv-moms-2015; "A Psychologist Ranks the 9 Worst Parents on TV," https://www.vulture.com/2015/05/psychologist-ranks-the-9-worst-parents-on-tv.html; "TV Moms We Love to Watch: The Good, the Bad, and the Ugly," https://www.pastemagazine.com/articles/2018/05/tv-moms-we-love-the-good-the-bad-and-the-ugly.html#elizabeth-the-americans; "The Worst TV Moms of All Time," https://mom.com/entertainment/24415-10-best-and-worst-tv-moms-2015; "The 50 Most Badass Female Characters on TV," https://www.revelist.com/tv/50-badass-female-tv-characters/1230.

5. Suzanna Danuta Walters and Laura Harrison, "Not Ready to Make Nice: Aberrant Mothers in Contemporary Culture," *Feminist Media Studies* 14:1 (2012): 38–55. DOI: 10.1080/14680777.2012.742919.

6. Margaret Tally, *The Rise of the Anti-Heroine in TV's Third Golden Age* (Newcastle-Upon-Tyne: Cambridge, Scholars Publishing, 2016), 8.

7. Joanna Robinson, "How a Lifetime Show Gave Us TV's First Pure Female Antihero," *Vanity Fair*, August 3, 2015, https://www.vanityfair.com/hollywood/2015/08/unreal-shiri-appleby-rachel-female-anti-hero.

8. Milly Buonanno, *Television Antiheroines: Women Behaving Badly in Crime and Prison Drama* (Chicago: University of Chicago Press, 2017), Kindle Edition.

9. Qtd. in Buonanno.

10. Laura Hudson, "Binge Watching Guide: *The Americans*," *Wired*, September 9, 2015, https://www.wired.com/2015/09/binge-guide-the-americans/.

11. *The Americans*, season 1, episode 13, "The Colonel," directed by Adam Arkin, written by Joseph Wiesberg and Joel Fields, aired May 1, 2013, HBO.

12. *The Americans*, "EST men," season 3, episode 1, directed by Daniel Sackheim, written by Joseph Weisberg and Joel Fields, aired January 28, 2015, HBO.

13. *The Americans*, season 1, episode 10, "Only You," directed by Adam Arkin, written by Joseph Weisberg and Bradford Winters, aired April 10, 2013, HBO.

14. *The Americans*, season 1, episode 2, "The Clock," directed by Adam Arkin, written by Joseph Weisberg, aired February 6, 2013, HBO.

15. *The Americans*, season 1, episode 1, "Pilot," directed by Gavin O'Connor, written by Joseph Weisberg, aired January 30, 2013, HBO.

16. *The Americans*, "The Colonel."

17. *The Americans*, season 5, episode 5, "Lotus 1-2-3," directed by Noah Emmerich, written by Joseph Weisberg and Joel Fields, aired April 4, 2017, HBO.

18. *The Americans*, season 6, episode 1, "Deadhand," directed by Chris Long, written by Joseph Weisberg and Joel Fields, aired March 28, 2018, HBO.

19. *The Americans*, season 4, episode 11, "Dinner for Seven," directed by Nicole Kassel, written by Joseph Weisberg and Joshua Brand, May 25, 2016, HBO.

20. *The Americans*, season 5, episode 2, "Pests," directed by Chris Long, written by Joseph Weisberg and Joel Fields, aired March 14, 2017, HBO.

21. *The Americans*, season 5, episode 3, "Cardinal," directed by Stefan Schwartz, written by Joseph Weisberg and Tracy Scott Wilson, aired March 21, 2017, HBO.

22. *The Americans*, season 5, episode 8 "Immersion," directed by Kevin Bray, written by Joseph Wiesberg and Tracey Scott Wilson, aired April 25, 2017, HBO.

23. *The Americans*, season 3, episode 6, "Born Again," directed by Kevin Dowling, written by Joseph Weisberg and Tracey Scott Wilson, aired March 4, 2015, HBO.

24. *The Americans*, season 4, episode 4, "Cloramphenicol," directed by Stefan Schwartz, written by Joseph Weisberg and Tracey Scott Wilson, aired April 6, 2016, HBO.

25. *The Americans*, season 6, episode 6, "Rififi," directed by Kevin Bray, written by Joseph Weisberg and Stephen Schiff, aired May 2, 2018, HBO.

26. *The Americans*, "Rififi."

27. *The Americans*, season 6, episode 7, "Harvest," directed by Stefan Schwartz, written by Joseph Weisberg and Sarah Nolen, aired May 9, 2018, HBO.

28. *The Americans*, season 6, episode 9, "Jennings, Elizabeth," directed by Chris Long, written by Joseph Weisberg and Joel Fields, aired May 23, 2018, HBO.

29. *The Americans*, "Jennings, Elizabeth."

30. *The Americans*, "Jennings, Elizabeth."

31. *The Americans*, season 6, episode 10, "START," directed by Chris Long, written by Joseph Weisberg and Joel Fields, aired May 30, 2018, HBO.

32. See, for example, Miriam Markowitz, "Madness in the Method," *Books and the Arts*, *The Nation*, April 22, 2013, https://www.thenation.com/article/archive/madness-method-homeland/; Elizabeth Fish Hatfield, "Motherhood and Mental Health: Carrie Mathison's *Homeland*," in *Mediated Moms: Contemporary Challenges to the Motherhood Myth*, eds. Heather Hudley and Sara Hayden, 33–52.

33. *Homeland*, season 1, episode 6, "The Weekend," directed by Micahel Cuesta, written by Alex Gansa and Howard Gordon, aired November 13, 2011, Showtime.

34. *Homeland*, season 3 episode 12, "The Star," directed by Leslie Linka Glatter, written by Alex Gansa and Howard Gordon, aired December 15, 2013, Showtime.

35. *Homeland*, season 3, episode 8, "A Red Wheelbarrow," directed by Seth Mann, written by Alex Gansa and Howard Gordon, aired November 17, 2013, Showtime.

36. *Homeland*, "A Red Wheelbarrow."

37. *Homeland*, season 3, episode 12, "The Star," directed by Lesli Linka Glatter, written by Alex Gansa and Howard Gordon, aired December 15, 2013, Showtime.

38. *Homeland*, "The Star."

39. *Homeland*, "The Star."

40. *Homeland*, season 4, episode 2, "Trylon and Persiphere," directed by Keith Gordon, written by Alex Gansa and Howard Gordon, aired October 5, 2014, Showtime.

41. *Homeland*, "Trylon and Persiphere."

42. Libby Hill, "A Shocking, Horrifying Act on Homeland Aims to Build Empathy for the Indefensible," *Vox*, October 6, 2014, https://www.vox.com/2014/10/6/6900651/homeland-carrie-drowns-baby.

43. Hayley Krischer, "Why the Bathtub Scene on Last Night's Homeland Was So Uniquely Disturbing," *Salon*, October 16, 2104, https://www.salon.com/2014/10/06/why_the_bathtub_scene_on_last_nights_homeland_was_so_uniquely_disturbing/.

44. Orna Donath, "Regretting Motherhood: A Sociopolitical Analysis," *Signs: Journal of Women in Culture and Society* 40, no. 2, 2 (Winter 2015): 362. DOI: 10.1086/678145.

45. *Homeland*, "Trylon and Persiphere."

46. *Homeland*, "Trylon and Persiphere."

47. *Homeland*, season 5, episode 1, "Separation Anxiety," directed by Leslie Linka Glatter, written by Chip Johannessen and Ted Mann, aired October 4, 2015, Showtime.

48. *Homeland*, season 5, episode 3, "Superpowers," directed by Keith Gordon, written by Gideon Raff and Alex Gansa, aired October 18, 2015, Showtime.

49. *Homeland*, season 6, episode 5, "Cassus Belli," directed by Alex Graves, written by Gideon Raff and Alex Gansa, aired February 19, 2017, Showtime.

50. *Homeland*, season 7, episode 1, "Enemy of the State," directed by Lesli Linka Glatter, written by Alex Gansa and Howard Gordon, aired February 11, 2018, Showtime.

51. *Homeland*, season 7, episode 7, "Andante," directed by Lesli Linka Glatter, written by Gideon Raff and Alex Gansa, aired March 25, 2018, Showtime.

52. *Homeland*, season 7, episode 10, "Clarity," directed by Daniel Attias, written by Gideon Raff and Howard Gordon, aired April 15, 2018, Showtime.

53. *Homeland*, "Clarity."

54. Walters and Harrison, "Not Ready to Make Nice," 14.

55. Elizabeth Fish Hatfield, "Motherhood and Mental Health: Carrie Mathison's Homeland Pregnancy," in *Mediated Moms: Contemporary Challenges to the Motherhood Myth*, eds. Heather Hudley and Sara Hayden (New York: Peter Lang, 2015), 49.

56. Tally, *The Rise of the Anti-Heroine*, 9.

57. Walters and Harrison, "Not Ready to Make Nice," 14.

BIBLIOGRAPHY

Buonanno, Milly, ed. *Television Antiheroines: Women Behaving Badly in Crime and Prison Drama*. Chicago: University of Chicago Press, 2017. Kindle edition.

Donath, Orna. "Regretting Motherhood: A Sociopolitical Analysis." *Signs: Journal of Women in Culture and Society*, 40, no. 2, (Winter 2015): 343–367.

Douglas, Susan J. and Meredith W. Michaels. *The Mommy Myth: The Idealization of Motherhood and How It Has Undermined All Women*. New York: Free Press, 2004.

Hatfield, Elizabeth Fish. "Motherhood and Mental Health: Carrie Mathison's *Homeland* Pregnancy." In *Mediated Moms: Contemporary Challenges to the Motherhood Myth*, edited by. Heather Hundley and Sara Hayden. New York: Peter Lang, 2015, 33–51.

Hill, Libby. "A Shocking, Horrifying Act on Homeland Aims to Build Empathy for the Indefensible." *Vox*, October 6, 2014. https://www.vox.com/2014/10/6/6900651/homeland-carrie-drowns-baby.

Homeland, season 1, episode 6, "The Weekend," directed by Micahel Cuesta, written by Alex Gansa and Howard Gordon, aired November 13, 2011, Showtime.

———, season 3, episode 8, "A Red Wheelbarrow," directed by Seth Mann, written by Alex Gansa and Howard Gordon, aired November 17, 2013, Showtime.

———, season 3 episode 12, "The Star," directed by Leslie Linka Glatter, written by Alex Gansa and Howard Gordon, aired December 15, 2013, Showtime.

———, season 4, episode 2, "Trylon and Persiphere," directed by Keith Gordon, written by Alex Gansa and Howard Gordon, aired October 5, 2014, Showtime.

———, season 5, episode 1, "Separation Anxiety," directed by Leslie Linka Glatter, written by Chip Johannessen and Ted Mann, aired October 4, 2015, Showtime.

———, season 5, episode 3, "Superpowers," directed by Keith Gordon, written by Gideon Raff and Alex Gansa, aired October 18, 2015, Showtime.

———, season 6, episode 5, "Cassus Belli," directed by Alex Graves, written by Gideon Raff and Alex Gansa, aired February 19, 2017, Showtime.

———, season 7, episode 1, "Enemy of the State," directed by Lesli Linka Glatter, written by Alex Gansa and Howard Gordon, aired February 11, 2018, Showtime.

———, season 7, episode 7, "Andante," directed by Lesli Linka Glatter, written by Gideon Raff and Alex Gansa, aired March 25, 2018, Showtime.

———, season 7, episode 10, "Clarity," directed by Daniel Attias, written by Gideon Raff and Howard Gordon, aired April 15, 2018, Showtime.

Hudson, Laura. "Binge Watching Guide: *The Americans*." *Wired*, September 9, 2015. https://www.wired.com/2015/09/binge-guide-the-americans/.

Hundley, Heather L. and Sara E. Hayden. *Mediated Moms: Contemporary Challenges to the Motherhood Myth*. New York: Peter Lange, 2015.

Krischer, Hayley. "Why the Bathtub Scene on Last Night's *Homeland* Was so Uniquely Disturbing." *Salon*, October 16, 2104. https://www.salon.com/2014/10/06/why_the_bathtub_scene_on_last_nights_homeland_was_so_uniquely_disturbing/.

Lotz, Amanda. *Redesigning Women: Television after the Network Era*. Urbana: University of Illinois Press, 2006.

O'Reilly, Andrea. *Twenty-First Century Motherhood: Experience, Identity, Policy, Agency*. New York: Columbia University Press, 2010.

Robinson, Joanna. "How a Lifetime Show Gave Us TV's First Pure Female Antihero." *Vanity Fair*, August 3, 2015. https://www.vanityfair.com/hollywood/2015/08/unreal-shiri-appleby-rachel-female-anti-hero.

Tally, Margaret. *The Rise of the Anti-Heroine in TV's Third Golden Age*. Cambridge Scholars Publishing, 2016.

The Americans, season 1, episode 1, "Pilot," directed by Gavin O'Connor, written by Joseph Weisberg, aired January 30, 2013, HBO.

———, season 1, episode 2, "The Clock," directed by Adam Arkin, written by Joseph Weisberg, aired February 6, 2013, HBO.

———, season 1, episode 10, "Only You," directed by Adam Arkin written by Joseph Weisberg and Bradford Winters, aired April 10, 2013, HBO.

———, season 1, episode 13, "The Colonel," directed by Adam Arkin, written by Joseph Wiesberg and Joel Fields, aired May 1, 2013, HBO.

———, season 3, episode 1 "EST men,," directed by Daniel Sackheim, written by Joseph Weisberg and Joel Fields, aired January 28, 2015, HBO.

———, season 3, episode 6, "Born Again," directed by Kevin Dowling, written by Joseph Weisberg and Tracey Scott Wilson, aired March 4, 2015, HBO.

———, season 4, episode 4, "Cloramphenicol," directed by Stefan Schwartz, written by Joseph Weisberg and Tracey Scott Wilson, aired April 6, 2016, HBO.

———, season 4, episode 11, "Dinner for Seven," directed by Nicole Kassel, written by Joseph Weisberg and Joshua Brand, May 25, 2016, HBO.

———, season 5, episode 2, "Pests," directed by Chris Long, written by Joseph Weisberg and Joel Fields, aired March 14, 2017, HBO.

———, season 5, episode 3, "Cardinal," directed by Stefan Schwartz, written by Joseph Weisberg and Tracy Scott Wilson, aired March 21, 2017, HBO.

———, season 5, episode 5, "Lotus 1-2-3," directed by Noah Emmerich, written by Joseph Weisberg and Joel Fields, aired April 4, 2017, HBO.

———, season 5, episode 8 "Immersion," directed by Kevin Bray, written by Joseph Wiesberg and Tracey Scott Wilson, aired April 25, 2017, HBO.

———, season 6, episode 1, "Deadhand," directed by Chris Long, written by Joseph Weisberg and Joel Fields, aired March 28, 2018, HBO.

———, season 6, episode 6, "Rififi," directed by Kevin Bray, written by Joseph Weisberg and Stephen Schiff, aired May 2, 2018, HBO.

———, season 6, episode 7, "Harvest," directed by Stefan Schwartz, written by Joseph Weisberg and Sarah Nolen, aired May 9, 2018, HBO.

———, season 6, episode 9, "Jennings, Elizabeth," directed by Chris Long, written by Joseph Weisberg and Joel Fields, aired May 23, 2018, HBO.

———, season 6, episode 10, "START," directed by Chris Long, written by Joseph Weisberg and Joel Fields, aired May 30, 2018, HBO.

Walters, Suzanna Danuta and Laura Harrison. "Not Ready to Make Nice: Aberrant Mothers in Contemporary Culture." *Feminist Media Studies* 14, no. 1, 38–55 (2012): 1–18.

Chapter Three

Tracking the Relationships between Postfeminism, Representations of Ageing Women, and the Rise of Popular Misogyny as Portrayed in FX's *Sons of Anarchy* (2008–2014)

Lucinda Rasmussen

The first decade of the twenty-first century saw a rise in the number of prestigious television programs featuring complex antiheroines: women characters in contemporary dramas who, as cultural critic Margaret Tally points out, often "engage in criminal acts that rival male anti-heroes."[1] FX's *Sons of Anarchy* (2008–2014), the story of a motorcycle gang called Sons of Anarchy Motorcycle Club Redwood Original (SAMCRO), is one example of such television programming. Although *Sons of Anarchy*'s (*SOA*) lead protagonist is Jax Teller (Charlie Hunnam), Jax's mother Gemma Teller Morrow (Katey Sagal) plays an almost equally important role as the motorcycle club's matriarch, a woman who was "as dangerous and volatile as any thug or criminal who's gone up against the club."[2] Despite Gemma's propensity for violence—or perhaps because of it—some viewers interpreted her role as evidence that the show's creators set out to embed a bit of "stealth feminism" in the narrative, the argument being that Gemma belonged to a new generation of complex antiheroines whose agency and autonomy reflect complicated, gendered social relations and power dynamics, instead of being cast as a "gangster's moll or compliant mob's wife or victim of male violence."[3] While it is possible at some points to suggest that several of the female characters in *SOA* are depicted so that the "masculine nature of heroism is called into question,"[4] it is also the case that traditional constructions of gender politics are reinforced by the series end.

Gemma's characterization does seem to challenge reductionist tropes because of her capacity to transgress normative ideas about femininity. For example, her transgressive agency is shockingly realized when she slays Jax's young wife Tara (Maggie Siff).[5] Gemma, who falsely believes that Tara plans to betray Jax by turning him over to law enforcement authorities, brutally attacks Tara, resulting in the younger woman's death. The affective horror of the scene is increased as the audience witnesses the effects of Tara's violent end on Jax, who is devastated to find his wife's battered corpse in the couple's home. Jax's grief is, of course, the audience's cue to sympathize with him, despite their having frequently witnessed his own capacity for violence as the club's leader. Indeed, the series invites the audience to understand him as having been thrust more deeply into crime because of his mother's insistence that he govern the motorcycle club in ways that ultimately protect her position as the club's matriarch.[6]

Kerry Fine optimistically observed (before the program's final two seasons) that *SOA* does not subject its major female protagonists to "narrative 'punishments'" such as being killed off at the end of an episode or season."[7] However, the episode "A Mother's Work," (S6, E13) in which Tara's murder takes place, paves the way for Jax's redemption for his past sins, complicates such critical commentary about the series' seemingly progressive representation of gender, as the differences between Gemma's death and Jax's death vindicate the patriarchal motorcycle club's many sexist practices while placing the responsibility for the the club culture's dysfunction on Gemma. That Gemma is brutally disposed of by the time of the series finale and that her death occurs in the service of Jax's character development suggests that she is not the sort of antiheroine who Milly Buonanno identifies as subverting certain "long-held ways of conceiving gender behavioural norms and the distribution of power within society."[8] Rather, she serves as an antiheroine by virtue of the complications her figure raises in the uniform acceptance of the unblushing male standard and the hypocritical and disenfranchising project of postfeminism. While it is possible at points to suggest that several of the female characters in *SOA* are depicted so that "the masculine nature of heroism is called into question,"[9] it is also the case that traditional constructions of gender politics are reinforced by the series' end. Thus, Gemma's moral lapses are not an indication of her depth or of the program creators' intention to create well-rounded female characters, but rather are a plot device by which Jax can be absolved of the atrocities that he has committed, while also seeking to situate his character (that of the young white male) at the top of the social hierarchy. While Jax does die in the *SOA* finale, thereby paying his own dues for crimes he has committed, his death is portrayed as that of the tragic hero. In contrast, Gemma's ignoble death (Jax executes his mother by shooting her in the back of the head) is understood as her just punishment for Tara's murder as well as her refusal to cede authority to her son. To fully explore what Gemma Teller Morrow's character represents, I argue that *SOA*'s treatment of Gemma as antiheroine must be understood as taking place in a postfeminist context. By doing so, I want to shift attention away from merely thinking about Gemma as a deviant mother to thinking more deeply about the ways in which her status as a middle-aged woman is foregrounded in the program. Women and gender studies scholar Julia Mason contends that programs such as *SOA* subject female characters to retribution on the basis of their failures to conform to an idealized understanding of maternal responsibilities; particularly, Mason argues, in cases where the character does not "put her children first."[10] Elsewhere, Amanda Lotz describes Gemma as an example of "monstrous motherhood," a woman who "destroys her offspring," but who can "defy conventional female portrayal in many ways."[11] Although Gemma's role in the series invites such analyses of motherhood, Gemma's age also deserves particular consideration when determining how gender is presented within this series, particularly because ageist rhetoric is deeply normalized throughout Western culture. Through such consideration, it becomes apparent that the program's storyline actually works to reify the patriarchy through its writers' reliance on ageist tropes.

Postfeminism is a term that is variably defined; however, in this chapter, its use aligns with the work of scholars such as Rosalind Gill who uses the term to refer to an ideology, a sensibility as she puts it, characterized by cultural practices and beliefs that disguise gendered forms of oppression under the guise that gender equality has been achieved.[12] For example, Gill explains how the postfeminist subject is socialized to believe that participating in practices such as painful cosmetic surgeries signifies her freedom of choice.[13] Angela McRobbie has adeptly argued that as subjects of postfeminism, young women are welcome to engage in hypermasculine cultural practices such as "heavy drinking, swearing, smoking, getting into fights, [and] having casual sex."[14] On the surface, women's freedom to partake in such stereotypically masculine behaviors might be interpreted as evidence that gender equality has been achieved. On closer examination, such behaviors ultimately serve to reify heteropatriarchal interests.[15] This reification of heteropatriarchy takes place because, in exchange for her freedom, the woman who is a subject of postfeminism must not criticize those institutions that objectify women.[16] As McRobbie puts it, postfeminism produces a "hostility to assumed feminist positions from the past, in order to endorse a new regime of sexual meanings based on female consent, equality, participation and pleasure."[17] However, the notion that postfeminism works by portraying feminism as redundant is only part of what is at stake in this analysis. Postfeminist ideology is, at its core, profoundly ageist, as noted by scholars who identify a "contemporary postfeminist culture in which, under the guise that equality has been achieved and within a consumerist society, the figure of the young woman represents an ideal of attainment."[18] Indeed, under postfeminism, even very youthful women are pressured to respond to what has been referred to as "time panic."[19] Since every woman inevitably grows older, ageism is the ultimate method through which a woman is disciplined and silenced and eventually stripped of those gains she may have been able to achieve as a youthful postfeminist subject.

One final aspect of postfeminism requires mention before Gemma's status as a middle-aged subject can be fully appreciated. *SOA* began production in 2008, the point at which the so-called decade of postfeminism[20] intersected with an economic downturn in the United States. In their introduction to *Gendering the Recession: Media and Culture in an Age of Austerity*, editors Diane Negra and Yvonne Tasker call attention to the ways in which the "semicollapse of the global financial system in 2007–2008 inaugurated a set of profound cultural shifts,"[21] one of which was to see postfeminist media evolve into an even more nuanced form of gender policing. The "recessionary culture" that these scholars identify as taking place at the time interrupted postfeminist media's tendency to glamorize conspicuous consumption, changing the tone, for instance, of the quintessentially postfeminist "chick flick" that once unquestioningly celebrated conspicuous consumption.[22] As literary scholar Suzanne Leonard shows, a different sort of narrative trope emerged in which "female gains [were] framed as occurring in relation to male losses."[23] In this way, "the recession also offered a convenient opportunity to recirculate and revalidate misogynist tropes about how feminist ideals have hurt boys and men."[24] Where postfeminist ideology initially celebrated a woman's capacity to consume extravagantly as the mark of gender equality having been achieved (thereby showing feminism had achieved its purpose and was no longer necessary)[25] the recession was used as a reason to revoke any cultural or economic gains. As a consequence, narratives that might once have celebrated a woman's capacity to have a lucrative career gets "underwritten or more precisely contextualized by a perception that equality is a luxury that can no longer be afforded," and that "equality is a concern to be reserved for times of plenty."[26] Just as cultural narratives suggested that the second-wave feminist was redundant in a more contemporary social order, so now could the empowered postfeminist subject also be dismissed, particularly when she could be connected to the disruption of patriarchal security by taking up too much space in the workforce. It is my contention that *SOA* presents its viewer with this very message. In this instance, the young white male hero, Jax, is unable to achieve his full potential due to his mother's position of authority in the motorcycle club, and because his feelings of inadequacy are connected to his young wife's professional success, as Tara is a skilled surgeon. In keeping with the paradox that is a part of postfeminist discourses, one in which younger women have been granted some limited privilege, it is the older Gemma who shoulders the bulk of the responsibility for the collapse of the social order. Tara's death, brought about by Gemma, becomes the ideal route to punishing both women for their independence, but it is significant that the series presents a young woman as a victim and a middle-aged woman as beyond redemption. It is noteworthy that Gemma, as a mature female character, ultimately must take responsibility for both Jax and Tara's demise, especially since, throughout the course of the series' trajectory, Tara also, behaves as a bad mother to her own child.[27] Her death at Gemma's hands, however, redeems her for viewers as a symbol of martyred motherhood.

Gemma's villainization is complicated by SAMCRO's history. SAM-CRO was founded by Jax's biological father (and Gemma's husband at the time) in 1967,[28] which ambiguously connects Gemma's authority in the club to the time of second-wave feminism while situating her in a story told during the time of postfeminism wherein that authority is undermined and vilified. By examining, then, the ways in which not only Gemma but also Jax and Tara fit within a postfeminist ideological context, it becomes clear that Gemma's status as the antiheroine has nothing to do with portraying gender equality. Nor is mother-blame the only narrative trope that the *SOA* writers draw upon. Rather, Gemma's status as a violent, powerful woman—coded early in the series as a woman who is ageing—serves only to bolster "a postfeminist culture [that] has tended to pay lip service to female individualism while [also] undercutting it."[29] This outcome is all the more apparent given that *SOA* concludes during a time when a larger cultural shift toward what, at the time of this writing, has been understood as the reemergence of a deeply misogynistic mind-set in the American public sphere.[30] As I will soon discuss, media scholar Sarah Banet-Weiser's exploration of popular misogyny and cultural critic Margaret Morganroth Gullette's analysis of midlife ageism can, when brought together, demonstrate the extent to which Western society's comfort with ageist storylines helps further a patriarchal agenda.[31] Viewed in this fashion, the narrative trajectory of this program might well be said to predict the American public's appetite for a nostalgic return to a very conservative social order, one that continues to rebuke feminism (even in its popular forms) while also normalizing the objectification of everyone who is not a heterosexual white male. As an antiheroine, Gemma functions not as a character who represents social progress, but as a call for the return to a particular form of hegemonic masculinity in which the young heterosexual white male is repositioned as the head of the dominant social order; under this regime, women of all ages who refuse to yield to this authority are violently suppressed. As both Banet-Weiser and Gullette focus on the tension between visibility and invisibility in their works, this analysis of *SOA* explores how the version of Gemma presented renders aspects of her identity as selectively perceptible on the basis of her age.

SOA's first season almost immediately foregrounds Gemma's age, a noteworthy observation because as the series creator Kurt Sutter states, the first season was "obviously about setting up the world and some of the primary relationships."[32] Within the first ten minutes of the pilot episode, Jax, who is awaiting the birth of his first child, teases his mother that soon she will be "Grandma." Gemma's response—she cheerfully calls Jax an "asshole"—is affectionate and in keeping with Gemma's outspokenness, but the message conveyed is that the character is slightly ill at ease about growing older.[33] Episode "AK-51," later in season 1, drives this point home forcefully.[34] Gemma, divulges in the episode that she is fifty-one and is depicted experiencing unpleasant menopause symptoms, a storyline which is significant given how infrequently menopause is represented in popular culture.[35] Although subtle, the program is postfeminist in the way it masks a seemingly progressive narrative within a larger one that ultimately ends up as repressive. Gemma's experiences and revelations in this episode effectively expose how women can feel silenced and shamed during this life change. Gemma endures a tactless pharmacist who, in front of other customers, loudly announces the name of the hormone replacement product that she has been prescribed to manage the vaginal dryness that has brought about changes in her sex life. This episode, in particular, is shot to show Gemma's humiliation over the pharmacist's lack of tact, a moment that speaks to ways in which older women can find themselves belittled within the medical system. Although there is some exploration of ageing identity and female heterosexuality in this episode, I do not read *SOA* as sidestepping intersecting ageist and gender stereotypes in the process, however. At best, the program takes a popular feminist approach to gender and ageing in this moment, with "popular feminist" understood here as a sort of feel-good feminism that, to cite media scholar Sarah Banet-Weiser, "accommodates men through its heteronormativity, which is of course defined by gendered norms that already prioritize the logic of heterosexuality."[36] Although the program gives some needed visibility to ageing and opens up a space for a discussion of what menopause can entail while also recognizing that middle-aged and ageing women are sexual beings, it is "the structural ground on and through which [this moment of being made visible] [is] constructed" which matters most.[37] As Banet-Weiser further notes, "Economies of visibility fundamentally shift politics of visibility so that visibility becomes *the end* rather than a means to an end." This is to say that Gemma's physical and mental struggle with her aging body is not exposed as a social construct to be critiqued, and therefore the program is not working to facilitate "a political process" that can be thought of as countering ageism.[38] What might have been a productive exploration of ways that ageing is felt in some relationships falls short when, in this same episode, Gemma savagely assaults a young woman named Cherry with whom her husband has had a sexual encounter. Notably, it is not Clay's infidelity that bothers Gemma; as a proper postfeminist subject, she is willing to accept that the male club members frequently engage in extramarital affairs and that these men frequently objectify women. Rather, the reason Gemma resents Cherry is because she is "so young."[39] That we see Gemma's capacity for physical violence during an episode where her emotions are heightened due to her anxieties over entering menopause is problematic. Gemma is, at this early point in the series, shown to be emotionally unstable and so compromised that she later regrets her decisions, as evidenced by the remorse she eventually feels for what she has done to Cherry. While her capacity for violence is part of what makes Gemma a complex character, her inability to control her emotions registers negatively in an episode that is also about menopause's impact on her sex life. Indeed, *SOA* seems only to reify Freud's anachronistic claim that after women have lost their "genital function," "[t]hey become quarrelsome . . . [and] exhibit sadistic . . . traits, which they did not possess earlier, during their period of womanliness."[40] Although *SOA* does not revisit Gemma's journey through menopause again, this episode serves as the narrative backdrop against which Gemma's other more violent crimes occur, the most heinous of which is Tara's murder in the penultimate season's finale, which Gemma carries out by stabbing Tara in the head with a carving fork. Thus, while the menopause storyline invokes an underlying hormonal instability and brings much-needed visibility to ageing, it also serves as the framework for Gemma's crimes throughout the remainder of the series. This makes it always possible to connect Gemma's age with her capacity for violence, which often she undertakes through clouded judgment. Gemma's depression over ageing also fits with well-established arguments regarding the postfeminist melancholic, defined as the postfeminist tendency to produce depictions of the middle-aged woman as "a figure of calculation, deceit, and insecurity."[41] When *SOA* writers represent Gemma's menopause symptoms in an episode that also features her attacking Cherry in broad daylight on a busy street, the series neatly positions Gemma as something of a hysteric, thereby making her experience of ageing visible while still failing to explore, in any adequate sense, the ways in which Gemma's shame over ageing is a socially constructed means to managing femininity.

While seeking to understand Gemma's role in *SOA*, it is important to consider how, from a collective standpoint, the narrative organizes the major characters into a hierarchy, suggesting that the most important characters are the ones who receive the greatest amount of redemption. Recent work on postfeminism points to how "young women of melancholic disposition are utilized [by filmmakers] as vehicles through which to explore the excesses of late capitalism and the failures of neoliberal post-feminism."[42] But what happens when the ageing woman is cast alongside those younger characters within these narratives? *SOA*'s early emphasis on Gemma's age is most significant when read against the representation of other characters in the program, particularly Jax and Tara, whose portrayals also fall within a range of postfeminist gender tropes, but who, because of their ages, are afforded more privilege in terms of their characters' development and their own capacities for redemption within this system. While Jaspreet Nijjar does not explicitly discuss postfeminism in her analysis of *SOA*, she does make the point that new critical assumptions must be utilized when interpreting Jax and characters like him. According to Nijjar, who coins the terms "Family-Oriented New Lad" and "Emotionally Inarticulate New Man" as she analyzes Jax Teller, these new versions of the lad grow out of the widely held perception that "a crisis of masculinity" exists.[43] Nijjar argues that her newly coined character types are a response to second-wave feminism, a claim that at its core must be connected to the ideology of postfeminism. Although Jax's crimes are just as heinous as Gemma's, after Gemma kills Tara, his redemption can be readily accepted because he can now be sympathetically represented as a grieving husband and father. Jax's capacity to be brutal toward those who cross SAMCRO is never disputed; however, throughout the series, *SOA* writers work to manage audiences' responses to Jax's destructive behaviors in part through depicting him as a loving father to his own sons. The sympathy that *SOA* writers invite the audience to feel toward Jax intensifies with Tara's death, as Jax must now parent both of his children alone. Film studies scholar Hannah Hamad uses Andrew Sarris's term "the male weepie" to describe a popular trope in postfeminist media whereby texts show widowed fathers left to care for children. Jax's depiction as a tender father who weeps for his children is meant to show that he is not disconnected from his humanity, irrespective of his violent behaviors. But as Hamad further explains, such representations often have the effect of "co-opt[ing] or reappropriat[ing] a certain femininity for the benefit of men and to the detriment of women."[44] In the process of constructing Jax as a sympathetic hero, the series reinforces the notion that Jax, as a young white male is entitled to wield violence in service of his goals, whereas Gemma, a middle-aged woman, is not. Additionally, in order for Jax to evolve into a sympathetic hero, the two most powerful female characters must be terminated. Though Jax also dies, his death plays out in radically different terms. First, he chooses the manner of his death, and second, he enacts his death plan only after he has been able to provide for the needs of his family and fellow motorcycle club members. In other words, Jax's death is noble, whereas Gemma's ignoble death by execution is presented as her just punishment.

Hamad's interrogation of the relationships between postfeminist discursive practices in popular culture and sympathetic representations of fatherhood enable deeper contemplation of how *SOA*'s plotline ultimately works not only to curtail Gemma's power but Tara's as well. Gemma's murder of Tara's is complex because of the way it cancels out various forms of female power in the program to privilege the restoration of a patriarchal social order, while at the same time working in accordance with postfeminist terms. In keeping with postfeminist ideology, Tara is read in this narrative as occupying a higher position in the social hierarchy than Gemma, and this is where ageism, again, plays a role. Whereas Gemma reads as a powerful, middle-aged woman, Tara is described by Kolb as representative of "a new generation of female power."[45] Certainly, much of her appeal rests in the fact that she is young, conventionally beautiful, and she loves her children, but Tara is also accomplished in terms of her education and professional success, which in postfeminist terms establishes her as a "subject worthy of investment," who is capable of achieving financial independence and autonomy.[46] Importantly, despite her complicated and often fraught relationship with Jax, Tara *chooses* to be with him, thereby fulfilling one of postfeminism's foundational principles, which is that gender equality has made it possible for a woman to select from a range of options, one of which is for her to place a heterosexual romantic relationship above professional ambition. Despite her loyalty to Jax, Tara's successes pose, at intervals throughout the series, a threat to his masculinity, along with what he perceives as his right to occupy a leadership role in his household. When Tara asks Jax to leave his motorcycle club, and reassures him that her physician's salary can support them, Jax is mortified and states he cannot "live off his wife." Although Jax desires a different sort of life, he claims that outlawing is his best option because he is only "an okay mechanic with a GED."[47] The couple's exchange resonates with the 2007 financial crisis in the United States, which by the episode's original airing has given rise to new forms of misogynistic backlash, this time targeted at the so-called woman of postfeminism who is supposed to have achieved equality at the expense of men; for instance, such backlash included the argument that "recessionary anxieties opened up space for a spate of . . . accounts that figure men and boys as significantly disadvantaged" because of the feminist-influenced attention girls have been receiving.[48] *SOA* implies this sort of imbalance through the dynamic between Jax and Tara, highlighting Jax's insecurities in relation to Tara's success.

However, to represent Jax as overtly chauvinistic toward Tara is not an option in postfeminist media terms. For Jax to remain sympathetic to audiences sensitized to crave postfeminist illusions of gender equality, Tara's power over Jax has to be undone by someone other than Jax himself. Gemma's murder of Tara, motivated by the older woman's neurotic fear that the younger woman will exert too much influence over her son, becomes the solution. Tara's death constitutes the removal of the threat that she poses to Jax's understanding of what masculine conduct should entail. The series' writers can thus demonstrate that Jax is supportive of what Tara represents—female empowerment—while using Gemma to remove the threat to masculinity that Tara's successes pose.

Ashley Donnelly argues that the *SOA* characters often straddle the line between outsider and Other with the latter signifying a character who does something that leaves them beyond redemption: according to Donnelly, a character becomes an outsider when they commit a crime so debased that they "cannot coexists with the ideology of a nation."[49] Gemma's sadistic murder of Tara, a young wife and mother to the future generation, renders her irredeemable in the way Donnelly suggests, not merely because she takes Tara's life, but because by doing so she also harms Jax as well as her grandsons who are toddlers at the time. Mother-blame plays a role in the narrative, but the power of this narrative also depends on the juxtaposition of two pervasive tropes found in North American media, one of which positions young white heterosexual males as leaders of the mainstream social order, and the second of which upholds the notion that ageing people a responsibility to step aside and sacrifice their own ambitions for a younger generation. Sociologist Erving Goffman drew attention to the first of these cultural ideals in 1963 when he published *Stigma*, in which he argues that there is only one American archetype who can be considered "unblushing" or free of negative association: in Goffman's terms this person is "a young, married, white, urban, northern, heterosexual Protestant father of college education, fully employed, of good complexion, weight and height, and a recent record in sports."[50] This definition of an ideal subject in American culture, so deeply tied to class privilege and racial identity, has prevailed to the present day, and has been explored extensively by theorists such as Rosemary Garland-Thomson who refers to the subject of Goffman's study as a "normate," or "the corporeal incarnation of culture's collective, unmarked, normative characteristics."[51] Garland-Thomson's assessment of privilege is useful in understanding how the audience is being encouraged to sympathize with Jax's dilemma: Jax's difficulties occur because he cannot be the unblushing male that he and those around him have been taught to believe he is entitled to become. The socialization process that encourages others to accept the normate as a cultural ideal is so deeply entrenched that individuals like Jax are granted enormous respect and lenience. Notably, the series invites the audience to regard Jax as having the capacity to become the very figure that Goffman describes. His character development upholds the supposition that gender and racial privilege serve as entitlement to the manifestation of the ideal and that challengers to the male subject's progression toward the ideal must be marginalized or defeated. To further adhere to this standard, Jax embodies the physical attributes of the normate insofar as he is fair-skinned, athletic, cisgendered, male, and young. However, Jax's failure to achieve a college education and with it the right kind of job means that Jax cannot achieve what dominant discourses socialize the general population to understand as his rightful destiny. Importantly, the storyline presents Gemma's interference in Jax's life as the reason Jax cannot leave the motorcycle club to pursue suburban life so that he might achieve this cultural ideal.

The narrative's treatment of its female characters shows how, in the wake of financial crisis where fewer opportunities exist, cultural rage at women intensifies, particularly when they are understood to be taking resources away from those men whom the general populace has been socialized to perceive as rightfully entitled. Even a cursory internet search reveals how the scene in which Jax executes Gemma has been read with great sympathy for Jax but little to no regard for Gemma. [52]

SOA represents a trend in television wherein middle-aged women serve as foils for young white males and viewers' tendency to accept such storylines often without question. The unquestioned belief that young men are the holders of privilege is so deeply entrenched that even Gemma ultimately accepts that she must relinquish her destiny to Jax when, just prior to him shooting her, she tells him he is "her sweet baby boy," and that she understands why he must kill her. [53] This reference to Jax as a "boy" is both the articulation of ageist privilege which furthers the narrative of "boys behaving badly" excusing young males' transgressions against social order assuming they will and can mature into men capable of leadership and moral stability. This confirmation of the privilege he is granted as a white male is a symptom of a phenomenon aptly described by journalist Alexandra Petri, who remarks on ways in which powerful grown American men are absolved of responsibility for the most heinous of acts because the rhetoric inscribing them as good boys draws attention away from what are their obvious moral lapses. [54]

SOA's storyline is one that works successfully within postfeminist tropes to perpetuate rhetorical practices that are superficially progressive yet ultimately espouse gender equality as the cause of social ills, yet all the while presenting a narrative that reifies a "traditional ideology of class difference, capitalist power, and . . . a deeply rooted hierarchy of patriarchy." [55] Naturally, in keeping with postfeminism's discursive formulae, *SOA*'s opposition to gender equality is never explicit. It is here that Gemma's age would seem to play a central role. The menopause episode against which all of Gemma's future actions are set is at once a progressive narrative for representing an ageing woman, while also encouraging the audience to read Gemma's desire to remain the matriarch of the motorcycle club as selfish because of its impact on Jax. The subtext here is that Gemma, as an ageing woman, ought to recede from visibility so that Jax can do as he wishes with the family business.

Gullette argues that midlife ageism is rampant in contemporary American culture and that it thrives because most people have internalized reductive beliefs about ageing people's capacities to perform in jobs that should, according to this logic, be rightfully given to younger people. As she puts it, "boomers can be held responsible for an increasing portion of the national crises (fiscal deficits, high youth unemployment), serving as a scapegoat." [56] Spelled out in this fashion, it is clear that midlife ageism is a serious social issue, and yet acceptance of this belief system underpins *SOA*, apparent in the ways writers depict not only Gemma, but also her husband Clay. Clay's age is also foregrounded in the series: his moral decline as the club's leader, which involves an obsession with money, runs parallel to his loss of physical prowess brought about by arthritic hands. While the scope of this chapter does not allow for space to analyze ageing masculinity the series' treatment of Clay's age only further confirms the argument that *SOA* relies on ageist tropes to present Jax, the young white male, as a tragic character denied the life he truly deserves as the older characters have selfish ambitions that thwart Jax's chances for the life that audiences are encouraged to believe he deserves.[57]

Jax has the capacity to become the ideal subject as defined by Goffman: he is a fair-skinned, conventionally handsome young man who is made to seem like a good man for the care he shows his children and his romantic partner. But for the machinations of a controlling older woman, this young man would be entirely fulfilled, a plot device which suggests that *SOA* is *deeply* misogynistic. "Much of the logic of popular misogyny revolves around twinned discourses of capacity and injury," writes Banet-Weiser, who goes on to state that "Expressions of popular misogyny often rely upon the idea that men have been injured by women."[58] The writers of storylines that construct ageing women as a young man's foil participate in more than the reification of straightforward mother-blame. *SOA*'s success stems, in part, from its audience's general indifference to ageism to pave way for the misogyny contained within them. Gemma is a criminal, certainly, but her fear of menopause and of ageing also suggests that she knows to expect and fear "ageist assaults," which are normalized within Western society and cause many people to feel shame over the ageing process.[59] When Jax shames Gemma for growing older in *SOA*'s first episode, his actions are downplayed. Jax's mockery of his mother's age when he teases her about becoming a grandmother is a light moment in the narrative that is intended to be humorous—even Gemma takes it in stride. However, as Gullette makes clear, many ageing people simply do not confront those who critique them for ageing, in part because rhetoric disparaging persons on the basis of their age is considered socially acceptable: as she puts it, the person who is subjected to ageism will generally remain silent as "no social movement has taught [those who endure an ageist slight] how to successfully respond."[60] The narrative pathway traced throughout this chapter suggests that mainstream culture's indifference to ageist beliefs can be readily deployed by television writers as a way to explain the wrongs endured by a young white male. The next step in interrogating the role played by ageing women such as Gemma in these dramatic television programs should be to examine how their racial identities as middle-aged white women intersect with that of the non-white characters. This chapter shows how normalized ageist tropes directed at middle-aged women can be used to bolster confidence in heteronormative patriarchy, particularly in those programs that grew out of the 2008 recession. To expose the misogyny at work within postfeminist narratives that rely on ageist tropes is to take a step forward in understanding and combating the hierarchies that dismiss the agency and autonomy of women. Through Gemma, the contradictory narratives scripted into *Sons of Anarchy* allow for auxiliary entries into our understandings of dominant discourses that reify heteronormativity, patriarchy, and ageism.

NOTES

1. Margaret Tally, *The Rise of the Anti-Heroine in TV's Third Golden Age* (Newcastle upon Tyne: Cambridge, 2016), 7, EBSCOhost. In addition, examples of popular programs featuring women who engage in criminal activities alongside men include *Breaking Bad* (2008–2013), *Weeds* (2005–2012), and *Orange Is the New Black* (2013–2019). In all of these examples, characters turn to crime to offset financial stress.

2. Tara Bennett, Sons of Anarchy: *The Official Series Guide* (New York: Time Home Entertainment, 2015), 28.

3. Thomas "*Sons of Anarchy*: A Little Stealth Feminism?" *Yes Means Yes! Visions of Female Sexual Power and a World without Rape*, November 15, 2010, https://yesmeansyesblog.wordpress.com/2010/11/15/sons-of-anarchy-a-little-stealth-feminism/. See also Milly Buonanno, "Editor's Introduction," in *Television Antiheroines: Women Behaving Badly in Crime and Prison Drama*, ed. Milly Buonanno (Chicago: Intellect, 2017), 13.

4. Kerry Fine. "She Hits Like a Man but She Kisses Like a Girl: TV Heroines, Femininity, Violence and Intimacy," *Western American Literature* 47.2 (Summer 2012): 153, JSTOR.

5. *Sons of Anarchy*, season 6, episode 13, "A Mother's Work," directed by Kurt Sutter, featuring Charlie Hunnam, Katey Sagal, and Maggie Siff, aired December 10, 2013, FX, DVD.

6. Bennett, "*Sons of Anarchy*," 30.

7. Fine, "She Hits Like a Man," 156.

8. Buonanno, "Editor's Introduction," 14.

9. Fine, "She Hits Like a Man," 153.

10. Julia M. Mason, "Mothers and Antiheroes: Analyzing Motherhood and Representation in *Weeds, Sons of Anarchy*, and *Breaking Bad*," *The Journal of Popular Culture* 52, no. 3 (2019): 659, SportDiscuss.

11. Amanda D. Lotz, "Really Bad Mothers: Manipulative Matriarchs in *Sons of Anarchy* and *Justified*," in *Television Antiheroines: Women Behaving Badly in Crime and Prison Drama*, ed. Millie Buonanno (Intellect, 2017): 138; 128.

12. Rosalind Gill, "Postfeminist Media Culture: Elements of a Sensibility," *European Journal of Cultural Studies* 10.2 (2007): 148. Gale.

13. Gill, "Postfeminist Media Culture," 153.

14. Angela McRobbie, *The Aftermath of Feminism* (London: SAGE Publications, 2009), 83.

15. McRobbie, *Aftermath*, 83–84.

16. McRobbie, *Aftermath*, 18.

17. McRobbie, *Aftermath*, 18.

18. Cathy McGlynn, Margaret O'Neill, and Michaela Schrage-Früh, eds. "Introduction," in *Ageing Women in Literature and Visual Culture* (Palgrave MacMillan, 2017), 10.

19. Diane Negra, *What a Girl Wants? Fantasizing the Reclamation of Self in Post-Feminism* (London; New York: Routledge, 2009), 47–85.

20. Angela McRobbie, "Post Feminism + Beyond," produced by Sebastian Richter, June 24, 2012, YouTube video, 0:10, youtube.com/watch=Wk-QIXx2wk.

21. Diane Negra and Yvonne Tasker, "Introduction," in *Gendering the Recession: Media and Culture in an Age of Austerity* (Durham, NC: Duke University Press, 2014), 1.

22. Negra and Tasker, "Introduction," 15–18.

23. Suzanne Leonard, "Escaping the Recession? The New Vitality of the Woman Worker," in *Gendering the Recession: Media and Culture in an Age of Austerity* (Durham, NC: Duke University Press, 2014), 36.

24. Leonard, "Escaping," 36.

25. McRobbie, "Post Feminism + Beyond."

26. Negra and Tasker, "Introduction," 4, 2.

27. Mason, "Mothers and Antiheroes," 659.

28. Ashley Donnelly, *Renegade Hero or Faux Rogue: The Secret Traditionalism of Television Bad Boys* (Jefferson, NC: McFarland, 2014), 57.

29. Tasker and Negra, "Introduction," 26.

30. For example, see Kate Manne, *Down Girl: The Logic of Misogyny* (New York: Oxford University Press, 2018).

31. Sarah Banet-Weiser, *Empowered: Popular Feminism and Popular Misogyny* (Durham, NC: Duke University Press, 2018); Margaret Morganroth Gullette, *Ending Ageism or How Not to Shoot Old People* (New Jersey: Rutgers University Press, 2017).

32. Sutter qtd. in Bennett, *"Sons of Anarchy,"* 158.

33. *Sons of Anarchy*, season 1, episode 1, "Pilot," directed by Allen Coulter and Michael Dinner, featuring Charlie Hunnam and Katey Sagal, aired September 3, 2008, FX, DVD.

34. *Sons of Anarchy*, season 1, episode 4, "Ak-51," directed by Seith Mann, featuring Katey Sagal, aired October 8, 2008, FX, DVD.

35. Sarah Falcus and Katsura Sako, "Women, Travelling and Later Life," in *Ageing, Popular Culture and Contemporary Feminism: Harleys and Hormones*, ed. Imelda Whelehan and Joel Gwynne (New York: Palgrave and Macmillan, 2014), 209–210.

36. Banet-Weiser, *Empowered*, 15.

37. Banet-Weiser, *Empowered*, 23.

38. Banet-Weiser, *Empowered*, 23.

39. *Sons of Anarchy*, "Ak-51."

40. Qtd. in Jan Campbell, *Freudian Passions: Psychoanalysis, Form and Literature* (London: Karnac Books, 2013), 96. Campbell discusses Freud's use of a "sexist stereotype" when, in this fashion, he refers to a woman who is experiencing menopause.

41. Negra, *What a Girl Wants?*, 75.

42. Kendra Marston, *Postfeminist Whiteness: Problematizing Melancholic Burden in Contemporary Hollywood* (Edinburgh: Edinburgh University Press, 2018): 3.

43. Jaspreet K. Nijjar, "Mutated Masculinities: A Critical Discourse Analysis of the New Lad and the New Man in *Sons of Anarchy* and *Ray Donovan*," *Journal of Men's Studies* 27, no. 1 (2019): 40.

44. Hannah Hamad, *Post-Feminism and Paternity in Contemporary U.S. Film: Framing Fatherhood* (London: Routledge, 2014), 25.

45. Leigh C. Kolb, "Mothers of Anarchy: Power, Control, and Care in the Feminine Sphere," in *"Sons of Anarchy" and Philosophy: Brains before Bullets*, ed. by William Irwin, George Dunn, and Jason T. Eberl (Malden: Wiley Blackwell, 2013), 183.

46. McRobbie, *Aftermath*, 57.

47. *Sons of Anarchy*, season 4, episode 1, "Out," directed by Paris Barclay, featuring Charlie Hunnam and Maggie Siff, aired September 6, 2011, FX, DVD.

48. Leonard, "Escaping," 36.

49. Donnelly, *Renegade Hero*, 56.

50. Erving Goffman, *Stigma: Notes on the Management of a Spoiled Identity* (Prentice Hall, 1963), 128.

51. Rosemarie Garland-Thomson, "Integrating Disability, Transforming Feminist Theory," *NWSA Journal*, 14, no. 3 (Autumn 2002): 10, JSTOR.

52. See viewer comments at "Gemma Death Scene—Sons of Anarchy," posted by Jay Cooper, December 2, 2014, YouTube video, https://www.youtube.com/watch?v=9SLh_Sr8QR8. Representative viewer responses posted beneath the Gemma execution scene include ones that refer to her as "egotistical witch," "snake," "Biaaaatch," "Spawn of Satan," and "the reason for all Jax's problems."

53. *Sons of Anarchy*, season 7, episode 12, "Red Rose," directed by Paris Barclay, featuring Charlie Hunnam and Katey Sagal, aired December 2, 2014. FX, DVD.

54. Alexandra Petri, "A 39-Year-Old Man Is Mysteriously Still a Kid," *The Washington Post*, July 13, 2017, https://www.washingtonpost.com/blogs/compost/wp/2017/07/13/a-39-year-old-man-is-mysteriously-still-a-kid/. Petri criticizes America for its tendency to refer to privileged white adult males as "boys" as a way of absolving them of accountability when they have done something wrong.

55. Donnelly, *Renegade Hero*, 69.

56. Gullette, *Ending Ageism*, 5. See also Margaret Morganroth Gullette, "Unwanted at Midlife: Not Old, but 'Too Old,'" *Los Angeles Review of Books*, February 20, 2019, https://lareviewofbooks.org/article/unwanted-at-midlife-not-old-but-too-old/.

57. Donnelly provides an overview of Clay's decline in *Renegade Hero*, 66–69. She accentuates that "Clay's mental state deteriorates as he . . . becomes obsessed with money, making a deal with Mexican drug cartel . . . once again ensnaring Jax."

58. Banet-Weiser, *Empowered*, 35.

59. Gullette, *Ending Ageism*, 179.

60. Gullette, *Ending Ageism*,184.

BIBLIOGRAPHY

Banet-Weiser, Sarah. *Empowered: Popular Feminism and Popular Misogyny*. Durham, NC: Duke University Press, 2018.

Barclay, Paris, director. *Sons of Anarchy*, season 4, episode 1, "Out." Featuring Charlie Hunnam and Maggie Siff. Aired September 6, 2011, FX, DVD.

Barclay, Paris, director. *Sons of Anarchy*, season 7, episode 12, "Red Rose." Featuring Charlie Hunnam and Katey Sagal. Aired December 2, 2014. FX, DVD.

Bennett, Tara. *Sons of Anarchy: The Official Collector's Edition*. New York: Time Home Entertainment, 2014.

Buonanno, Milly. "Editor's Introduction." In *Television Antiheroines: Women Behaving Badly in Crime and Prison Drama*, edited by Milly Buonanno, 2–23. Chicago: Intellect, 2017.

Campbell, Jan. *Freudian Passions*. London: Karnac Books, 2013. EBSCOhost.

Cooper, Jay. "Gemma Death Scene—*Sons of Anarchy*: Comments." December 2, 2014, YouTube. https://www.youtube.com/watch?v=9SLh_Sr8QR8.

Coulter, Allen and Michael Dinner, directors. *Sons of Anarchy*, season 1, episode 1, "Pilot." Featuring Charlie Hunnam and Katey Sagal. Aired September 3, 2008, FX, DVD.

Donnelly, Ashley M. *Renegade Hero or Faux Rogue*. Jefferson, NC: McFarland, 2014. EBSCOhost.

Falcus, Sarah and Katsura Sako. "Women Travelling and Later Life." In *Ageing, Popular Culture and Contemporary Feminism: Harleys and Hormones*, edited by Imelda Whelehan and Joel Gwynne, 203–218. New York: Palgrave MacMillan, 2014.

Fine, Kerry. "She Hits Like a Man, but She Kisses Like a Girl: TV Heroines, Femininity, Violence, and Intimacy." *Western American Literature* 47, no. 2 (2012): 152–173. https://doi:10.1353/wal.2012.0058.

Garland-Thomson, Rosemarie. "Integrating Disability, Transforming Feminist Theory." *NWSA Journal* 14, no. 3 (2002): 1–32. JSTOR.

Gill, Rosalind. "Postfeminist Media Culture: Elements of a Sensibility." *European Journal of Cultural Studies* 10, no. 2 (2007): 147–166. https:// doi:10.1177/1367549407075898.

Goffman, Erving. *Stigma: Notes on the Management of Spoiled Identity*. NJ: Prentice-Hall, 1963.

Gullette, Margaret Morganroth. *Ending Ageism: Or, How Not to Shoot Old People*. New Brunswick, NJ: Rutgers University Press, 2017.

———. "Unwanted at Midlife: Not Old, but 'Too Old.'" *The Las Angeles Review of Books*. February 20, 2019. https://lareviewofbooks.org/article/unwanted-at-midlife-not-old-but-too-old/.

Gunn, Anna. "I Have a Character Issue." *New York Times*. August 23, 2013. https://www.nytimes.com/2013/08/24/opinion/i-have-a-character-issue.html.

Hamad, Hannah. *Post-Feminism and Paternity in Contemporary U.S. Film: Framing Fatherhood*. New York: Routledge, 2014.

Kohan, Jenji, writer. *Weeds*. Season 8, episode 12, "It's Time." Featuring Mary-Louise Parker. Aired September 16, 2012, Showtime, DVD.

Kolb, Leigh C. "Mothers of Anarchy: Power, Control, and Care in the Feminine Sphere." In *"Sons of Anarchy" and Philosophy: Brains before Bullets*, edited by William Irwin, George Dunn, and Jason T. Eberl, 175–186. Chichester; Hoboken: Wiley-Blackwell, 2013.

Lagerwey, Jorie. *Postfeminist Celebrity and Motherhood: Brand Mom*. New York: Routledge, 2017.

Leonard, Suzanne. "Escaping the Recession? The New Vitality of the Woman Worker." In *Gendering the Recession: Media and Culture in an Age of Austerity*, edited by Diane Negra and Yvonne Tasker, 31–58. Durham, NC; London: Duke University Press, 2014.

Lotz, Amanda. "Really Bad Mothers: Manipulative Matriarchs in *Sons of Anarchy* and *Justified*." In *Television Antiheroines: Women Behaving Badly in Crime and Prison Drama*, edited by Milly Buonanno, 125–140. Chicago: Intellect, 2017.

Mann, Seith, director. *Sons of Anarchy*, season 1, episode 4, "Ak-51." Featuring Katey Sagal. Aired October 8, 2008, FX, DVD.

Manne, Kate. *Down Girl: The Logic of Misogyny*. New York: Oxford University Press, 2018.

Marston, Kendra. *Postfeminist Whiteness: Problematising Melancholic Burden in Contemporary Hollywood*. Edinburgh: Edinburgh University Press, 2018.

Mason, Julia M. "Mothers and Antiheroes: Analyzing Motherhood and Representation in *Weeds*, *Sons of Anarchy*, and *Breaking Bad*." *Journal of Popular Culture* 52 no. 3 (2019): 645–662. Wiley Online Library.

McGlynn, Cathy, Margaret O'Neill, and Michaela Schrage-Früh, editors. "Introduction," *Ageing Women in Literature and Visual Culture: Reflections, Refractions, Reimaginings*, 1–20. Cham, Switzerland: Palgrave Macmillan, 2017.

McRobbie, Angela. *The Aftermath of Feminism: Gender, Culture and Social Change*. Los Angeles; London: Sage, 2009.

———. "Post Feminism + Beyond." Posted by Sebastian Richter. June 24, 2012. YouTube video, 40:50. https://www.youtube.com/watch?v=Wk-QIXlx2wk.

Negra, Diane. *What a Girl Wants? Fantasizing the Reclamation of Self in Post-Feminism*. London; New York: Routledge, 2009.

Negra, Diane and Yvonne Tasker. *Gendering the Recession: Media and Culture in an Age of Austerity*. Durham, NC; London: Duke University Press, 2014.

Nijjar, Jaspreet K. "Mutated Masculinities: A Critical Discourse Analysis of the New Lad and the New Man in *Sons of Anarchy* and *Ray Donovan*." *Journal of Men's Studies* 27, no. (2019): 24–44. https://doi10.1177/1060826518782196.

Petri, Alexandra. "A 39-Year-Old Man Is Mysteriously Still a 'Kid.'" *The Washington Post*. July 13, 2017. https://www.washingtonpost.com/blogs/compost/wp/2017/07/13/a-39-year-old-man-is-mysteriously-still-a-kid/.

Stache, Lara C. *Breaking Bad: A Cultural History*. Lanham, MD: Rowman & Littlefield, 2017.

Sutter, Kurt, director. *Sons of Anarchy*, season 6, episode 13, "A Mother's Work." Featuring Charlie Hunnam, Katey Sagal, and Maggie Siff. Aired December 10, 2013, FX, DVD.

Tally, Margaret. *The Rise of the Anti-Heroine in TV's Third Golden Age*. Newcastle upon Tyne: Cambridge Scholars Publishing, 2016.

Thomas. "*Sons of Anarchy*: A Little Stealth Feminism?" *Yes Means Yes: Visions of Female Sexual Power and a World without Rape*. November 15, 2010. https://yesmeansyes-blog.wordpress.com/2010/11/15/sons-of-anarchy-a-little-stealth-feminism/.

Chapter Four

"As Bad as Him"

Reframing Skyler White as Breaking Bad's
Overlooked Antiheroine

Melanie Piper

"Ozymandias," the third-to-last episode of *Breaking Bad*, is bookended by two lies that Walter White tells his wife, Skyler. The first flashes back to the beginning of his journey, the one that creator Vince Gilligan first pitched as "turning Mr. Chips into Scarface."[1] Shortly after being diagnosed with cancer, Walt turns his chemistry expertise into his first meth cook in a bid to secure his family's financial future. It's a simple lie, the first of many, as Walt calls Skyler to tell her that he will be home late from work. The last lie comes later in the episode after the tragic fall of Walt's drug empire: his DEA agent brother-in-law, Hank, is dead, and his family is irrevocably broken. After kidnapping his infant daughter in his escape, Walt calls home. Aware that the police are listening in to the phone call, Walt berates Skyler, minimizing her involvement in the financial side of his criminal activities. His voice harsh, his words vitriolic, he mocks Skyler's initial reaction to finding out he is a drug dealer, her old arguments in favor of the law and morality. With tears streaming down his face, Walt spits insults at her: "You stupid bitch. How dare you. . . . You have no right to discuss anything about what I do. What the hell do you know about it anyway? Nothing." A silent agreement takes place between husband and wife as she picks up on his game and plays along, meekly agreeing with him. This is Walt's final attempt to help his family before he disappears into hiding, to get on the record the lie that his wife was his helpless victim and not one of his last remaining co-conspirators.[2] This lie and its characterization of Skyler echoes the first impressions many *Breaking Bad* viewers had of the character which shaped

57

the way she has been interpreted. This chapter intends to go beyond readings of Skyler White as a foil for or victim of Walter White to consider how the antihero's wife can be considered an antiheroine in her own right.

Television critic Emily Nussbaum wrote that the words Walt leaves his wife with in their final phone call could very well have come from some of *Breaking Bad*'s online fan community.[3] A segment of the *Breaking Bad* audience expressed such overwhelming hatred for Skyler White at the height of the show's popularity that Anna Gunn, the actress who played Skyler, was prompted to pen a *New York Times* editorial addressing the misogyny that Skyler seemed to bring out in some of its viewers.[4] In a series filled with morally gray characters, Skyler has been criticized for her hypocrisy. Her narrative arc takes her from the suspicious wife attempting to get to the source of her husband's drastically changed behavior, to throwing him out of the house and demanding a divorce when he admits to cooking crystal meth, to taking over the financials of Walt's empire and working with him to launder tens of millions of dollars in drug money. Some of her behavior such as smoking while pregnant and sleeping with her boss has led viewers to complain that Skyler is a hypocrite whose moral compass applies to every-one but herself.[5]

This chapter revisits those cracks in Skyler's moral armor to offer a counter to the dominant reception of *Breaking Bad*'s most prominent female character. Rather than reading Skyler as a nagging bitch wife, a reality check against the antihero protagonist,[6] or a tragic victim,[7] this interpretation in-tends to unpack Skyler's potential as an antiheroine. Here, I reexamine Skyler White's narrative journey and propose that her arc traces a seismic shift in her relationship to criminality on par with that of the series' male leads. The morally and legally dubious choices she makes while attempting to assert her agency and push back against the boundaries of victimhood make for a fascinatingly flawed character who is all too often relegated to the margins of one of the most critically and popularly revered series of contem-porary television. Through the example of Skyler White, the role of the antihero's wife in contemporary television is reevaluated to shed light on the often-strict moral standards to which women are held.

As an antiheroine, Skyler's characterization is firmly rooted in a distinctly feminine domestic space.[8] As a possible explanation for why the wives of television antiheroes are so often maligned, Margrethe Bruun Vaage argues that in the contemporary antihero television series, home and family are constructed as the boring, staid life that the male antihero wants to escape.[9] Our first introduction to Skyler comes as she hands Walt his breakfast on his fiftieth birthday, forcing the family to eat veggie bacon, and inquiring about Walt's persistent cough.[10] She is visibly pregnant and immediately shown in a caretaker role as a wife and mother. The maligning of the domestic space in a male antihero series like *Breaking Bad*, and Skyler's stereotypically feminine role of "home" and "family" in the series, could account for some of the antipathy directed toward her character. When Skyler begins her moral transformation, it is done within the construct of this feminine gender role. She uses her sexuality as a weapon through her infidelity, controls Walt's access to the family home and their children and extends her everyday management of household finances to managing Walt's drug money. Zach Blumenfeld notes the unique power that Skyler draws from her femininity, and how she uses her gender to her advantage, whether it is faking labor to get out of a possible arrest, or faking a suicide attempt to get her children out of the house and away from Walt.[11] This analysis takes an approach to the antiheroine that shares some overlap with established understandings of the male antihero. As Margaret Tally writes, the contemporary television antihero behaves in ways that are morally, legally, or ethically dubious in order to achieve a goal that is seen as justifiable, given the character's circumstances.[12] Gender roles and their associated expectations are where this analysis deviates from this basic definition. Tally goes on to note that the male antihero's behavior often stems from broader questions of male identity that works to amplify the character's hypermasculine coding to the point of toxicity. In considering the antiheroine, Tally finds these kinds of gendered characteristics too limiting an understanding.[13] The type of antiheroine under consideration in this chapter, however, relies on gendered characteristics and transgresses the acceptable standards of her traditionally feminine role, rendering her as the difficult woman her antihero partner must contend with.

In reframing Skyler White as an antiheroine, I will first examine how the narrative constructs Skyler as an antagonist early on in the series and examine some of the potential reasons behind the negative reception discourses surrounding the character, and what this has done to block potential readings of Skyler-as-antiheroine. Then, I move on to looking in detail at two key points in Skyler's journey of moral compromise: her affair with her boss, Ted Beneke, and her decision to stay with Walt and begin laundering his drug money. By examining the motivations behind these actions, my goal is to demonstrate how Skyler's deliberate use of her femininity, her professional and creative skills, and her desire to control the domestic sphere drives her to commit moral and legal transgressions. Through this example, possibilities emerge for considering the antihero's wife as an antiheroine in her own right.

SKYLER THE ANTAGONIST

Breaking Bad would not work if the audience were not on Walt's side from the very beginning of the series. If we are to go along on this journey, we must understand why Walt makes the decisions that he does, why Mr. Chips stays on the road to becoming Scarface. But before that final transformation;

before the challenges, threats, and complications put in Walt's way; before the drug world leads Walt to Tuco Salamanca, Gustavo Fring, and Jack Welker; and before Hank becomes aware that Walt is the kingpin he has been chasing all along, Mr. Chips needs his first antagonist. This is how we are initially positioned to view Skyler White: the object standing in the way not only of Walt's goals, but our viewing pleasures of experiencing Walt's "enjoyable transgressions."[14]

When Walter is diagnosed with inoperable lung cancer in the series' pilot episode, he partners up with his former student and street-level dealer, Jesse Pinkman, and puts his chemistry expertise to work manufacturing high purity methamphetamine. Walt's goal is clear: earn whatever money he can in the time he has left in order to provide for Skyler; Walter Jr., their teenage son with cerebral palsy; and Holly, the surprise baby with whom Skyler is pregnant for the majority of the first two seasons. Outside of Walt and Jesse's early misadventures and setbacks in the meth trade, Skyler is the primary threat to Walt's goals. Skyler questions and attempts to investigate his frequent long absences from home, threatening Walt's secrets as he initially tries to keep both his cancer diagnosis and his newly found criminality under wraps. Once Walt reveals his diagnosis to appease her, Skyler insists he seek the best (and, therefore, most expensive) treatment available. After Walt agrees to undergo treatment, his plan becomes even more complicated. Gone is the hope of a nest egg for his family and a quick death on his own terms. Now he must go further down the criminal path to pay for his additional healthcare costs and continue to conceal his double life from an increasingly suspicious Skyler.

From the viewer's vantage point, Skyler is an antagonist, the one from whom secrets must be kept while also standing in the way of Walt's criminal life. In Murray Smith's typology of character engagement, we are primarily "aligned" with Walt: by virtue of Walt being the focus of the narrative, we have more access to the character in terms of what behaviors we witness and how we are led to understand his interiority.[15] As Jason Mittell notes, it is rare in television that we as viewers get direct access to a character's interiority as a reader would in literature through conventions such as inner voices or descriptions of emotion and thought. Therefore, most of the cues of a character's interiority in television come from witnessing and reading external cues such as appearance, behavior, and dialogue.[16] Given the amount of screen time we spend with Walt, we can see shifts in the external cues of his self-performance in different contexts he balances: at home with his family, out cooking in the RV with Jesse, at work as the underappreciated chemistry genius trapped in a high school classroom filled with indifferent teenagers. We see both his public and private behaviors and accumulate evidence that guides us toward understanding his interiority, his emotions and thought processes. In order to keep the audience engaged throughout Walt's moral decay and criminal transformation, the viewer's alignment with and access to Walt is essential.

Skyler, on the other hand, does not occupy as much screen time or narrative space as Walt. Not only is the viewer's time with her less, but the way our time with her is positioned is almost exclusively in terms of what our protagonist, Walt, does. Robert Blanchet and Margrethe Bruun Vaage argue that television's narrative structure of repeated encounters with characters that span across episodes and seasons permits repeated and extended exposure to television characters, which fosters deep engagement and parasocial connections through familiarity.[17] Malcolm Turvey offers a counter to this theory, pointing out that while familiarity brings pleasure, it also "breeds contempt."[18] I propose that it is Skyler's initial positioning as an antagonist to Walt that has contributed to some of the negative reception toward the character, and the frequent oversight of Skyler as a complex, morally compromised character and antiheroine. Turvey writes that if an initial impression of a character is positive, familiarity and repeated exposure can facilitate the pleasures of a parasocial connection. However, if we view them as having unattractive qualities, repeat exposure to the character only amplifies this negative reaction.[19] For viewers positioned to see Skyler as a roadblock to Walt's initial goals in the first season—her repeated questioning of his disappearances, her insistence that he pursue costly cancer treatment, her disclosure of his cancer diagnosis to the rest of their family—this first impression frames the reception of what might be seen as her future bad acts in later seasons, long after her antagonist position is usurped by other, more deliberately villainous, characters that Walt encounters in the drug trade.

The vitriol directed toward Skyler White—and, often, in turn, actor Anna Gunn—on platforms such as Facebook and Reddit has been frequently addressed in critical and scholarly consideration of the character.[20] In her *New York Times* op-ed, Gunn herself addresses the hatred of Skyler by proposing it is laced with a thread of misogyny directed at a strong female character who does not fit the ideals of what a wife should be.[21] Lara C. Stache proposes that fan misogyny is not entirely to blame for the vocal hatred of Skyler, instead arguing that Skyler is, on first encounter in the early seasons of the show, simply unlikeable. Stache herself even notes that it took until her fifth viewing of the series to begin to see the character differently.[22] Rather than approaching Skyler as the antagonist of the early episodes, Stache proposes that as a character she suffers from being underwritten in the first few seasons, "a one-note character whose primary focus is telling Walt what he should be doing and constantly suggesting he fails as a partner by shutting her out."[23] Melissa Vosen Callens makes a similar argument that it is a lack of character development and backstory in the female partners of television's male antiheroes that suppresses them being popularly accepted as operating in a similar antihero role.[24] This early "underwrittenness" means that it is not only that Skyler is Walt's roadblock that renders her unlikeable, but how she goes about it. Stache cites moments such as Skyler investigating a phone call Walt receives from Jesse and acting on the explanation Walt gives her that Jesse is selling him marijuana. Skyler's approach to telling Jesse to quit selling pot to her husband makes her seem like "a naïve prude, unaware of how the world really works, and [she] treats Walt like a child."[25] Without a clear backstory or motivation being written into Skyler's behavior early in the series, her only function is to impede Walt and she does so in an unlikeable manner that is pushy, clueless, and condescending. It is moments like this that accumulate throughout the early episodes of the series to create the first encounters with Skyler that, upon repeat exposure begin to engage the more negative, contemptuous aspects of familiarity that Turvey describes for some viewers.

This baseline of Skyler's rigid moral framework, however, does serve to lay the foundation for her descent into compromised criminality and the opening of her complexity as a potential antiheroine in later seasons. Early on, we see that Skyler is adamantly opposed to any infraction against institutions of the law and the family, from Walt's hypothetical marijuana use and long afternoon disappearances, to her son Walter Jr.'s attempts at underage drinking, to her sister Marie's shoplifting. However, with repeated negative encounters establishing the character as unlikeable for many viewers, when Skyler begins to stray from her strict moral code it is seen as a distasteful act of blatant hypocrisy rather than burgeoning complexity and character development. Even when Skyler's bad acts are framed in connection to and contrast with Walt's, the balance of negative reception is tipped toward Skyler. Take, for example, Skyler's smoking while pregnant, a transgression that is often cited as a particularly immoral and selfish act in fan criticisms of Skyler.[26] As Elliott Logan observes, in the moment when Walt confronts Skyler about her covert smoking, Skyler mirrors Walt's behavior as she hardens and shuts down and sarcastically adopts Walt's "fugue state" excuse as her own in order to avoid exposure and protect herself against shame.[27] Although Skyler's actions are often purposefully aligned with Walt's, there is a marked contrast in how they are received in terms of reading the character as an antihero.

In order to reframe the discussion of Skyler's character arc, I will be approaching my analysis of key moments in her development by applying what Carl Plantinga outlines as the understanding of fictional characters as "moral agents." This requires the consideration of characters *as if* they are real people, overlooking their functions as narrative constructs to consider them as "intentional beings with desires, beliefs, anticipations, and motivations for their actions."[28] In doing so, my aim is to engage in a version of reception discourse that evaluates the character's motivations, behavior, and reactions in a way that attempts to remove potential limitation—such as narrative bias toward empathizing with Walt—to understanding Skyler White as a rounded, complex, and morally flawed character.

In order to reframe Skyler's motivations and journey into moral compromise, I will be closely examining two narrative events that constitute transgressions against the family and the law that are done with the purpose of getting what she wants out of the situation that Walt has created. First, I will be looking at Skyler's affair with her boss, Ted Beneke, in early season 3 and the subsequent decisions she makes to stay with Walt. This then leads to the second major event in Skyler's antiheroine arc, as she becomes actively involved in Walt's criminal activity by taking responsibility for laundering his money in the latter part of the third season and into the fourth.

SHE FUCKED TED: WEAPONIZED INFIDELITY

One recurring criticism of Skyler is her affair with Ted, owner of the fabrications company where she works part-time as a bookkeeper.[29] At this point in the narrative, Skyler is aware that Walt manufactures methamphetamine, has banished him from the family home, and has initiated divorce proceedings. In the season 3 episode "I.F.T.,"[30] Walt breaks into the White residence to resume family life as if nothing has happened. Upon discovering Walt has returned against her wishes, Skyler threatens and eventually follows through with calling the police on her husband. Without any restraining order in place, without any evidence of family violence, and with Skyler unwilling to reveal Walt's criminal activity to the authorities, there is nothing that the police can do about Walt's presence in the home. Skyler is rendered powerless as Walt performs the role of dutiful husband and father, offering to soothe baby Holly when she starts to cry and making grilled cheese sandwiches for Walter Jr., who is ecstatic to see his father has returned and bewildered that his mother has called the police on him.

After days of being ignored, Walt confronts Skyler with a duffle bag full of half a million dollars in drug money laid out on their living room floor. Gunn's performance in this scene shows Skyler as both transfixed and terrified by the money and what it represents: she appears to exert great effort in tearing her eyes away from the bundles of cash to look at Walt, visibly shaking. Walt implores her to accept the money. He earned it, and the things he has done to earn it will be for naught if Skyler refuses to use it for its intended purpose to support herself and the children once he is gone. Skyler is forced to listen silently, hands knotted in her lap, her breathing labored and eyes glassy with tears as she shakes her head almost unconsciously. "I'll be here when you get home from work," Walt tells her. "You can give me your answer then."[31]

It is under these circumstances that Skyler actively pursues the simmering flirtation with Ted that has been building since the previous season and, it is implied, existed before the timeline of the series. Unable to reinforce and uphold the boundaries of her domestic sphere, Skyler uses her sexuality and bodily autonomy outside of the home to regain some of the control that Walt has eroded. When she sleeps with Ted for the first time, Skyler's subsequent actions indicate that her purpose is not to engage in subterfuge or create her own secret life separate from Walt. The first thing she does after sleeping with Ted is to tell Walt, in the bluntest of terms, what she has done. This suggests that Skyler's intention behind the affair was for Walt to know about it, the infidelity thus becoming a strategic move designed to make Walt leave.

When Skyler returns home that evening, once again Walt sets the tone for what will take place within their home. By unexpectedly inviting Walter Jr.'s friend, Louis, to stay for dinner, any kind of confrontation between Walt and Skyler must be put on hold to maintain a front for their son and his friend. In the kitchen, Skyler once again stands in silence as Walt prepares dinner, reflecting on their conversation about the money from that morning, extolling the virtues of the new honesty and openness in their relationship. Calmly and quietly, Skyler steps forward to stand across from him, and softly tells him: "I fucked Ted." She picks up the salad Walt has been preparing and takes it to the table, calling the boys to dinner. Skyler has turned Walt's tactic of keeping up a front for Walter Jr. and Louis back on him, leaving him to simmer in angry silence before the episode cuts to black.

Melissa Vosen Callens observes that infidelity a common trait of antiheroine wives that sees women assert their agency and challenge gender role stereotypes, often to the detriment of their likeability.[32] Taken from the point of view of audience allegiance with Walt, Skyler's affair is seen as showing a lack of gratitude for the lengths that her husband has gone to secure the family's financial future, callously cheating on a man battling cancer. To reframe Skyler's choice to sleep with Ted as the act of an antiheroine, her motivation for doing so must be considered. In the argument that follows Skyler's revelation, she tells Walt, "If you don't like it then *leave*. And take your drug money with you."[33] In a later episode, she confesses to her divorce lawyer that she is sleeping with her boss and that deep down she might be doing it to get Walt to leave her, but also expresses that being with Ted is the only moment in her day she does not "feel like [she's] drowning."[34] Understanding Skyler's motivation for her affair with Ted, the act becomes a moral transgression done to assert her autonomy and control where it was otherwise being suppressed, her sexuality turned into a weapon to use against Walt to try to make him leave her. The affair is a transgression that goes against not only what is expected of Skyler's role as a wife and mother, but which goes against her own established moral code. For a time, she commits, without apparent remorse, an act that she herself would likely have found reprehensible earlier in the series. She compromises her morality to reclaim her agency in an attempt to achieve a desired outcome.

Skyler's decision to stay with Walt and to not file their divorce papers is another choice that sees her compromising and further eroding her established moral framework. There are two moments that we as viewers have access to that give an indication of Skyler's interiority and motivation behind the decision. The first moment is part of a phone call with her sister Marie as Skyler is parked outside Ted's house, about to embark on another rendezvous. Marie has called to talk about Hank, who has been recently traumatized by an encounter with the Mexican drug cartel while on assignment in Juárez. "Facing death, it changes a person," Marie tells Skyler. "It has to; don't you think? I guess you've noticed a change in Walt."[35] This comment from Marie seems to trigger Skyler into looking at their situation with a sense of empathy for Walt that the revelation of his criminal activity has thus far prevented: at dinner that night, she offers to let Walt take care of a crying Holly, which Walt gratefully accepts. Later in the same episode, the second hint of Skyler's interiority comes as she is putting away laundry and comes across Walt's bag of cash. She turns away and abruptly stops and reconsiders. As she takes a second look, we see Skyler battling her "repulsion for and attraction to" the money[36] as she slowly opens the bag, her hands sliding cautiously over the fabric she pulls back the zipper. She picks up one of the bundles of cash for closer examination, her lips parted and eyes wide for a moment before she exhales in a rush. The shot cuts back to her hands and she suddenly drops the cash bundle back in the bag, fingers splayed as if in resistance to her first impulse. Skyler is clearly curious enough to entertain the money's possibilities on her own before she pulls herself back from the edge.

Skyler changed her moral standards for Ted when she not only entered a relationship with him, but, as his bookkeeper, agreed to cover up his embezzlement and tax fraud. Her standards shift once again in order to protect her family as she begins to come to terms with Walt's meth manufacturing. When Skyler reveals to both Walt and the audience that she never finalized their divorce, she explains that married couples cannot be compelled to testify against each other. The fact of their continuing marriage soon becomes convenient for the cover story and money laundering that Skyler works to take control of.

CLEAN CARS, CLEAN MONEY, DIRTY HANDS

The season 3 finale, "Full Measure,"[37] takes us sixteen years or so into the past with a cold open flashback that shows Walt and Skyler inspecting the house that will become their home. This Walt is different from the one we are first introduced to in the series. This Walt is cocky, ambitious, and dreams big. Skyler tempers his desire for a five-bedroom house for the three children he eventually wants with caution and pragmatism. The Skyler-as-antagonist to Walt's desires dynamic is present even in the flashback, although its execution is softened by the apparent newlywed bliss of their relationship. The flashback reveals Skyler's pragmatism as an inherent trait of her character that helps to explain a narrative development of the late third season that carries over into the fourth, as Skyler becomes involved in creating a plausible cover story for the existence of Walt's money and, eventually, takes responsibility for laundering it.

After Hank is injured in a cartel shooting that Skyler correctly suspects has something to do with Walt's criminal enterprise, she offers to help Marie pay for Hank's physical therapy using Walt's money.[38] In order to explain the money's existence, Skyler invents a cover story that Walt earned the money through gambling. As Skyler presents this story to Marie, Walt is also hearing it for the first time, sitting forward in his chair and hanging on Skyler's every word. While Skyler tells Walt that the lie came about because she "learned from the best" (once again aligning Walt and Skyler's transgressive behavior), her ability to create and control a narrative gestures toward a piece of backstory introduced early in the series. Skyler is a writer, and it is a skill she puts to use in her capabilities as a liar and the importance she places on constructing and upholding a plausible narrative. Following from the intricate creation of the gambling cover story, Skyler's desire for caution resurfaces to temper Walt's excesses by setting in motion a plan to buy the carwash that Walt formerly worked at, rather than the less plausible money laundering options of a laser tag arcade or a nail salon proposed by their lawyer, Saul Goodman. Her role in managing the carwash and Walt's money utilizes her skills as a bookkeeper, not only in the actual process of money laundering, but in maintaining the plausibility of their cover story that protects Walt's money from attracting the attention of the IRS or the suspicions of their family.

At this point, Skyler has come to tolerate the idea that Walt is bringing in millions of dollars as a methamphetamine manufacturer, and that he is not going to stop. She takes the step to begin actively engaging in illegal activity herself in order to reassert some control over a situation where she otherwise has none. It has been decided that this is how Walt makes his money and that she will accept the money he makes. Skyler's primary concern is preventing her children, particularly Walter Jr., from finding out about Walt's criminal activity. Going to the authorities is out of the question for her: all she can do is try to stop the authorities from finding them. Skyler's skills in storytelling and money management, along with her pragmatic nature, are what she draws upon in her efforts to control the situation as much as she can, thus officially entering into a criminal partnership with Walt. These skills that were formerly attached to the feminine domestic space—publishing short stories as a hobby and to bring in extra money, working part-time as a bookkeeper around her duties as a mother—become refocused in the interests of criminality.

Her desire to keep her children from finding out about Walt's crimes is Skyler's ultimate undoing that drives her further into criminality. Rather than actually protecting her children, Skyler's motivation leads her to become "the bad mother," another common theme of antiheroine wives that transgresses the boundaries of acceptable femininity.[39] Skyler goes to great lengths in her attempts to prevent the children from finding out about Walt, and in doing so, also potentially brings harm to her children by disrupting their home life with little to no explanation. In early season 3, as Skyler begins the process of separating from Walt and directs him to move out of the house, Walter Jr. is left in a state of anger and confusion: from what he has experienced, his father has just recovered from cancer surgery and suddenly his mother has thrown his father out of the house for seemingly no reason. The introduction of the gambling cover story offers some explanation, but, as Skyler tells Walt, the cover story paints her as "the bitch Mom who wouldn't cut [him] any slack" to their son.[40] The confusion and disruption is repeated in season 5, after Skyler stages an emotional breakdown by walking into the pool during Walt's fifty-first birthday dinner.[41] What appears to be a possible suicide attempt to Marie and Hank is Skyler's tactic to get the children out of the house after she finds out that Walt is not only involved in the drug trade, but is a murderer. Subsequently, Skyler purposefully performs the role of an emotionally unstable and unfit mother so that Marie and Hank will take Walter Jr. and Holly into their care, separating the White family for what ends up being a three-month period of story time.

Throughout Skyler's negotiation of her place in Walt's criminal life, her actions toward her children could be seen to be done for the greater good, to, as she puts it "protect this family from the man who protects this family."[42] However, the futility of maintaining Walt's cover for the sake of the kids becomes apparent at the moment Walt's empire falls apart.[43] When Marie receives a phone call from Hank to tell her he has Walt in custody, she goes to Skyler to tell her that it is over. Marie demands that Skyler tell Walter Jr. everything so that he hears the news from his family. Skyler is shocked out of a near catatonic state to tearfully and emphatically plead with Marie: "No. No. No, he cannot know." The truth is inescapable at this point, however, and Junior is understandably shocked into disbelief. In between his denials are some pointed accusations levelled at Skyler. First, he asks, "How could you keep this a secret . . . why would you go along?" to which she responds through tears, "I'll be asking myself that for the rest of my life." Later, he condemns her as Walt's equal: "If all this is true and you knew about it, then you're as bad as him." Skyler accepts the judgment in silence.

With her criminal behavior so inextricably linked with Walt's, and both the motivation and consequences of her criminal behavior tied to her children, Skyler fits further tropes of the contemporary television antiheroine. Margaret Tally writes that often the antiheroine's moral transgressions take place as part of a married unit, and that the antiheroine's behavior is frequently conflated with being a bad mother.[44] Although Skyler's motivation for joining Walt's criminal empire is repeatedly expressed as being a means of protecting her children, the outcomes paint her not only as a bad mother to Walter Jr. himself, but eventually completely destroys their home life with Skyler potentially facing federal prison.[45] The moment that Skyler loses control over her idea of protecting the children from criminal life is illustrated by a literal role reversal of protector/protected. When she suspects that Walt has killed Hank, she pulls a knife from the kitchen and blocks Walter Jr. from coming any closer as she brandishes it at Walt, demanding he leave the house. In the struggle that ensues, Walt gets control of the weapon and pins Skyler to the ground. It is Walter Jr. who pulls his father from his mother and calls 911, now serving in the role of protector as his arm barricades a weeping Skyler from Walt. It is Walter Jr. who notices that Walt has picked up baby Holly, and Skyler who ineffectually runs after Walt as he drives away with their daughter.[46] In the end, Skyler's complicity in Walt's crimes is revealed to cause more harm than the "higher good"[47] it was ostensibly driven by.

As with many of *Breaking Bad*'s characters, Skyler has a fatal flaw that proves to be her undoing: her belief that the space she carves out for herself using what resources she has—whether that be her sexuality as a weapon, her skills as a liar and a storyteller, or her ability to take Walt's children from him—is enough to provide a cover of control and safety. As she repeatedly adjusts her moral boundaries to take account of Walt's own moral descent and how it affects her ability to keep their children unaware of their criminal life, she goes so far that by the final episodes of the series, she has destroyed her relationship with her sister by helping Walt blackmail Hank.[48] Ultimately, in what is perhaps the rock bottom of Skyler's moral decay, she actively encourages Walt to commit murder. After Jesse breaks into the Whites' house and attempts to burn it down, Skyler does not understand why Walt values Jesse's life over his family's safety, telling him coldly, "We've come this far. For us. What's one more?"[49] What was once a strict moral code that baulked at the comparatively minor crime of Marie's shoplifting has become so compromised that toward the end of the series, Skyler is arguably a closer criminal partner to Walt than Walt is to Jesse. By that point, for her, murder is simply a necessary means to what proves to be an unattainable end.

CONCLUSION

Throughout the series, Skyler's motivation for becoming increasingly complicit in Walt's criminal activities is presented in much the same terms as his own: they do it for the family. Walt's motivation is dismantled in the series finale as he finally admits to Skyler, "I did it for me. I liked it. I was good at it. And I was, really—I was alive."[50] However, Skyler's motivation of keeping Walt's secrets from their children until the situation can resolve itself with Walt's death from cancer is exposed as a delusion without specifically clarifying any underlying self-serving motivation. As Vaage notes, the direct access we get to Skyler's thought process and motivation for staying with Walt is limited, with the conversations with her divorce lawyer in season 3 the only real opportunity Skyler has to verbally express what she is going through.[51] In these scenes, Skyler is given the advice to immediately divorce Walter and go to the police, with her lawyer spelling out what will happen if she does not: consequences are ultimately what happens as Skyler and her kids lose their home and everything they own. Skyler expresses her paralysis and inability to make a decision in any direction and rationalizes her reluctance to divorce Walt as the fact that she "didn't marry a criminal."[52] Working through her thoughts in front of her lawyer's judgment creates a performative screen to Skyler's words that renders them potentially insincere. Despite her denials to the contrary, there is a sense that Skyler wants to justify keeping the money not only so that what Walt has done is not for naught, but so the suffering she has endured means something too.[53] Rebecca Price-Wood's analysis of Skyler White as a believable and accurate portrayal of a postpartum woman emphasizes the need for stability and drive to protect her newborn baby underlying many of Skyler's choices.[54] This reading is a valuable one that helps to contextualize and reinforce the plausibility of Skyler's moral compromise when it comes to Walt's criminality. Nevertheless, there is some ambiguity in the moments that Skyler first encounters Walt's money. That ambiguity and the gusto with which she throws herself into creating and maintaining their cover story, on closer examination of the character, raise some questions about the seemingly clear-cut nature of Skyler's motivation. Was Skyler drawn to the money? Did her pragmatic nature take over when Walt pointed out that the money would be necessary to support the children after his death? Did her failed dream of being a writer finally get a chance to flourish? Were some of the reasons behind her own criminal behavior as self-serving as Walt's, cloaked beneath the guise of doing it for the family? These kinds of questions about character motivation are perhaps vital to the contemporary complex serial television narrative. Mittell describes "narrative statements" as the events in a television narrative that make us question what is going to happen next, and "narrative enigmas" as elements of uncertainty as to what happened, how it happened, why it happened, or whether it happened at all.[55] Once the narrative is resolved, however, in the age of archived television through platforms such as Netflix perhaps questions of narrative enigmas related to character motivation become vital to sustaining the shelf life of a television series. Questions like the exact nature of Skyler White as an antiheroine are ones that can never quite be completely resolved long after everyone knows what happens in the story.

Some scholars writing about Skyler White have noted their initial dislike of the character that was overcome through subsequent repeat watching of the series[56] and, likewise, some of the fan response to Skyler has softened in the years since *Breaking Bad* ended. Prompted by the 2019 release of the Jesse Pinkman-focused epilogue *El Camino: A Breaking Bad Movie*, fans returned to *Breaking Bad* to re-watch in preparation for the film's release. On Reddit, some responses took a more empathetic view of Skyler this time around.[57] This is evidence of the value of re-watching complex television in order to negotiate alternate readings and points of ambiguity. The narrative initially constructs Skyler as an antagonist and the bastion of the domestic, stagnant life that Walt is escaping through his criminal transgressions. Perhaps it is only once the outcome of Walt's story is known that focus can be given to Skyler's role in it, and her motivations more readily understood. In the era of binge-watch consumption of a series like *Breaking Bad*, the compressed window of screen time spent with a disliked character does not give the viewer's initial responses the time and space between episodes to evolve and change.

Antiheroine wives like Skyler White, Carmela Soprano, and Betty Draper have been judged by different standards than their husbands. By representing the domestic space that the male antihero escapes through moral or criminal transgressions, the antihero's wife and her feminine-coded existence becomes all that is uninteresting about a male antihero's double life. Turvey argues that it is our fascination for the antihero, not our sympathy or empathy, that keeps us engaged.[58] In the case of Skyler White, being the opposite of Walter White's enjoyable transgressions means that the fascination factor may be lacking enough for the majority of viewers to readily accept her as an antihero in her own right, albeit in a supporting role to a male protagonist. There is perhaps an inherent unlikability and difficulty to the antiheroine in a male-driven narrative, particularly one such as Skyler whose transgressions are enmeshed with her use of femininity as a means of power and control. To transgress what is considered acceptable behavior for a wife and mother, through acts such as infidelity, inserting herself into her husband's criminal activity, and bringing harm to her children, is to break with gendered expectations, linking the concepts of "anti" and "female" in the female antihero. By reframing Skyler as an antihero and examining her moral arc on its own merits, perhaps we can see that, just like Walt, she was good at being bad.

NOTES

1. Vince Gilligan, interviewed by Terry Gross, *Fresh Air*, October 11, 2019, https://www.npr.org/2019/10/11/769312766/breaking-bad-creator-vince-gilligan-reflects-on-meth-and-morals.

2. *Breaking Bad*, "Ozymandias," directed by Rian Johnson, written by Moira Walley-Beckett, AMC, September 15, 2013.

3. Emily Nussbaum, "That Mind-Bending Phone Call on Last Night's *Breaking Bad*," *New Yorker*, September 16, 2013, https://www.newyorker.com/culture/culture-desk/that-mind-bending-phone-call-on-last-nights-breaking-bad.

4. Anna Gunn, "I Have a Character Issue," *New York Times*, August 23, 2013, https://www.nytimes.com/2013/08/24/opinion/i-have-a-character-issue.html.

5. Joke Hermes and Leonie Stoete, "Hating Skyler White: Audience Engagement, Gender Politics and Celebrity Culture," *Celebrity Studies* 10, no. 3 (2019), 417–418, https://doi.org/10.1080/19392397.2019.1630155.

6. Margrethe Bruun Vaage, *The Antihero in American Television* (New York, Routledge, 2015), 167.

7. Zach Blumenfeld, "Why TV Finally Caught Up to *Breaking Bad*'s Skyler White," *Consequence of Sound*, October 8, 2019, https://consequenceofsound.net/2019/10/breaking-bad-skyler-white-op-ed/.

8. Lara C. Stache, *"Breaking Bad": A Cultural History* (Lanham, MD: Rowman & Littlefield, 2017), 101.

9. Vaage, *The Antihero*, 154.

10. *Breaking Bad*, "Pilot," S01E01, directed and written by Vince Gilligan, AMC, January 20, 2008.

11. Blumenfeld, "Why TV Finally Caught Up."

12. Margaret Tally, *The Rise of the Anti-Heroine in TV's Third Golden Age* (Newcastle-Upon-Tyne: Cambridge Scholars, 2016), 5.

13. Ibid., 103.

14. Vaage, *The Antihero*, 151.

15. Murray Smith, *Engaging Characters: Fiction, Emotion, and the Cinema* (Oxford: Clarendon, 1995), 142–143.

16. Jason Mittell, *Complex TV: The Poetics of Contemporary Television Storytelling* (New York: NYU Press, 2015), 130.

17. Robert Blanchet and Margrethe Bruun Vaage, "Don, Peggy, and Other Fictional Friends? Engaging with Characters in Television Series," *Projections* 6, no. 2 (Winter 2012): 22–24. DOI: 10.3167/proj.2012.060203.

18. Malcolm Turvey, "Familiarity Breeds Contempt: Why Fascination, rather than Repeat Exposure, Better Explains the Appeal of Antiheroes on Television," in *Screening Characters: Theories of Character in Film, Television and Interactive Media*, ed. Johannes Riis and Aaron Taylor (New York: Routledge, 2019), 231.

19. Turvey, "Familiarity Breeds Contempt," 236.

20. For the scholarly take, see: Stache, *A Cultural History*, 95–112; Vaage, *The Antihero*, 150–169; Hermes and Stoete, "Hating Skyler White." For discussion in the blogosphere, see, for example: Blumenfeld, "Why TV Finally Caught Up"; Nussbaum, "That Mind-Bending Phone Call,"; Ellen E. Jones, "Skyler White: The *Breaking Bad* Underdog Who Set the Template for TV's Antiheroine," *The Guardian*, January 13, 2018, https://www.theguardian.com/tv-and-radio/2018/jan/13/breaking-bad-how-skyler-white-created-the-modern-aniheroine.

21. Gunn, "I Have a Character Issue."

22. Stache, *A Cultural History*, 96.

23. Stache, *A Cultural History*, 98.

24. Melissa Vosen Callens, "AMC's Infamous Criminal Partnerships: Suppressing the Female Antihero," *Dialogue* 6, no. 2 (2019), 55–57, http://journaldialogue.org/issues/v6-issue-2/amcs-infamous-criminal-partnerships-suppressing-the-female-antihero/.

25. Stache, *A Cultural History*, 98.

26. Hermes and Stoete, "Hating Skyler White," 417.

27. Elliott Logan, *"Breaking Bad" and Dignity: Unity and Fragmentation in the Serial Television Drama* (Houndmills: Palgrave, 2016), 63–64.

28. Carl Plantinga, "Ethical Criticism and Fictional Characters as Moral Agents," in *Screening Characters: Theories of Character in Film, Television and Interactive Media*, ed. Johannes Riis and Aaron Taylor (New York: Routledge, 2019), 192.

29. Hermes and Stoete, "Hating Skyler White," 417–418.

30. *Breaking Bad*, "I.F.T.," season 3, episode 3, directed by Michelle MacLaren, written by George Mastras, AMC, April 4, 2010.

31. *Breaking Bad*, "I.F.T."

32. Callens, "AMC's Infamous Criminal Partnerships," 52–53.

33. *Breaking Bad*, "Green Light," season 3, episode 4, directed by Scott Winant, written by Sam Catlin, AMC, April 11, 2010.

34. *Breaking Bad*, "Más," season 3, episode 5, directed by Johan Renck, written by Moira Walley-Beckett, AMC, April 18, 2010.

35. *Breaking Bad*, "Más."

36. Plantinga, "Ethical Criticism," 191.

37. *Breaking Bad*, "Full Measure," season 3, episode 13, directed and written by Vince Gilligan, AMC, June 13, 2010.

38. *Breaking Bad*, "Kafkaesque," season 3, episode 9, directed by Michael Slovis, written by Peter Gould and George Mastras, AMC, May 16, 2010.

39. Callens, "AMC's Infamous Criminal Partnerships," 53–54.

40. *Breaking Bad*, "Bullet Points," season 4, episode 4, directed by Colin Bucksey, written by Moira Walley-Beckett, AMC, August 7, 2011.

41. *Breaking Bad*, "Fifty-One," season 5, episode 4, directed by Rian Johnson, written by Sam Catlin, AMC, August 5, 2012.

42. *Breaking Bad*, "Cornered," season 4, episode 6, directed by Michael Slovis, written by Gennifer Hutchinson, AMC, August 21, 2011.

43. *Breaking Bad*, "Ozymandias."

44. Tally, *The Rise of the Anti-Heroine*, 17.

45. *Breaking Bad*, "Granite State," season 5, episode 15, directed and written by Peter Gould, AMC, September 22, 2013.

46. *Breaking Bad*, "Ozymandias."

47. Tally, *The Rise of the Anti-Heroine*, 9.

48. *Breaking Bad*, "Confessions," season 5, episode 11, directed by Michael Slovis, written by Gennifer Hutchinson, AMC, August 25, 2013.

49. *Breaking Bad*, "Rabid Dog," season 5, episode 12, directed and written by Sam Catlin, AMC, September 1, 2013.

50. *Breaking Bad*, "Felina," season 5, episode 16, directed and written by Vince Gilligan, AMC, September 29, 2013.

51. Bruun Vaage, *The Antihero*, 160.

52. *Breaking Bad*, "Más."

53. Alan Sepinwall, *Breaking Bad 101: The Complete Critical Companion* (New York: Abrams Press, 2017), 110; Stache, *A Cultural History*, 111–112.

54. Rebecca Price-Woods, "Breaking Bad Stereotypes about Postpartum: A Case for Skyler White," in *The Methods of "Breaking Bad": Essays on Narrative, Character and Ethics*, ed. Jacob Blevins and Dafydd Wood (Jefferson, NC: McFarland, 2015), 132–146.

55. Mittell, *Complex TV*, 24–25.

56. See Stache, *A Cultural History*, 96; Vaage, *The Antihero*, 163. In the interests of full disclosure, I greatly enjoyed Skyler's passive-aggression on my first watch of the series, despite it being a less than admirable character trait.

57. See, for example: rxtc, "I changed my mind about Skyler," Reddit thread, August 21, 2019, https://reddit.com/r/breakingbad/comments/ctc9rb/i_changed_my_mind_about_skyler/; WhiteWolfofUtah, "It didn't really click until this last rewatch but . . . Skyler got dealt such a shit hand," Reddit thread, September 24, 2019, https://reddit.com/r/breakingbad/comments/d8h2bn/it_didnt_really_click_until_this_latest_rewatch/; clearsurname, "On my 2nd rewatch, I'm finding Skyler is an amazing character," Reddit thread, October 8 2019, https://reddit.com/

r/breakingbad/comments/df4q7q/on_my_2nd_rewatch_im_finding_skyler_is_an_amazing/.
This is not to say that fan response to Skyler has taken a complete turnaround over the years: within these and similar threads, as well as on other pre-*El Camino* rewatch posts, Skyler hate still has a place on the r/breakingbad subreddit.
   58. Turvey, "Familiarity Breeds Contempt," 232.

BIBLIOGRAPHY

Blanchet, Robert, and Margrethe Bruun Vaage. "Don, Peggy, and Other Fictional Friends? Engaging with Characters in Television Series." *Projections* 6, no. 2 (Winter 2012): 18–41. DOI: 10.3167/proj.2012.060203.
Blumenfeld, Zach. "Why TV Finally Caught Up to *Breaking Bad*'s Skyler White." *Consequence of Sound*, October 8, 2019. https://consequenceofsound.net/2019/10/breaking-bad-skyler-white-op-ed/.
Breaking Bad. Created by Vince Gilligan. Sony Pictures Television, AMC, 2008–2013.
Callens, Melissa Vosen. "AMC's Infamous Criminal Partnerships: Suppressing the Female Antihero." *Dialogue* 6, no. 2 (2019): 49–61. http://journaldialogue.org/issues/v6-issue-2/amcs-infamous-criminal-partnerships-suppressing-the-female-antihero/.
Clearsurname. "On my 2nd rewatch, I'm finding Skyler is an amazing character." Reddit, October 8 2019, https://reddit.com/r/breakingbad/comments/df4q7q/on_my_2nd_rewatch_im_finding_skyler_is_an_amazing/.
Gilligan, Vince. "*Breaking Bad* Creator Reflects on Meth and Morals." Interview by Terry Gross. *NPR*, October 11, 2019. https://www.npr.org/2019/10/11/769312766/breaking-bad-creator-vince-gilligan-reflects-on-meth-and-morals.
Gunn, Anna. "I Have a Character Issue." *New York Times*, August 23, 2013. https://www.nytimes.com/2013/08/24/opinion/i-have-a-character-issue.html.
Hermes, Joke, and Leonie Stoete. "Hating Skyler White: Audience Engagement, Gender Politics and Celebrity Culture." *Celebrity Studies* 10, no. 3 (2019): 411–426. https://doi.org/10.1080/19392397.2019.1630155.
Jones, Ellen E. "Skyler White: The *Breaking Bad* Underdog Who Set the Template for TV's Antiheroine." *The Guardian*, January 13, 2018. https://www.theguardian.com/tv-and-radio/2018/jan/13/breaking-bad-how-skyler-white-created-the-modern-aniheroine.
Logan, Elliott. *"Breaking Bad" and Dignity: Unity and Fragmentation in the Serial Television Drama*. Houndmills: Palgrave, 2016.
Mittell, Jason. *Complex TV: The Poetics of Contemporary Television Storytelling*. New York: NYU Press, 2015.
Nussbaum, Emily. "That Mind-Bending Phone Call on Last Night's *Breaking Bad*." *New Yorker*, September 16, 2013. https://www.newyorker.com/culture/culture-desk/that-mind-bending-phone-call-on-last-nights-breaking-bad.
Plantinga, Carl. "Ethical Criticism and Fictional Characters as Moral Agents." In *Screening Characters: Theories of Character in Film, Television, and Interactive Media*, edited by Johannes Riis and Aaron Taylor, 191–208. New York: Routledge, 2019.
Price-Wood, Rebecca. "*Breaking Bad* Stereotypes about Postpartum: A Case for Skyler White." In *The Methods of "Breaking Bad": Essays on Narrative, Character, and Ethics*, edited by Jacob Blevins and Dafydd Wood, 132–146. Jefferson, NC: McFarland, 2015.
Rxtc. "I changed my mind about Skyler." Reddit, August 21, 2019. https://reddit.com/r/breakingbad/comments/ctc9rb/i_changed_my_mind_about_skyler/.
Sepinwall, Alan. *"Breaking Bad" 101: The Complete Critical Companion*. New York: Abrams Press, 2017.
Smith, Murray. *Engaging Characters: Fiction, Emotion, and the Cinema*. Oxford: Clarendon, 1995.
Stache, Lara C. *"Breaking Bad": A Cultural History*. Lanham, MD: Rowman & Littlefield, 2017.
Tally, Margaret. *The Rise of the Anti-Heroine in TV's Third Golden Age*. Newcastle-Upon-Tyne: Cambridge Scholars, 2016.

Turvey, Malcolm. "Familiarity Breeds Contempt: Why Fascination, Rather than Repeat Exposure, Better Explains the Appeal of Antiheros on Television." In *Screening Characters: Theories of Character in Film, Television, and Interactive Media*, edited by Johannes Riis and Aaron Taylor, 231–247. New York: Routledge, 2019.

Vaage, Margrethe Bruun. *The Antihero in American Television*. New York: Routledge, 2015.

WhiteWolfofUtah. "It didn't really click until this last rewatch but . . . Skyler got dealt such a shit hand." Reddit, September 24, 2019, https://reddit.com/r/breakingbad/comments/d8h2bn/it_didnt_really_click_until_this_latest_rewatch/.

Part II

Women to Watch (Out For)

Chapter Five

The Other's Hero

*The Importance of Annalise Keating and Olivia Pope
as Black Antiheroines*

Melanie Haas

The antihero has always been an important part of Western literature, giving us a character with whom we can identify—one who is not perfect, but who still manages to accomplish heroic deeds. More recently, though, they have been one of the most popular character archetypes showcased on our television screens, and these newer antiheroes have been the focus of cultural popularity and critical discussion. For example, in her discussion of the evolution of the antiheroine, Margaret Tally explains that the antihero has been "understood to represent the damaged American male in the post-Vietnam period of American history . . . [and] were portrayed as attempting to navigate a world where corruption and the misuse of power had become the norm in many American institutions. This meant that their actions, though morally suspect, could be justified, given the world they lived in."[1] However, in the last few decades, we have seen the rise of a new archetype: the anti*heroine*. While antiheroes have long been a staple of Western literature, examples of antiheroines are few and far between, with a few famous examples being Medea, Lady Macbeth, and Scarlett O'Hara. Since about 2008, though, we have welcomed growing numbers of antiheroines into our homes via our television screens.[2] The list of the post-millennial antiheroines who have garnered audience support and academic discussion is much longer than at any other time in history, including *Weeds'* Nancy Botwin; *Orange Is the New Black'*s Piper Chapman; *Nurse Jackie'*s Jackie Peyton; *Homeland'*s Carrie Mathison; *House of Cards'* Claire Underwood; *Game of Thrones'* Cersei, Arya, and Sansa; and many of the characters on *American Horror*

Story, . . . the list seems almost inexhaustible. Tally points out that, generally, antiheroines are defined as female antiheroes, which is reductive, as this definition demands audiences to view women as the same as men and ignores the complex and nuanced differences between men and women. Tally goes on to explain that more than a simple gender flip, antiheroines are complex representations of the reality of what it means to be a woman in our Western patriarchal culture.[3] Tally's working definition of an antiheroine is that she is:

> a deeply flawed, yet at the same time, sympathetic character. She is one who is neither uniformly good nor evil, but has qualities that mark her as being capable of doing bad things for good reasons. She is usually "edgy" in the sense that her actions and her personality do not obey the conventions of traditional femininity, though she may or may not behave at times in conventionally masculine ways either.[4]

Antiheroes generally behave in conventionally masculine ways. Tally explains that "one way of understanding the anti-hero is to examine them in terms of gender. . . . The qualities we find compelling in these characters are generally associated with masculine traits such as pride, violence or seduction."[5] Tally goes on to explain that antiheroines must be able to interweave the conventions of femininity and masculinity, and use the tools most beneficial for the situation.[6]

While antiheroines are on the rise, the list of recent and current television antiheroines is not as inclusive nor as progressive as it might seem on the surface, as there is a significant lack of women of color. A simple Google search for "antiheroines" + "women of color" results primarily in popular articles that lament the lack of women of color in such important roles, rather than a list of women who occupy them. A Google Scholar search using the same terms returns just twenty-seven results of varying degrees of currency and relevance. Just as television was slow to warm to the idea of casting women of color in leading roles, there appears to be some resistance in casting women of color in these antiheroine roles as well. The *Hollywood Diversity Report* explains "The marginalization of diverse groups in Hollywood is an old story, one dating back to the origins of the film industry over a century ago. Hollywood has always been a 'bastion of whiteness,' a highly lucrative and insular industry in which White men dominate the positions of power."[7] People of color, and particularly Black women, have a long history of negative representations in media. Apryl Williams and Vanessa Gonlin state that "Black women are frequently portrayed in media as unattractive, threatening, hypersexualized, and inferior to all others,"[8] and this media representation mirrors current negative gender and racial social constructs. According to Imani Cheers:

Until the 1980's television shows with predominantly Black casts that focused on Black themes were under the creative control of White studio and network executives . . . [and] [t]hese White producers and executives depicted Black women through a prism that was rooted in the point of view of middle-class White Americans who primarily viewed and encountered African-American women as domestic servants and entertainers. [9]

Additionally, the shows curated by white producers and executives were those that were shown on the "Big 3" networks, NBC, ABC, and CBS, and it was only additional networks, such as Fox and UPN, that began airing shows with more varied roles for Black women. [10] In 1990, Patricia Hill Collins asserted that there were five types of roles for Black women, the mammy, the matriarch, the jezebel, the Black lady, and the welfare mother, each of which was one-dimensional and allowed white producers and executives "to rationalize oppression of U.S. Black women and to maintain dominance" [11] Marquita M. Gammage echoes this position, saying "Media productions of Black women can result in the colonization of Black women's images because it is the primary venue through which Black women's images are transmitted to society. Misogynistic and materialistic images of Black womanhood in the media aid in the reduction of the Black female to a sexual product used to export negative stereotypical imagery to society." [12]

In response to Collins's analysis that white men have used their privileged positions to maintain oppressive social constructs, A. N. Wissah believes that it is "logical to conclude that if Black women gain institutional power to produce cultural products, they would disrupt rather than perpetuate the status quo." [13]

In the twenty-first century, representations of the Black woman have expanded beyond stereotypical lines throughout literary media, television, and cinema culture to explore diverse forms of blackness throughout the world. Wissah explains that *Scandal*'s appearance on ABC in 2012 started a "trend of 1-hour scripted television programs produced by Black women, featuring Black female leads." [14] *Scandal* was the first of its kind, scripted and aired on one of the "Big 3" during prime time since the mid-1970s. The show enjoyed mainstream success, but was also "the top-rated, scripted series among Black women in 2013, according to The Nielsen Company." [15] Following the success of *Scandal*, several other networks followed suit and added "scripted programming featuring Black women in lead roles such as *Deception* in 2013, *Being Mary Jane* in 2013, and *How to Get a Way with Murder* in 2014." [16] Since Black women have only been represented in lead roles on television recently, we have only just begun to see Black antiheroines in media as the film and television industries work to keep up with the demands our changing culture is making. While marginalized groups are still woefully underrepresented, the *Hollywood Diversity Report* explains that

"Today's diverse audiences, the evidence shows, prefer film and television content populated with characters to whom they can relate and whose stories drive the narrative" and reports that there has been an increase in diverse racial and cultural representation on-screen.[17] This increase in characters who have depth and complexity is allowing for better representations of intersectionality in characters and helps to cultivate social constructs which celebrate the marginalized, instead of working to maintain outdated and oppressive norms.

Two of the most well-known characters who occupy the intersections of antiheroines and women of color are *Scandal*'s Olivia Pope and *How to Get Away with Murder*'s (*HTGAWM*) Annalise Keating. *Scandal* is a political drama that follows the prominent crisis management specialist, or "fixer," Olivia Pope. The show explores the Washington, DC, political landscape as it follows Olivia through her relationships with the president (Fitzgerald Grant) the First Lady (Melly Grant), and many other politically powerful people. Over the course of the series, Olivia, handles politically complex situations for her clients, in the midst of dealing with her own complicated life as the owner of her own company, intense romantic entanglements, and convoluted family relationships. *HTGAWM* is a legal drama centered on Annalise Keating, a prominent lawyer and law school professor, her students, and their clients. Beginning with a season which primarily focuses on the murders of Annalise's husband and one of his students, Lila Stangard, while Annalise and her students work to defend their clients, *HTGAWM* reveals the complexity of Annalise's life as the audience learns of her struggles with infertility and the loss of her infant son, her husband's infidelity, the abuse she suffered as a child, and her alcoholism, as well as her complicated romantic and professional relationships.

These shows were created by one of the most popular showrunners of the last few decades, Shonda Rhimes, who has made history on several occasions. For example, "On September 25th, 2014, [she] made an historic turn as the first African American showrunner ever (female or male) to have an entire primetime programming bloc of three consecutive hours for three different shows on a single night, a night ABC dubbed 'Thank God It's Thursday' (TGIT)."[18] As a showrunner, Rhimes has creative and managerial control over most aspects of a series, and while she may not be the writer for every episode or make every wardrobe decision, Rhimes is, as Anna Everett argues, the auteur of most of her series, and creates primarily "proud women-centric narratives that feature professional women-in-charge or women (many of color) as bosses in the workplace; and narratives of audacious and racy sexualities, both heteronormative and queer, that operate inside and beyond the workspace."[19] Rhimes's characters Olivia and Annalise represent such minority characters who are multifaceted, unique, and complex.

Olivia and Annalise are antiheroines, and, as such, add much more complexity to the shows than if they were traditional heroes. However, for these characters, their role as antiheroine has an even more important benefit to the audience, as they also challenge current negative gender and racial social constructs and present realistic and flawed, but still powerful and successful Black women with whom the audience can relate. Olivia's and Annalise's role as antiheroine has an even more important benefit to the audience, as they provide representations of the intersectional Other, the Black woman, subverting the patriarchal system which has marginalized her, as she manages to achieve incredible personal power against all odds. As antiheroines, Olivia and Annalise challenge constructions of powerlessness and disenfranchisement, not just for women of color, but for all women who live under social constructs that maintain women of color as the ultimate Other and which prevent any woman from recognizing her own agency and autonomy. As audiences watch Olivia and Annalise thwart patriarchal norms, many of them can, perhaps, imagine a world in which they have more agency and autonomy.

While it would seem that the importance of the intersectionality of these characters as Black women and antiheroines would have been previously discussed at length, this is not the case. Much has been written about both Olivia and Annalise. The majority of that writing is published in the popular sphere, but there are some scholarly offerings as well. There are some popular articles, such as Meghan Gallagher's "*Scandal*'s Olivia Pope and the Rise of the Female Antihero" and Kelsey Wallace's "*How to Get Away with Murder* Gives Us a Female Antihero We Can Root for." Both of these are popular articles, and they explain that Olivia and Annalise are antiheroines, but they both touch only briefly on the fact that these are Black women, which brings another intersection to the mix, and adds further complexity to the character. As for scholarly sources, Tally comes the closest to examining these intersections, as she focuses more on the importance of Shonda Rhimes's role in creating Olivia and Annalise, and then on the importance of Olivia and Annalise as Black women in title roles, rather than their importance as Black antiheroines. Many other books and articles have been written about Rhimes's characters, about her importance as the showrunner for these shows, and various aspects of Olivia and Annalise, but none of these offer a focused examination on the importance of Olivia and Annalise as Black antiheroines.

Based on common definitions of antiheroines, it is quite clear that both Olivia and Annalise are antiheroines. Olivia possesses many characteristics which are generally thought of as "good." Her company is staffed by people who she has "rescued" from a bad situation. Olivia's initial team included Harrison Wright, who was unfairly convicted of insider trading and Olivia helped get him released early and then employed him; Huck, who was emotionally destroyed by the covert agency B613 and homeless when Olivia encountered and then employed him; Abby Whelan, who was a survivor of domestic abuse; and Quinn Perkins, who had been drugged, kidnapped, transported across the country and then had to assume a new identity. Olivia also, generally, works to achieve justice, not just to clear her clients' names. For example, in one episode, her client is an accused rapist. Olivia learns that her client is guilty, not of the rape of which he stands accused, but of the rape of his accuser's friend, a rape which resulted in the victim's suicide. Olivia's response to this is to offer the client a chance to admit his guilt, and, when he chooses not to do so, she gives the information to the police and he is arrested for his crime. Several times over the course of the series, Olivia demonstrates that justice and all that is "good" is truly important to her. She even calls her group "the white hats," showing that she believes them to be the "good guys." However, Olivia is far from a static, one-dimensional character, as she also engages in behaviors which do not mesh well with her "good guy" persona. In the pilot episode of *Scandal*, the audience learns of Olivia's affair with the married president, Fitzgerald Grant. In later episodes, we find out that she fixed the presidential election which made Fitz president, and she beat the man who orchestrated her kidnapping to death with a chair, never mind the fact that he was a paraplegic. Near the end of the series, Olivia has taken over control of B613, and proves to be no more of a benevolent leader than previous Commands, as she gives orders that show a single-minded determination to protect herself, those close to her, and the Republic at all costs. For example, she gives the order to blow up a plane to kill the president of a Middle Eastern country because of difficulties in obtaining a nuclear weapons treaty. The fact that her order also resulted in the deaths of several innocent people does not appear to have been a factor in her decision. These villainous behaviors Olivia commits are in pursuit of some form of justice; for herself, for her friends and family, or for victims of some kind of patriarchal oppression. As the series reveals more about Olivia, it becomes clear that, for her, the ends almost always justify the means.

Annalise is just as clearly an antiheroine. Annalise has a much more "hard as nails" persona initially than does Olivia, but as the series goes on, we find that she truly cares about her students and her friends and family and works very hard to protect them. The audience learns that Annalise represented Wes Gibbons's mother before she died and has been acting as something of a guardian angel ever since. Annalise met Bonnie when Annalise was defending a client accused of rape. Bonnie was the accuser in that case, and after Annalise had to cross-examine her, Annalise felt terribly guilty, quit her job, started her own firm, and hired Bonnie to be a part of it. She also helps Bonnie get into law school and become a lawyer. In a more morally grey area, she helps her students cover up some major crimes, such as Sam Keating's and Emily Sinclair's murders, which demonstrates the lengths she will go to in order to protect those she cares about. Just as is the case with Olivia, though, Annalise operates under her own moral code, one in which the ends clearly justify the means. Annalise "rewards students for illegally obtaining evidence, lying to police and members of the court, blackmailing witnesses, and using any and all means to exonerate defendants guilty of heinous crimes. We hear her profess that all clients lie and that all people, including law students and attorneys, are capable of committing terrible deeds."[20] Annalise, like Olivia, also has an affair with a married man, although in Annalise's case, she is also married, the wife of the man with whom she has an affair is terminally ill, and her husband has committed several similar sins against her, making a simple affair even more morally complex to critique. Annalise is manipulative on a level to which most could only aspire, and she lies and doctors evidence to defend her clients. According to Cherrelle Brown, Annalise "is an anti-hero, an archetype usually reserved for brooding, white men on television—she's a Jack Bauer, a Dr. Gregory House, a Walter White, or a Don Draper."[21] Annalise's, and therefore Olivia's, subversion of a typically male character type is just one aspect of how these depictions of Black antiheroine characters help construct narratives which work to supplant the current marginalization of many groups by the Western patriarchy.

Further evidence of this narrative is the number of prominent characters which represent marginalized groups, as both *Scandal* and *How to Get Away with Murder* include a varied cast of such characters. Olivia, who is a Black woman, owns a crisis management firm and uses her power in this position to hire others who represent marginalized groups. Two of her "gladiators in suits" are young Black men, Harrison Wright and Marcus Walker. In addition to their racial marginalization, both Harrison and Marcus have pasts which are often vilified. Harrison grew up in foster homes and later served time in prison for insider trading. Marcus was falsely accused of murder, an accusation which was partly responsible for ending his political career. Another member of Olivia's team is Huck, a Latinx man, who is a former operative for B613 and, as a result, carries many emotional scars that sometimes significantly hinder his ability to function. Abby Whelan, a white woman, was hired by Olivia not long after Olivia helped save Abby from her abusive husband. Quinn Perkins, another white woman, joined the team after arriving in Washington, DC, as the result of being kidnapped and forced to assume a new identity. There are also regular appearances by James Novak and Cyrus Beene, who are gay white men, and David Rosen, who is Jewish. Most of these characters represent more than one marginalized group, depending on their race, gender, and personal backgrounds. In addition, these characters, while not entirely realistic, do represent the complexity of marginalized people. Not all of the women or men are alike, they all have different goals and complex identities, and none of them fit well within any of the standard tropes which are so often imposed on characters in these groups. We see this same type of complex representation of marginalized groups in *How to Get Away with Murder*. Annalise is the primary character, and a bisexual Black woman. Her full-time staff consists of Bonnie, a white woman, and Frank, a white male, but there is more racial diversity in her students. Those students include two young, Black lawyers-in-training, Michaela Pratt and Wes Gibbins, the Latinx Laurel Castillo, and Connor Walsh, a gay white man. As with *Scandal*, some of these characters occupy more than one area of marginalization. For example, Bonnie was sexually abused as a child by her father and several men who paid her father to have sex with her. Frank, who is Annalise's investigator, who was convicted and imprisoned for the murder of his abusive father. Annalise helped Frank get parole and then hired him when he was released from prison. Michaela is Black, a woman, and was raised in poverty and in the foster system. Wes is also Black and had a difficult childhood as his mother was murdered when he was young. Laurel is an immigrant from Mexico and has mostly cut ties with her father because of his shady business dealings. The inclusion of these characters who represent marginalized groups continues the narrative of the subversion of the patriarchy as it provides a complex representation of these marginalized people with whom the audience can identify. These are characters who do not fit easily into any one mold, but, much like the real people in these marginalized groups, the characters are complicated and deal with the difficulties they face in different ways, have different goals than what would be expected of static characters, and different means of achieving those goals. However, whether despite or because of the aspects that place them in the margins of a patriarchal culture, these characters are successful and powerful.

By their very existence as Black antiheroines, Olivia and Annalise challenge negative constructs regarding gender and race. One cultural norm that Olivia and Annalise challenge is that women need to rely on a man in order to be powerful. Both women are incredibly powerful in their own right. Olivia is the most famous fixer in DC, and Annalise is the best defense attorney and the most sought out law professor in Philadelphia. Both women have relationships with powerful or strong men. Olivia has romantic relationships with powerful men, such as the president and a senator. Her father is the head of B613 for several seasons, and she has a romantic relationship with the man who takes over when her father is removed. Annalise is married to a psychology professor who is well respected in his field, and she has an affair with a police detective. Unlike many other representations of women on television, Olivia and Annalise do not have to rely on their significant others to support them as they pursue their goals, but, instead, actively resist any involvement of their significant others in any aspect of their lives other than the truly personal. Neither Olivia nor Annalise accept unsolicited assistance from their male intimates, sometimes rejecting their help to their own detriment. They do both go to one of the men and either request or demand help, but these moments are rare, and limited to requesting help when the situation demands some kind of specific advantage that the man has. For example, Olivia goes to the president once in a while and asks him to make sure that a certain bill makes it to a vote, or to provide her with information to which she otherwise would not have access. Annalise uses her police detective boyfriend to win a case on which he was the lead detective. Questioning him on the stand is harmful to his career, but Annalise is willing to put him and their relationship in peril to save her client. Olivia and Annalise are both willing to use whatever tools they have at their disposal, including their relationships, but their power is not derived from these relationships. Their powerful positions also challenge racial constructs. One common representation of Black women in television is that they are inferior to all others and that they are powerless to control their lives. This is not how Rhimes chose to present Olivia and Annalise. Both of these characters are the lead for their show, and these characters are certainly not powerless. They run their own successful businesses, they manage employees, they are financially stable without the income of a partner, and they are regarded by others as the top in their field. These characters which refute common constructions of Black women as inferior and powerless challenges the audience's understanding of Black women and offers a different representation, one which places Black women in more advantageous positions.

Olivia and Annalise also challenge notions of beauty and femininity. Olivia visually adheres to traditional standards of beauty and femininity, as she is relatively light skinned, typically wears her hair straightened or with a slight wave, she often wears "power suits" but with more delicate blouses underneath, and wears her signature five-inch heels to help produce her trademark power strut. Annalise strays further from these constructs as she is darker skinned and less "classically" beautiful, she wears pencil skirts and dresses frequently, but walks in a way that demonstrates her "unladylikeness" in her heels, a walk intentionally developed by Viola Davis to further the representation of Annalise as "real."[22] Regardless of this typical construction on-screen, both are shown at some point in their series without all of the physical trappings that typically go along with being a Black woman in a Western patriarchal culture. In season 4 of *Scandal*, Olivia is kidnapped and, within just a day or so, her hair goes from the straightened long locks to which audiences have become accustomed to natural, curly coils, and she is without her makeup and her couture wardrobe. Annalise is shown one night as she gets ready for bed removing her wig, her eyelashes, and her drawn-on eyebrows. These images of Olivia and Annalise with all of the socially required beauty entrapments removed gives the audience a more realistic vision of Black women. In their article on Olivia's hair in the one hundredth episode of *Scandal*, Jihan Forbes says "There has been a fair share of discussion on the significance of Olivia's hair, and how she usually straightens it for the workplace. Plenty of black women feel pressure to do so for the sake of their careers, thanks to lingering biases against black hair."[23] Julia Robins suggests that Rhimes's "was purposefully constructing a critical commentary of our society: that our society only allows black women to be natural in a hyper-sexual, far off, foreign realm—and that to really be successful, they must conform to arbitrary beauty standards put in place by the white establishment."[24] Williams and Gonlin refer to Annalise's on-screen removal of her makeup and wig "the big reveal" and goes on to explain that this scene portrays "a ritual that most women perform . . . daily. The imagery of taking off the wig to reveal natural, kinky hair underneath is something specific to Black women."[25] Williams and Gonlin's examination of tweets in response to this scene reveals that this move is one of which audiences approve. They explain that the scene "sparked intense emotions via the co-viewing discourse of tweeters. Some of the most prevalent words associated with Annalise taking off her wig include *real, raw, powerful,* and *inspiring.*"[26] One tweet they provide as an example of audience support for this scene reads "Annalise just took off her wig, eyelashes and makeup on national TV. Does anyone realize how revolutionary this is?!?!"[27] Viola Davis herself wanted a scene in which she removed her wig: "So often I see women on the screen, and I don't recognize them. They're not women that I know. It's like a woman who's been through a filter, and then she comes out, and there's pieces that I recognize, but mostly it's a Mr. Potato Head of male desirability."[28] These images of Olivia and Annalise without makeup or "white" hair challenge notions that only those who conform to standards of white beauty are worthy or capable of success.

More importantly, what these characters do while they do not have these trappings demonstrates that they are at least as strong, perhaps stronger, than they are when they have them. When Olivia is kidnapped, she rips the underwire out of her bra and uses it as a tool to attempt to escape from her captors, thus using one of the tools used to constrict women to fight for her freedom. She also does this with her natural hair and the appearance of no (or at least minimal) makeup. Annalise confronts her husband with her knowledge of his affair with his student. Annalise's determination to confront Sam even stripped of her hair and makeup shows the audience that her power is not tied to her conventionally determined beauty, but instead is a power that comes from within. Olivia's and Annalise's possession of strength and power, even in the absence of traditional beauty conventions, offers up a challenge to the validity and necessity of such constructs and is a demonstration of their willingness and ability to challenge such constructions.

Olivia's and Annalise's realness construct a sense of relatability in these characters, and their realness also challenges the victim construct that is so prevalent in our culture. Both of these women have suffered immensely in their lives, have histories of trauma and abuse, and yet they do not behave in a manner consistent with our ideas of how a victim is "supposed" to act. Even with all of this trauma in their past, these women are able to act with incredible levels of courage, especially when it is in the defense of another marginalized person.

One prime example is an episode of *Scandal*, "The Lawn Chair," in which we see Olivia face down the systemic racism present in the Washington police department.[29] A young Black man was killed by the police, who deceptively claim the young man had a knife and threatened them, causing them to use lethal force. The young man's father sets up a lawn chair, and guards his son's body with a shotgun, insisting on his son's innocence. Olivia steps headlong into the conflict between the father and the police, even though she has PTSD as a result of her recent kidnapping. After the father levels his shotgun at her, she returns to the police barrier, trembling . . . but only after she has promised the father that she would fight to find the truth for his son. Olivia's fear is evident in this scene, and in several others, particularly those in which she is being held captive. And yet she never stops fighting. Whether she is fighting for her own safety or to find out the truth of a case which will eliminate a corrupt police officer and restore the reputation of his slain victim, Olivia charges in valiantly.

Annalise is just as devoted to protecting others, although the others she is generally protecting are her students. In season 2 of *HTGAWM*, Annalise is shot, and narrowly survives her injury. Over the season, the audience learns that Asher, one of Annalise's students, had killed Emily Sinclair, the attorney opposing Annalise and her team in one of their major cases. Annalise concocted a rather convoluted plan to protect Asher. This plan involves framing one of their clients, who is actually guilty of murdering her parents, but Annalise and her team cannot provide the information needed for a conviction to the prosecution without implicating themselves for Emily Sinclair's murder. Part of the plan requires that Annalise gets shot, and in the season finale (which is typical of the series) we find out that Annalise asked her students, as a group, for one of them to shoot her, and one by one, they all refused, except for Wes, who shoots Annalise after she provokes him. Annalise realized that there was no other way out for Asher, who would be facing a murder charge if Annalise did not step in, so Annalise chose what was, for her, the lesser of two evils. She preferred facing possible death and certain immense pain over the potential damage to a member of her team. These characters exhibit extraordinary courage as they fight for the rights to which they believe they and those they care about are entitled. This courage helps situate these characters as antiheroines, as courage is necessary to overcome fear and stand up for oneself and others. However, it also helps challenge social constructs which paint women, and women of color even more so, as weak, inferior, and in need of protection. These characters' actions prove that they are capable and willing to protect themselves and others.

Constructing Olivia and Annalise as antiheroines created characters who are complex and somewhat unpredictable, just as are real people. Rhimes gave these characters the strength, grit, and the ability to overcome obstacles in their path. This allows Olivia and Annalise to often get the upper hand, which is another way they challenge current negative gender and racial social constructs. Olivia and Annalise have reasons to fight, and they fight to win, even if that means they have to fight dirty. Audiences root for them to win because Olivia and Annalise fight against the same oppressive constructs as many audience members are faced with every day. While there are actual villains in these shows, these villains are typically a member of a very privileged group and are symbolic of the oppressive social constructs that are ultimately responsible for the difficulties faced by Olivia and Annalise, their associates, innocent clients, and the victims of their guilty clients.

Olivia's clients are often straight white men who are far from innocent. While Olivia fixes the problems of these men, and therefore reinforces some of the cultural expectations for women to step in and clean up whatever mess a man has made, the audience is also made aware of the depth of their guilt as Olivia works to keep their reputations intact. For example, in "Hell Hath No Fury," the third episode of the first season, Olivia Pope & Associates' client is Travis Harding, the white, college-aged son of Sandra Harding, a multi-millionaire CEO, who stands accused of rape. Eventually, it is revealed that Travis did not commit the rape for which he is currently on trial but did rape a different woman. He paid the victim a large settlement for her silence. Olivia uncovers this, and speaks to Sandra, convincing her to hold him responsible for his actions. Travis's case culminates in Olivia and Sandra confronting Travis in Olivia's office, Travis confessing to the rape he has committed and his subsequent arrest for that crime. In this episode, Olivia walks in a grey area where attorney/client privilege is concerned, but her actions lead to the arrest of one of those who are frequently responsible for harming the disenfranchised: a young, white, financially stable, and well-educated male who uses his position of privilege to take whatever he wants from those who are marginalized. Thus, Olivia's willingness to occupy that grey area and her subsequent win against white male privilege challenges the current misogynistic rhetoric which so often surrounds rape accusations.

Not all of Olivia's battles against such an enemy are so explicitly successful, though. In "All Roads Lead to Fitz," Olivia's client is Samuel Reston, Fitz's former presidential rival, who has killed a man. He supposedly walked into his home and saw a man attacking his wife, Joan, who cried out that he was raping her. The audience learns by the end of the episode, however, that Samuel knew that his wife was having an affair with the man he killed, and used his wife's cries, which were fake, and he *knew* they were fake, as his motive for murder. Once Olivia, and the audience finds this truth out, the depth of Samuel's guilt is revealed, but we also know that Olivia has no legal recourse, as he is her client and enjoys attorney/client privilege, and, though she has been willing to drift across that line a bit in the past, she knows that violating Samuel's privilege will bring her down as well. Olivia must, therefore, allow Samuel to literally get away with murder, at least for the time being, and Joan ends up taking the fall for the murder. However, true to her antiheroine nature, Olivia gets her vengeance, perhaps even justice, as she initiates a cunning plan that culminates in Samuel's political disgrace and his subsequent withdrawal from the presidential race. Thus, even when Olivia is not immediately successful in her fight against white male privilege, she refuses to yield the field, and instead uses her "behind the scenes" power to challenge the idea that those with privilege always win.

This struggle against the patriarchal system is also evident in *HTGAWM*. The majority of the clients Annalise successfully defends are charged with crimes against those in power. While we may, at first, identify with the victim, as Joan Faber McAlister explains, "In each case, a potential path to identification with a white male heterosexual figure of rank is closed as the character is deemed deserving of punishment or even death."[30] In both shows, the audience realizes that the "good" people, usually represented by straight, white men, are not really "good" at all, but are instead the enemy. Regarding *How to Get Away with Murder*, McAlister explains that:

> By challenging common televisual fantasies with real struggles endured by those at the margins of society, this legal melodrama creates revelatory reflections of U.S. culture. As its mirror image of our own society reverses conventional morality, *How to Get Away with Murder* challenges categories of victim and villain and aligns audiences with widely vilified figures who are perennial targets of misogyny and bigotry. Although we witness their depravity and misdeeds, audiences are nonetheless compelled to forgive them as we learn to see our legal system as a corrupt social order that requires skill without scruple.[31]

We regularly watch Annalise, even from the first episode, take on clients who are accused of committing a crime, usually a crime against a person who enjoys a large amount of privilege. The case revolves around a wealthy, older, white man, whose secretary (and mistress) is accused of attempting to murder by using aspirin, to which he is allergic. He suffered anaphylactic shock and subsequent brain damage, leaving him significantly impaired. During the trial, though, the audience is treated to an interaction between the accused and the injured man's wife in which they are in the ladies room and the wife reaches over, takes the accused's hand, and gently squeezes it in what appears to be a gesture of support. Because of the clandestine interaction between the wife and the mistress, not only is the audience aware that the mistress is guilty, but also that the wife was aware of the mistress's guilt, or perhaps even a conspirator. While the victim in this case is by no means the worst of the privileged white males featured on the show, he is also not a complete innocent, as he uses his position to manipulate his assistant into a sexual relationship, as well as being a philanderer. As a wealthy white man who uses his privilege in ways that hurt others, he is an example of the well-educated, financially stable, straight, white male which is a frequent representation of Western patriarchal values. As the case ends with Annalise's client's acquittal, the writers set the series up as one in which the motivations of the characters are much more important than the outcome of the situation, which fits well with Annalise's position as an antiheroine.

While it is so very common for men, especially white, financially privileged men, to betray and mistreat women, there is a clear theme running throughout these shows that men who choose to treat these antiheroines in such a manner will suffer for those crimes, one way or another. In *Scandal*, Olivia confronts Andrew Nichols, the man who orchestrated Olivia's kidnapping.[32] Although Andrew has since become a paraplegic, in this scene, he threatens to reveal many secrets that would be devastating to Olivia, her friends, and Fitz, and then threatens to have her kidnapped again. At this point, Olivia picks up a metal chair and beats Andrew to death, eliminating the threat that he poses. Olivia is clearly not a simple villain, so we cannot write this off as being just another action of a truly bad person. Instead, Olivia metes out the punishment she feels Andrew deserves for his crimes against her and his threats to those she cares about. In the first season of *HTGAWM*, the audience gradually discovers that Annalise's husband, Sam, poses a threat to Annalise in several ways. Sam had an affair with one of his students, impregnated her, and, when she refused to get an abortion and threatened to reveal their relationship to Annalise, he blackmailed Frank into murdering her and disposing of her body. He was also negligent in other ways, being, at best, nonchalant when he realized that Annalise was having another miscarriage, and he encouraged Annalise, who is an alcoholic, to drink. He is also verbally abusive, at one point telling Annalise "You want the truth? You're nothing but a piece of ass. That's what I saw when I first talked to you in the office that day. Cause I knew you'd put out. That's all you're really good for: dirty, rough sex that I'm too ashamed to tell anyone about. That's how foul you are, you disgusting slut."[33] Just like Andrew in *Scandal*, Sam is killed as one of Annalise's students fights Sam as Sam tries to strangle one of Annalise's clients, and, thus, the audience again sees a man punished for his abuse against a woman. This trend of showing, not just men, but wealthy, powerful, white men, be held accountable for the damage they have caused further challenges current constructs. Currently, in many countries, women who are attacked by men are far more likely to be blamed for that attack than the man is to be held responsible for his crime. *Scandal* and

HTGAWM provide an alternate ending for such occurrences, one which audiences may be more willing to fight for just as did Olivia and Annalise.

The audience tends to forgive Olivia and Annalise for the means they use, most of which are either blatantly in opposition to accepted social action or occupy a grey area between the ethical and the unscrupulous, to challenge social constructs which help perpetuate oppression. Once the audience learns of the personal crises and professional difficulties that Olivia and Annalise have faced, we are more willing to accept the ways that Olivia and Annalise accomplish their goals, whether those goals are personal or professional. When we add to their backstories the understanding that Olivia and Annalise are women of color, and as such there are difficulties that they have faced that are not often overtly demonstrated in the storylines of the shows. Harassment, discrimination, disrespect, and possibly abuse are the experiences of almost all women, and even more so for women of color. In *Scandal*, Rowan, Olivia's father, frequently reminds her that she has "to be twice as good as them to get half of what they have." In his analysis of the show, Neil Drumming tells us that this sentiment is not unique to the Pope family but is part of the shared experience of people of color:

> More than simply a family motto, the sentiment is one with which almost every African-American of my generation and before is all too familiar. Notice the them and the they—that's white folks. The you is every black kid who has ever brought home a bad grade or failed to study hard enough for a test being told by their concerned parents that they might never succeed if they don't work harder and smarter than their white peers. Maybe not everyone will accept this assertion as true, but in *Scandal*'s choppy ocean of absurdity, it felt like rock-hard reality.[34]

As for Annalise, McAlister explains that "We see Annalise encounter racism and sexism on a daily basis as she is persecuted, disrespected, and disparaged as a token by those with more power. After overhearing white women describe Annalise as an inhuman animal, the deceptions she employs to humiliate her (nearly always white and usually male) opponents seem justified."[35] Though neither of the shows overtly focus on the lifetime of negative racial experiences Olivia and Annalise have faced, both shows provide enough implicit information and examples to help the audience understand their plight as Black women is more than what is shown on-screen, which adds to our ability to forgive them for their actions. Rhimes's choice to make characters with which the audience can sympathize further challenges the current negative gender and racial constructs. If the audience can understand what motivates a character to behave like Olivia and Annalise, then, perhaps, they can develop a better understanding of their coworkers, their neighbors, their family, or even a stranger on the street. A better understanding of the difficulties marginalized people face forces audiences to reconsider their socially influenced ideas of those groups.

More than just forgiving them, though, audiences love these antiheroines and watching them challenge social constructs which consistently marginalize anyone who is not a straight, white, heterosexual, college-educated, and financially stable male. The audience's appreciation for these characters is clear in the high ratings and awards these shows have won, as well as the audience's response to the show in online communities. Henry Jenkins explains that "Online fan communities might well be some of the most fully realized . . . and expansive self-organizing groups focused around the collective production, debate, and circulation of meanings, interpretations, and fantasies in response to various artifacts of contemporary culture."[36] While there has been some social media backlash against both characters, in general, the social media viewer response, such as live tweeting along with the show, to these characters has been mostly positive. After mentioning Viola Davis's Emmy win for Outstanding Lead Actress for *How to Get Away with Murder*, Merryn Johns, the editor in chief of *Curve* magazine says "the culture has changed, and we've changed it. Audiences—rather than being titillated by an on-screen kiss that lasts a few seconds—are welcoming characters and storylines that span seasons."[37] Both of the shows were also part of ABC's popular TGIT (Thank Goodness It's Thursday) Shondaland lineup, and both shows have won numerous awards, including Emmys and the distinguished Peabody award. Further evidence of our love for these characters is the *Scandal*-inspired clothing line that Lyn Paolo and The Limited launched in 2015. The success of this line further proves that viewers feel a strong connection to Olivia and want to emulate her.

The social and political climate in the United States also adds to the audience's acceptance of Olivia and Annalise. Jonathan Michael explains that antiheroes often arise in response to ongoing crises in a culture.[38] Michael goes on to say "If we consider the 21st century so far—9/11 terrorist attacks, the Iraq War, Enron, Hurricane Katrina, the economic recession, Hurricane Sandy, the Newtown shootings, the Boston Marathon attacks—there's been a steady stream of terrible events to shake our faith in humanity. The promise of hard work resulting in economic prosperity and a stable future is no longer trustworthy."[39] The future to which Michael refers is one which is promised to men, particularly white, straight men, who are raised believing that if they work hard they can achieve any dream. Marginalized people are not made such promises, and, in fact, their futures are almost always uncertain and unstable. It follows, then, that the rise of antiheroines who represent marginalized people must be in response to some other impetus. Recently, there has been a dramatic increase in awareness of the disparity between those with privilege and those in the margins, and how that disparity affects the marginalized. Just in the last few years, we have seen many highly publicized examples of how those with privilege are able to exert their desires over those who do not. There have been many unjustified attacks and murders of young Black men by police. A woman who won the popular vote by almost three million votes still lost the election to a misogynist. Women marched on the capitol to protest the inauguration of that misogynistic president. That misogynistic president also instituted policies in which immigrant children are taken from their parents and locked in abhorrent conditions, and their parents are imprisoned as criminals. That president also fought to implement a ban on people from Middle Eastern countries entering the country, and, most recently at the time of this writing, referred to a deadly viral pandemic as being caused by a "Chinese virus," which increased violence committed against those of Asiatic descent. A man who was credibly accused of rape was confirmed as a Supreme Court Justice. Perhaps the most qualified Democratic hopeful for the 2020 race, and who also happened to be a woman, was easily defeated by two ageing, white men, both of whom have been accused of sexual harassment and sexism. There have been several social media movements intended to bring attention and support to those who have been victimized and to bring further awareness to the victimizers, such as #blacklivesmatter, #sayhername, #metoo, and #muterkelly. All of these examples have created varying degrees of outrage, outrage which ended up having little to no effect, as regardless of public outcry, those with privilege continued to carry out their plans. This, in turn, created further outrage, as those who protested felt powerless against the Western patriarchal system that blatantly ignored their pleas. It is into such a conflicted culture that we have witnessed this recent rise of antiheroines, and intersectional antiheroines in particular. As antiheroes are more common when the future which has been promised to men appears unstable, it appears that antiheroines are becoming more common in the hopes of *preventing* the promise of further marginalization and abuse. While we cannot pinpoint which came first, the anger and frustration or the antiheroine, there is clearly some connection between the rise of both at this time in our culture.

In this discussion, it has been demonstrated that the enemy that these antiheroines are fighting is the Western patriarchal system in general, and, more specifically, heterosexual, college-educated, financially stable, normally abled, white men, the intersections of which form the most privileged group in our culture. If these straight white men are the enemies, then, all of the marginalized people represented in these shows, and especially Olivia and Annalise, must, therefore, be the allies of the marginalized. These characters occupy the marginalized intersectional spaces of race, gender, and, in Annalise's case, sexual orientation. As the audience watches Olivia and Annalise subvert the patriarchy and win against all of the odds that are stacked against them, the audience gains exposure to the idea that those who are marginalized *can* fight back and win their agency and autonomy. Olivia and Annalise are only able to fully realize their agency after sometimes using tactics that most would place in either a moral grey area or outside of the bounds of moral behavior. While even Kerry Washington has said that having a character such as Olivia as a role model is "misguided,"[40] the audience may be inclined to examine the ways that they fight to gain agency and autonomy for themselves and others. Though murder and other felonies are beyond what most would be willing to do in pursuit of this, the audience may be inspired to speak up in the defense of themselves or others more often, participate in public protests, volunteer to help those who have less privilege, or work on the campaign of someone who is committed to helping marginalized groups. We, those of us who are members of marginalized groups, cheer for them, regardless of what acts they commit that fall outside of accepted moral and cultural norms. While Olivia and Annalise may have lives that are vastly different from those of their audiences, they provide a form of representation that is unique in that they allow the audience to not focus on their weaknesses, but instead focus on the strengths they could possess.

While much credit has been given to Shonda Rhimes for adding so much diversity to television both on-screen and behind the scenes, Griffin and Meyer explain that "exasperated by the reductive attention paid to her positionality as an African-American woman,"[41] Rhimes has openly stated that she "hate[s] the word *diversity.*"[42] Rhimes explains:

> I am what I have come to call an F. O. D.—a First. Only. Different. . . . We all have the same weary look in our eyes. The one that wishes people would stop thinking it remarkable that we can be great at what we do while black, while Asian, while a woman, while Latino, while gay, while a paraplegic, while deaf . . . when you are a F. O. D., you are saddled with that extra burden of responsibility—whether you want it or not.[43]

Griffin and Meyer explain that "the domination of media by white industry professionals creates a lack of representation in both the creation of television content and character performance in television narrative."[44] Just as we need stronger and more representative examples of people of color and other marginalized groups, we also need better representations of marginalized people who are willing to stand up, not just for themselves, but for each other. This representation helps demonstrate ways that audience members who are also marginalized can challenge their oppressors and offer a helping hand to those who are marginalized around them. The unity of marginalized people and the protection that Olivia and Annalise offer them far outweighs the morally ambiguous means with which Olivia and Annalise achieve their goals. Further, Rhimes claims that instead of *diversifying* television, she is *normalizing* television as she states "I am making TV look like the world looks. . . . I am NORMALIZING television."[45] By providing us with characters such as Olivia and Annalise, Rhimes is doing more than normalizing women, women of color, or even strong women of color. She is normalizing those who are willing to use whatever means they have at their disposal to prevent or remove marginalization. Rhimes's antiheroine creations challenge typical representations of marginalized people as one-dimensional, instead creating characters who are complex and, therefore, more representative of the reality which marginalized people face. By creating Olivia and Annalise, Rhimes has provided a space where all who occupy the margins of a patriarchal system can imagine, and perhaps create, a world in which they can achieve agency and autonomy.

NOTES

1. Margaret Tally, *The Rise of the Anti-Heroine in TV's Third Golden Age* (Newcastle-Upon-Tyne: Cambridge, 2016), 5.
2. Tally, *The Rise of the Anti-Heroine*, 5.
3. Tally, *The Rise of the Anti-Heroine*, 7.
4. Tally, *The Rise of the Anti-Heroine*, 8.
5. Tally, *The Rise of the Anti-Heroine*, 6.
6. Tally, *The Rise of the Anti-Heroine*, 7.
7. Darnell Hunt, Ana-Christina Ramón, and Michael Tran, *Hollywood Diversity Report 2019* (UCLA College of Social Sciences 2019), 62.
8. Apryl Williams and Vanessa Gonlin, "I Got All My Sisters with Me (on Black Twitter: Second Screening of *How to Get Away with Murder* as a Discourse on Black Womanhood," *Information, Communication and Society*, Vol. 20, No. 7, 984–1004, 2017.
9. Imani Cheers, *The Evolution of Black Women on Television: Mammies, Matriarchs, and Mistresses* (New York: Routledge, 2018), 2.
10. Assatu Wisseh (2018), "Mapping Mammy 2.0: Insecure and the Middle-Class Black Woman's Burden," *Howard Journal of Communication*, 2.
11. As qtd. in Wisseh, 1.
12. Marquita M. Gammage, *Representations of Black Women in the Media* (New York: Routledge, 2016).
13. Wisseh, 2.
14. Wisseh, 2.
15. Wisseh, 2.
16. Wisseh, 2.
17. Hunt, Ramón, and Tran, *Hollywood Diversity Report 2019*, 50–51.
18. Anna Everett, "Scandalicious: *Scandal*, Social Media, and Shonda Rhimes' Auteurist Juggernaut," *The Black Scholar*, Vol. 45, No. 1, 34.
19. Everett, "Scandalicious," 36.
20. Joan Faber McAlister, "Wounded Detachments, Differential Alliances: Beyond Identity and Telos in Shondaland's Heterotopia," in *Adventures in Shondaland*, eds. Rachel Alicia Griffin and Michaela D. E. Meyer (New Brunswick, NJ: Rutgers, 2018), 47.
21. Cherrell Brown, "Black, Queer and Powerful: Annalise Keating is TV's Most Overdue Anti-Hero," *Paste*, November 12, 2015.
22. Diane Gordon, "Viola Davis Wouldn't Have Played Annalise Keating If Her Wig Didn't Come Off," *New York Vulture*, May 30, 2015.
23. Jihan Forbes, "Olivia Pope Wore Her Hair Natural for *Scandal* 100," *Allure*, April 14, 2017.
24. Julia Robins, "Kerry Washington's 'Professional' Hair," *Ms. Magazine*, February 3, 2015.
25. Williams and Gonlin, 985.
26. Williams and Gonlin, 993.
27. Williams and Gonlin, 994.

28. Newnam as qtd. in Williams and Gonlin, 994.
29. *Scandal*, "The Lawn Chair," directed by Tom Verica, air date March 5, 2015.
30. McAlister, "Wounded Detachments, Differential Alliances," 49.
31. McAlister, "Wounded Detachments, Differential Alliances," 43.
32. *Scandal*, "Thwack!" Directed by Tony Goldwyn, air date April 7, 2016.
33. *HTGAWM*, season 1, episode 9, "Kill Me, Kill Me, Kill Me."
34. Neil Drumming, "*Scandal*'s Racially Charged Motto: "You Have to Be Twice as Good as Them," *Salon*, October 4, 2013.
35. McAlister, "Wounded Detachments, Differential Alliances," 49.
36. Henry Jenkins, *Fans, Bloggers, and Gamers: Exploring Participatory Culture* (New York: NYU Press, 2016), 137.
37. Merryn Johns, "Queering the Culture," *Curve*, November 2015, 4, https://ezp.twu.edu/login?url=https://search-proquest-com.ezp.twu.edu/docview/1729733820?accountid=7102.
38. Jonathan Michael, "The Rise of the Anti-Hero," *Relevant*, April 26, 2013, https://relevantmagazine.com/culture/rise-anti-hero/.
39. Michael, "The Rise of the Anti-Hero."
40. Nardine Saad, "*Scandal*'s Olivia Pope Is No Role Model, Kerry Washington Says (but OK to Dress Like Her)," *Los Angeles Times*, August 5, 2015.
41. Rachel Alicia Griffin and Michaela D. E. Meyer, "Introduction," in *Adventures in Shondaland*, eds. Rachel Alicia Griffin and Michaela D. E. Meyer (New Brunswick, NJ: Rutgers, 2018), 7.
42. Lacy Rose, "Hollywood's Most Powerful Black Female Showrunner," *Hollywood Reporter*, October 17, 2014, as qtd. in *Adventures in Shondaland*, eds. Rachel Alicia Griffin and Michaela D. E. Meyer (New Brunswick, NJ: Rutgers, 2018), 7.
43. Shonda Rhimes, *Year of Yes: How to Dance It Out, Stand in the Sun, and Be Your Own Person* (New York: Simon & Schuster, 2015), 138–39.
44. Griffin and Meyer, "Introduction," 7.
45. Rhimes, *Year of Yes*, 235.

BIBLIOGRAPHY

Brown, Cherrell. "Black, Queer and Powerful: Annalise Keating Is TV's Most Overdue Anti-Hero." *Paste*, November 12, 2015.
Castillo, Michelle. "Netflix Only Takes Up 8 Percent of the Time You Spend Watching Video, but the Company Wants to Change That." *CNBC*, July 17, 2018. https://www.cnbc.com/2018/07/17/netflix-small-portion-of-overall-watch-time-and-competition-is-stiff.html.
Cheers, Imani. *The Evolution of Black Women on Television: Mammies, Matriarchs, and Mistresses*. New York: Routledge, 2018.
Drumming, Neil. "*Scandal*'s Racially Charged Motto: 'You Have to Be Twice as Good as Them.'" *Salon*, October 4, 2013.
Everett, Anna. "Scandalicious: *Scandal*, Social Media, and Shonda Rhimes' Auteurist Juggernaut." *The Black Scholar*. Vol 45, No. 1. p. 34.
Forbes, Jihan. "Olivia Pope Wore Her Hair Natural for *Scandal* 100." *Allure*, April 14, 2017.
Gammage, Marquita M. *Representations of Black Women in the Media*. New York: Routledge, 2016.
Gordon, Diane. "Viola Davis Wouldn't Have Played Annalise Keating If Her Wig Didn't Come Off." *New York Vulture*, May 30, 2015.
Griffin, Rachel Alicia and Michaela D. E. Meyer. "Introduction," in *Adventures in Shondaland*, eds. Rachel Alicia Griffin and Michaela D. E. Meyer. New Brunswick, NJ: Rutgers, 2018.
HTGAWM. "Kill Me, Kill Me, Kill Me," season 1, episode 9.
Hunt, Darnell, Ana-Christina Ramón, and Michael Tran. *Hollywood Diversity Report 2019* (UCLA College of Social Sciences 2019), 50–51.
Jenkins, Henry. *Fans, Bloggers, and Gamers: Exploring Participatory Culture*. New York: NYU Press, 2016.

Johns, Merryn. "Queering the Culture." *Curve*, November 2015, 4. https://ezp.twu.edu/login?url=https://search-proquest-com.ezp.twu.edu/docview/1729733820?accountid=7102.

Madrigal, Alexis. "When Did TV Watching Peak?" *The Atlantic*, May 30, 2018. https://www.theatlantic.com/technology/archive/2018/05/when-did-tv-watching-peak/561464/.

McAlister, Joan Faber. "Wounded Detachments, Differential Alliances: Beyond Identity and Telos in Shondaland's Heterotopia," in *Adventures in Shondaland*, eds. Rachel Alicia Griffin and Michaela D. E. Meyer. New Brunswick, NJ: Rutgers, 2018.

Michael, Jonathan. "The Rise of the Anti-Hero." *Relevant*, April 26, 2013. https://relevantmagazine.com/culture/rise-anti-hero/.

Rhimes, Shonda. *Year of Yes: How to Dance It Out, Stand in the Sun, and Be Your Own Person*. New York: Simon & Schuster, 2015, 138–39.

Robins, Julia. "Kerry Washington's 'Professional' Hair." *Ms. Magazine*, February 3, 2015.

Rose, Lacy. "Hollywood's Most Powerful Black Female Showrunner." *Hollywood Reporter*, October 17, 2014. As qtd. in *Adventures in Shondaland*, eds. Rachel Alicia Griffin and Michaela D. E. Meyer. New Brunswick, NJ: Rutgers, 2018, 7.

Saad, Nardine. "*Scandal*'s Olivia Pope Is No Role Model, Kerry Washington Says (but OK to Dress Like Her)." *Los Angeles Times*, August 5, 2015.

Newnam as qtd. in Williams and Gonlin, 994.

Scandal. "The Lawn Chair." Directed by Tom Verica. Air date March 5, 2015.

———. "Thwack!" Directed by Tony Goldwyn. Air date April 7, 2016.

Tally, Margaret. *The Rise of the Anti-Heroine in TV's Third Golden Age*. Newcastle-Upon-Tyne: Cambridge 2016.

"TV's Golden Age is Real." *The Economist*, November 24, 2018. https://www.economist.com/graphic-detail/2018/11/24/tvs-golden-age-is-real.

Williams, Apryl and Vanessa Gonlin. "I Got All My Sisters with Me (on Black Twitter: Second Screening of *How to Get Away with Murder* as a Discourse on Black Womanhood." *Information, Communication and Society*, Vol. 20, No. 7 (2017): 984–1004.

Wisseh, Assatu. (2018). "Mapping Mammy 2.0: Insecure and the Middle-Class Black Woman's Burden." *Howard Journal of Communication*, 1–20.

Chapter Six

Where the Streets Have No Shame

*Queen Cersei Lannister's Journey to
Alternative Patriarchy*

Louise Coopey

The growing complexity of television narratives has expanded the scope of development of female characters, allowing them to challenge the boundaries of socially imposed gender roles and heteronormative expectations. Margaret Tally's examination of the twenty-first-century antiheroine notes that television leads the way with the cultural construction of new female leads, positioning the antiheroine as a woman who is presented as morally flawed, complex, and multi-layered.[1] The trope, thus defined, breaks away from the conventions of the heroine by categorizing characters as difficult, reclaiming this loaded term and subverting its usage as a means of criticizing and disempowering women who do not adhere to the gendered expectation of passivity. They are complicated, often unlikeable, but still sometimes able to elicit sympathy: women who exhibit reckless behavior, choose cynicism over idealism, and, at times, transgress normative female attributes.[2] This broad set of traits allows for nuance, providing scope for the creation of flawed but varied characters who are far more realistic than the extremes of hero and villain. *Game of Thrones'* (2011–2019) female characters certainly adhere to Tally's broad categorization of new but multifaceted female leads and none easily sit within broad categories, instead challenging established modes of representation.[3] They refuse to conform to gendered expectations and push the boundaries of the identities that are imposed on them. They question why they should fulfill certain roles and embrace their imperfections. In effect, they resonate with modern television audiences who also challenge modes of representation that encourage them to fulfill specific gendered roles.

"When you play the game of thrones, you win or you die."[4] Cersei Lannister's ominous warning to Ned Stark is remembered as one of the iconic lines of *Game of Thrones*. Closely associated with the role that King Robert Baratheon's soon-to-be widow played in the death of Stark, the line also acts as a warning to the hegemonic masculine status quo. Powerful men have been expected to play the game of thrones in order to gain more power, status, and influence in Westeros, but it is also a game that women are expressly forbidden from playing because of the strict imposition of gender roles in the pseudo-Medieval society. Despite that, Cersei is one of the most adept players, having learned to play it from one of the most powerful men in Westeros: her father, Tywin Lannister. His knowledge and her determination provide Cersei with the opportunity to take full advantage of the chaos visited on Westeros by the War of Five Kings to become the first woman to ever sit on the Iron Throne. She is an antiheroine who is morally flawed because she refuses to conform to the restrictions that are set within and enforced by patriarchal structures in her own society and in ours. She relishes the challenge she presents to the hegemonic patriarchal hierarchies of Westeros and navigates the political complexities of limited gendered expectations and expected moral standards with aplomb and ruthlessness in pursuit of her own ends within the *Game of Thrones* storyworld. For viewers, she provides a complex device through which it is possible to navigate the structural constraints that women still face. Cersei is relevant to television audiences simply because the binaries and gendered norms that are designed to hold her in an expected role can no longer contain her. Her antiheroism is an important reminder of the complexity of modern identities and the need for every individual to forge their own path.

The patriarchal structures and values that are prevalent within the Westerosi social order are created, promoted, and maintained by the powerful white male members of the nobility who act as protectors of the status quo.[5] For the purpose of this chapter, "patriarchy" specifically refers to the overarching male-dominated cultural structures that are founded on gendered norms that maintain men's power over their wives and children and confine women to domestic roles. When the status quo declines, as is the case after the deaths of Robert Baratheon and Ned Stark in season 1, such structures come under attack, predominantly by female assailants. Cersei Lannister is one of those assailants and also one of twenty-first-century television's most complex, manipulative, determined, and malevolent characters. She is an antiheroine because she refuses to conform to the expectations imposed on women in Westeros, but does so without embracing the chivalric codes of honor that masculinized warrior women like Brienne of Tarth do.[6] Brienne is portrayed as heroic and capable of fighting her own battles physically. Cersei is not. She is aesthetically feminine and does not engage in physical fights, but she is willing to occupy the in-between space and flaunt the structural restrictions placed on women. The men in her life have always objectified and oppressed her, because her gender defines her within the patriarchal system of Westeros. However, her quest for power is always bound up with the need for autonomy, agency, and self-determination, particularly over her own body.[7] Further, she tests the notion that "a woman must forfeit her femininity to be taken seriously in a male dominated world."[8] This is not unique to the fantasy storyworld of *Game of Thrones* and is a struggle that the show's female viewership can identify with. That Cersei refuses to relinquish her femininity to fit into broader societal structures that are designed to exclude women is admirable, and yet Cersei is not always constructed as an admirable figure. As a trailblazer, she should be considered heroic, but the ruthless and often vindictive way she challenges the validity of the Westerosi patriarchy suggests otherwise. This, in turn, complicates her representation and positions her as an antiheroine—not honorable enough to be a heroine, but not indiscriminately dangerous enough to be a villain.

Cersei's evolution as an antiheroine can be divided into three overlapping phases. The first is her subjugation as a wife and mother, the second is her apprenticeship, and the third is her queenship. Each phase is examined here. Drawing upon close textual analysis of the episodes "Blackwater," "And Now His Watch Is Ended," and "Winds of Winter," I contend that Cersei expressly uses the lessons she learns from the patriarchy to challenge its validity. I also argue that Cersei is an antiheroine precisely because she is unlikeable, stubborn, and morally flawed and yet uses the skills and tools at her disposal to reject typical gender roles, claiming a form of masculine power that she co-opts for her own benefit. In claiming Tywin's experience, wisdom, and knowledge of how to use the hegemonic structures and institutions in place to gain power, Cersei forges a destiny outside of the norms and expectations that should, and would, have confined her. As such, my analysis of Cersei Lannister contributes to the discussion of antiheroines as a device that challenges the validity of the patriarchal norms and highlights the hypocrisy of modern gender roles in both the Westerosi storyworld and the real world.

THE SUBJUGATION AND PERFORMANCE OF
CERSEI LANNISTER

Cersei Lannister is the eldest Lannister child and, had she been male, would have been the heir to the house. As it is, her twin Jaime is the heir to House Lannister and Cersei is used as a pawn to be married off in service to her father Tywin's strategic power play. The strict gender roles in place define her and subjugate her by depriving her of a path to independent agency that extends beyond her role as queen. Considered to be inferior to Jaime because she is female, the primary value she can add to her house is the function of reproduction through her marriage to King Robert Baratheon. In fact, she bears three children to ally the Lannisters with the throne and consequently increases the family's social and political power. In doing so, she fulfills her role as a wife and her function as a Lannister, but neither Tywin nor Robert consider her to be compatible with leadership and power within the social order of Westeros in her own right.

At this point in the series, Cersei's public performance of femininity in line with societal expectations serves to undo her personhood because she is expected to conform to the role of queen in line with the stereotypical passive lady. During the first season, she has little agency over the version of herself that she presents as Robert's queen, facing violence if she does challenge her husband's masculinity and control over her as the consequences of stepping out of line. Her public persona is subject to the expectations of the Westerosi patriarchy in the first season and imposes a construct on her that stifles her individuality. However, she does have a measure of agency that allows her to create space for a private persona, which sets her apart from other female characters. For instance, Sansa, the eldest Stark daughter, is unable to form a private persona until she has personal experience of the power dynamics of Westeros and returns to her home, the North, in season 6. Cersei's private persona is present from the outset and indicative of her struggles in terms of her own expectations and identity, thus establishing the challenges she must overcome as an antiheroine who engages the dichotomies between women's roles in the public versus private spheres and exercising self-determination to achieve personally satisfying ends rather than those scripted by patriarchal hegemony as socially acceptable.

Cersei's private struggle is visible to viewers and casts her as an antiheroine because it stems from her moral flaws, albeit through adultery and incest that is considered to be unacceptable both on the show and in the real world, and demonstrates that she is willing to transgress every boundary for her children (something that every parent can identify with and viewers are drawn to her as a result of). Her focus on her children is constant and an element of her femininity, but it is also through them that we see the struggle between her public persona and private self as she subverts the role of queen as limited to breeding stock and social ornament from within. Cersei forms an incestuous relationship with her twin, Jaime, and cuckolds Robert by allowing herself to become pregnant by her brother. In doing so, she undermines the patriarchal structure of male-preference cognatic primogeniture by giving birth to Lannister children, usurping the Baratheon line of succession by installing illegitimate children as publicly legitimate heirs.[9] She also routinely schemes in a "Machiavellian" way against the patriarchal power that both defines and confines her. This is exemplified by her clash with Ned Stark in "You Win or You Die." As Elizabeth Beaton argues, "Her coup accords with Machiavelli's advice that a prince should assume control completely, rather than allowing others to 'become powerful.'"[10] She limits Ned's power by scheming against him and performing in a public forum, that of the Throne Room, to discredit him. She requests Ned's presence in the Throne Room the moment Robert Baratheon's death is confirmed, though Cersei knows that Ned will move to block her eldest son Joffrey's ascension to the throne because he made the mistake of informing her that he was aware of Joffrey's parentage. This knowledge empowers her to preempt Ned's attack, preparing a trap that makes him appear to be a traitor as he presents a letter from Robert declaring his brother, Renly, his heir. Cersei dramatically rips the letter up and makes Ned an offer she knows he will refuse: "Is this meant to be your shield, Lord Stark? A piece of paper. We have a new king now. Lord Eddard, when we last spoke you offered me some counsel. Allow me to return the courtesy. . . . Bend the knee and swear loyalty to my son."[11] On multiple levels this is a performance, but it is also indicative of her using her status to privately scheme while maintaining her public persona as a woman with limited power (able to negotiate power through her son rather than through her own standing).

Gerald Poscheschnik observes that safeguarding her family is a priority for Cersei and a key element of her identity. As such, her actions here are unsurprising.[12] It also irrevocably links her to Tywin's philosophy of family first as the absolute dictum of the Lannisters. Although the relationship between Cersei and Tywin cannot fully be assessed until he arrives in King's Landing at the end of season 2, both are framed as scheming, devious, and manipulative prior to his installment at court. It would be a mistake to assume that such characteristics are Lannister family traits because Jaime and their younger brother Tyrion do not exhibit such deep investment in self-serving machination, and yet the female child confined to marriage and motherhood by the gender expectations championed by Tywin does. The parallel between Cersei and her father's quest for power and control illuminates ambition as individual rather than gendered traits, but it also highlights the hypocrisy of modern gender roles because the treatment of Tywin and Cersei as individuals could not be more different.

Cersei's internal struggle between her prescribed role and her personal desires and ambitions is palpable twelve episodes later in "Blackwater." Tasked with leading the ladies of Westeros into the Red Keep, the royal residence and focal point of Westeros, for their protection as her brother-in-law, Stannis Baratheon, attacks King's Landing, she ostensibly fulfills her role as Queen Mother while the menfolk fight. Cersei's resentment toward her very feminine role of keeping the ladies calm until the battle is over becomes more apparent the longer she is confined. She exhibits her antiheroine credentials as a difficult woman in this scene and underscores her disregard for convention. Cersei stakes an initial claim to a warrior's identity by wearing body armor that symbolizes her personal desire to be something more than a wife and mother, but her scorn for her fellow ladies highlights her contempt for the gendered roles prescribed by the hegemonic masculine order: "I should've been born a man. I'd rather face a thousand swords than be shut up inside with this flock of frightened hens."[13] In response, Sansa points out that the "frightened hens" are her guests, to which Cersei bitterly stresses that she is simply doing what is expected of her. Although Tywin is not there at that stage, the patriarchal values he upholds, specifically the primacy of men and the fixity of gender roles, are woven into the fabric of this scene. As a queen, she must perform the duty of maintaining domestic order and unity where possible,[14] mirroring her role as mother and position at the heart of the family. The body armor and the plinth she is sat upon, slightly apart from the rest of the ladies, visually and symbolically separate her from the other women. It manifests a discourse that posits Cersei's strength in opposition to the assumption of women's frailty, feebleness, and inability to engage the physicality of violence and battle as offensive or defensive agents. It also positions her between the world she longs to occupy and the one she is situated within. Both are examples of Patel's "political prostheses," or substitutions for the female body that project masculine power[15] that "allow the female ego to enter into the patriarchal order of political struggle."[16] The armor provides scope for a dual reading. It may be read as a breastplate and a literal representation of the female body, but it is significant that she is the only woman in the room who has it. Although it is not comparable with the full armor worn by Brienne of Tarth, its presence in a war situation demonstrates its symbolic value as an indication of a preparedness to fight. By adopting prostheses that are coded as male and rejecting the weakness of the female body, she symbolically reinforces her desire to be something other than just a woman. This signals her intent to challenge the validity of patriarchal norms and expectations because it marks the start of her overt challenges to established modes of representation. Westerosi queens do not wear armor because their place is not in battle, and yet Cersei's attire challenges that principle despite being confined to a highly gendered space. Her desire to push the boundaries of her role emphasizes that it is male control that maintains those boundaries, thus heralding a more visible form of resistance that appeals to viewers by demonstrating that possibilities to instigate change emerge from within.

CERSEI, STUDENT OF TYWIN

Cersei's inner struggle is contextualized within the broader landscape of the patriarchy during the first two seasons of *Game of Thrones* but not in terms of her relationship with her father. The two are separated until he rides in like her paternal knight in shining armor to save King's Landing in the chaotic final scene of "Blackwater." In these earlier episodes, Tywin's influence over his daughter is not apparent to the extent that it is in the third and fourth seasons. Her father's arrival is deeply significant because of the shift it causes in her behavior. Between Robert's death and Tywin's arrival, Cersei's strategic confidence grows, but that is replaced by a need for her father's approval as her position as his student becomes clear. She seeks his approval precisely because she has no female role model after the death of her mother and absence of other women during her childhood. In aspiring to learn about politics and strategy from Tywin, she works against the models other women present. For instance, Ned's wife, Catelyn Stark, teaches Sansa how to become a lady by epitomizing the idealized version of the role, specifically a passive and broadly silent figure who acquiesces to the control of her husband. Cersei does not have access to that teaching and, in working against such role models, she subverts the social order and destabilizes prescribed roles. Although there is evidence of Cersei already having traits that are conducive to achieving her goals despite her gender, and indeed, that emphasize her status as a morally flawed, cynical and difficult antiheroine, she learns to harness them from Tywin.

Just as the process of cultural indoctrination by which Cersei initially began to learn from Tywin became active via studying him and his methods, her "apprenticeship" is a process of learning through active observation and self-directed study rather than active or direct teaching. Tywin does not intend her to progress beyond her prescribed gender-based social role as he chronically underestimates Cersei; her "education" is not a process of reciprocity. Representing dominant masculinity, Tywin is indifferent to his daughter, believing that she is tightly bound by her gender and unable to access and adopt masculinities or the power invested in maleness through hegemonic patriarchy. As such, Cersei also highlights the blatant hypocrisy of his refusal to educate her in the principles of leadership when she is far more suited to it than either of her sons, both of whom ultimately inherit the Iron Throne and Tywin seeks to mentor. In bucking gendered norms, Cersei also rejects the validity of patriarchal structures and institutions. Such dismissal is reinforced by excessive male supremacy but, in choosing observation and self-directed study for the purpose of effecting her own agenda, Cersei rejects the limitations of Tywin's indifference, exhibiting a stubbornness that reinforces her status as an antiheroine.

Tywin's refusal to confer recognition on Cersei is evident in their one-on-one conversations. He deliberately withholds recognition as a result of the norms of the Westerosi patriarchy and women's place within it, thus maintaining power over her. The episode "And Now His Watch Is Ended" provides the site of an important conversation between Cersei and Tywin in this respect, illustrating the tensions in the father-daughter relationship and the deviation in attitudes toward the patriarchally-imposed limitations that underpin it. Cersei approaches Tywin to ask how he is trying to resolve Jaime's imprisonment by Ned's eldest son, Robb Stark, but must wait for the first twenty seconds of the scene before he pays her attention. Tywin, for his part, is patiently writing letters to orchestrate Jaime's release and his own revenge on the Starks, the quill scratching on the parchment throughout in contrast to his daughter's fidgeting impatience as she waits to receive his attention. At this point, she appears almost childlike in her desire to seek her father's approval as well as exasperated that he does not truly see her or recognize her potential. Cersei asks whether Tywin is doing everything he can to free Jaime. Tywin answers the question without confiding his strategic plans to her. Despite a brusque dismissal, she remains seated and demands a justification for ignoring her:

> Did it ever occur to you that I might be the one that deserves your confidence and your trust? Not your sons. Not Jaime or Tyrion, but me. Years and years of lectures on family and legacy, the same lecture really just with tiny, tedious variations. Did it ever occur to you that your daughter might be the only one listening to them, living by them? That she might have the most to contribute to your legacy that you love so much more than your actual children?[17]

The tone and content of her riposte are equally significant. Her clipped tones betray her bitterness and the hurt she feels at Tywin's dismissal of her value beyond that as a wife and mother. Similarly, the questions she asks are rhetorical; she knows that it has not, in fact, occurred to him that Cersei deserves confidence and trust, nor does he believe that she has more to contribute to his legacy than Jaime or Tyrion. However, it does draw his, and the audience's, attention to the fact that she has been listening to his lessons on social values and power, absorbing them and putting them into practice in her own life to subvert the patriarchal values that Tywin holds so dear.

Ultimately, Tywin's final dismissal of Cersei is damning, if entirely contradictory: "I don't distrust you because you're a woman. I distrust you because you're not as smart as you think. You've allowed [Joffrey] to ride roughshod over you and everyone else in this city."[18] Each sentence is delivered in an even, measured tone as Tywin pauses his correspondence and glares at her, underlining his displeasure at her direct challenge. The first sentence confirms that he does not trust her, whereas the second offers a damning indictment of her high opinion of her abilities. He subtly acknowledges that she has some intelligence and capacity for strategic thought, but she overestimates herself. Although Tywin views overconfidence as one of Cersei's primary weaknesses, her constant desire for his approval projects a different impression. She is arrogant in her belief that she knows what is best for her children, but there is a dissonance between Tywin's perception of her as a know-it-all and her representation as a child desperately craving acceptance that is withheld on the basis of gender, which elicits sympathy for her. This is evidenced by the final sentence contradicting the first because it is explicitly linked to her womanhood, suggesting that she is a bad mother who is unable to control her son. Tywin's observation is correct but her inability to control Joffrey reflects on her aptitude for leadership, reinforcing the message that gender is an obstacle that must be overcome if she wants to rule. Further, her children provide a marker by which she is judged and block her path to wielding power in her own right. Finally, Tywin reminds her she must trust her own abilities and intelligence, seeking to develop them outside of the obstructive assumptions of gender-based roles because she will continue to be judged by the patriarchal claim that women are unfit to rule because they simply cannot control men. Cersei is capable of recognizing that the ability to rule is not dependent on gender, but this is meaningless in the context of this scene because Tywin controls the message. He points out her weaknesses, but he also underestimates her ability to act on the articulation of her self-awareness and agency.

The lessons that Cersei takes from Tywin are, at least in part, reinforced by her ability to learn from mistakes. She is fallible and recognizes the need to change to mitigate her weaknesses, unlike the controlling paternal order who pit themselves against her. It also conforms to the antiheroine trope of imperfection rather than idealization. Her imperfections and moral flaws are highlighted by the High Sparrow, leader of the Faith Militant religious fundamentalist group that converges on Westeros in season 5. Proclaiming to be the moral saviors of Westeros, the Faith Militant members impose their own religious moral values on the population and Cersei falls short. Some of her immoral acts, like adultery and incest, are breaches of the social orders within the storyworld and that of the viewers, but her rejection of the limits of the Westerosi social system renders her a threat to its coherence and control on a much grander scale. That her husband, Robert Baratheon, routinely engaged in adultery and went unpunished contrasts with the consequences that Cersei has to endure, illuminating the abject hypocrisy of the Westerosi social system and patriarchal controls. That she engages in such immoral behaviors flaunts established modes of representation of female characters as passive and happy to perform in the role of the good wife and mother. It is therefore Cersei's determination to challenge the validity of the structures of the patriarchy that encourages the High Sparrow to push back in the first instance.

Having arrested Cersei on the charges of adultery and incest with her cousin, Lancel Lannister, and regicide, the High Sparrow sentences her to a walk of atonement—a naked walk of shame through the streets of King's Landing—in "Mother's Mercy." The High Sparrow chooses this method of shaming her to force Cersei to retreat from her opposition to the remaining institutions that do not bend to her will.[19] She is pushed out to stand in front of a hostile crowd, her femininity compromised as her hair is shorn and her clothes replaced with a sack (which is eventually removed), and she is condemned by the High Sparrow as a liar and fornicator. Despite her devious, petty, and often malicious nature, this moment does elicit sympathy for the broadly hated Cersei from the TV audience. Cersei bears the walk stoically. Despite being covered in rotting vegetables and bodily fluids, her feet bloodied and skin torn, she refuses to shed a tear or drop her head throughout her ordeal, only revealing her emotions when among allies, safely behind the door of the Red Keepisode The walk of atonement was designed to deprive her of her dignity, pride, and self-respect. Her refusal to be publicly broken by it evokes sympathy and admiration from the TV audience, which is a key trait of the antiheroine. The sentence imposes nudity to emphasize the inherent shame scripted on women's bodies, shame rooted in inferiority and to force her to "demonstrate her repentance, [by] cast[ing] aside all pride, all artifice, and present herself as the gods made her."[20] In reality, her exposed body signifies the power difference within the interaction.[21] When faced with the challenge of a power play from the High Sparrow, Cersei is not equal to it. She falls for his games, her own weakness of overconfidence getting the better of her. Despite learning her father's methods, she does not learn about how to oppose patriarchal power in situations that pose a direct threat. She must learn that lesson herself, just as viewers learn that Cersei cannot be broken by the patriarchy that seeks to bring her under control.

Tania Evans's reading of Cersei's early attempts to accumulate power and test the parameters of gendered norms contends that she is largely unsuccessful: "Almost all of Cersei's decisions are hastily made and poorly considered, which may suggest . . . that female masculinities are poor imitations of male masculinities, or worse, that women should be excluded from power because they cannot rule effectively."[22] There is, however, an alternative reading. Although some of her decisions backfire and many do not show evidence of thought beyond the immediate present, they are based on strategic considerations and test the application of Tywin's philosophies on power. All decisions she makes draw on what she has learned from him, blurring the boundary between the gendered performances that were traditionally expected in Westeros. There is a case to be made for female masculinities being more experimental than male masculinities as Cersei searches for an identity that is removed from the double standards of patriarchally-imposed gender roles. Cersei makes serious errors in judgment, not least her decision to trust the High Sparrow, but she takes full lessons in masculinity from the master then shifts those trappings of masculinized power so she may inhabit and exert authority as a woman. She is an antiheroine and trailblazer precisely because she recognizes the need to use the tools and strategies of the patriarchy to challenge its validity and undermine the justification for her exclusion from power based on her gender. This resonates with female viewers precisely because the structural constraints that bind Cersei are recognizable within their lived experiences. Cersei's approach to her perpetual struggle does not appeal to audiences in order to make them like her, but it does strike a chord with which they can identify.

QUEEN CERSEI, FIRST OF HER NAME

Cersei's education comes to fruition in the moments before she becomes queen, using her skills and the knowledge she acquired through watching Tywin. There is a marked shift in her attitude and behavior as she embraces her own form of masculinity. The framing of the first eighteen minutes of "Winds of Winter" focuses on the action within the Sept of Baelor and allows it to build to a crescendo to provide an insight into the sheer scale of the plan that Cersei has put into action. The episode sees Cersei fully embrace her self-determination and seize power. Her previous attempts at putting Tywin's teachings into practice may not have yielded the results she wanted, but the strategic planning and execution of her grand plan to eliminate her enemies—the High Sparrow and Faith Militant, her uncle Kevan Lannister, her daughter-in-law Margaery Tyrell, and many other nameless nobles that oppose her—and seize power is successful. She does so in a single act of violence—the use of wildfyre positioned under the Sept of Baelor to effectively bomb it with the elite of King's Landing in it. The plan is elaborate and relies on several of the city's street children to ignite the wildfyre, but the camera credits Cersei with responsibility immediately. The first shot of the episode positioning her looking out of a window in the Red Keep at the Sept and the final shot of the sequence bookend the scenes with a much-changed physical, political, and social landscape. It is the moment the camera shifts from juxtaposing women's experiences with male perspectives,[23] framing a female perspective and marking the shift in the dynamics of power. As Hand of the Queen Qyburn muses, "sometimes before we can usher in the new, the old must be put to rest."[24] This demonstrates that Cersei paid attention to Tywin's insistence that the Lannisters should trust themselves alone.

In choosing to eliminate her enemies, Cersei chooses to no longer engage with the patriarchal expectations that held her back. Having been accused of incest by her cousin and member of the Faith Militant, Lancel Lannister, the Sept is the site of Cersei's trial at that moment. It is full of lords and ladies serving as witnesses to her humiliation. As the walk of atonement had already punished her indiscretions, the persecution of Cersei by the establishment under the Faith Militant generates sympathy for her. The trial would have cemented the High Sparrow's male absolutism and fulfilled the desire to cast Cersei out of society on a more permanent basis. Instead, she reverses the dynamic, using her knowledge of the High Sparrow's desire to create a dramatic spectacle, like her earlier walk of atonement, when punishing sinners and exerting control. Her awareness of how he will conduct the trial allows her to lay a trap, using the wildfyre that is stored under the Sept as a weapon and choosing to reset the balance of power. Her ingenuity and resoluteness in the face of continued persecution not only establishes that she is an antiheroine, but it also challenges the true purpose of the Faith Militant as a vehicle for the patriarchy. It is their desire to disempower her and force her into passivity, but Cersei is able to use the qualities she learned observing Tywin, particularly how to deal with enemies, to challenge the validity of the structures that seek to contain her.

The explosion resets the patriarchal order but does not serve to make it more inclusive. The removal of the elites who would not support her is an example of the resulting short-term thinking that often drives Cersei in *Game of Thrones.* Although choosing to take a short-term approach is one of Cersei's weaknesses, it allows her to grasp power within a social order that she knows and can maneuver within. In "Hardhome" (5.08), Cersei's eventual rival for the Iron Throne, Daenerys Targaryen, states her intention to "break the wheel"[25] by removing every vestige of the hegemonic social order and installing a society based on equality and inclusivity in its place. This is diametrically opposed to Cersei's intentions and desires. Cersei desires only power for herself and intends to maintain power on her own terms, embracing characteristic self-interest as opposed to heroic altruism out of a concern for the greater good. However, Daenerys does not seek power purely out of a selfless need to liberate either and therefore is also an antiheroine. Both women seek power because they believe they are entitled to it, and both are morally flawed and perceived as difficult by their male relatives and enemies, many of whom seek to disempower them. Both women retain their aesthetic femininity, wearing outfits that highlight the female body because they believe that gender and the associations invested in women's bodies should not stop them. They are ultimately enemies because Daenerys's feminist empowerment is the natural enemy of the patriarchal tools and strategies co-opted by Cersei.[26] Although both characters co-opt masculine and often violent approaches to gaining power, Cersei embraces the reinforcement rather than subversion of the hegemonic masculine norms that her rival expressly rejects. Despite their oppositional approaches to achieving their goals, the fact that both Cersei and Daenerys occupy the same space as antiheroines demonstrates how diverse, complex, and nuanced the category is.

Although the outcome of Cersei's attack on the Sept directly challenges the notion that women are not strong enough to rule, she reinforces patriarchal power by implementing Tywin's philosophy. She orchestrates her plan with the intelligence and scheming that Tywin prides, employing the masculine norms of violence and strength with little regard for the collateral damage. The opening scene of "Winds of Winter" serves as Cersei's final test for her apprenticeship with the patriarchy, confirming that she has passed it with flying colors. She shows no mercy for her enemies and offers no reprieve for those who have wronged her. In the Westerosi storyworld, mercy is coded as feminine and framed as indicative of weakness. In the very first episode, Ned Stark demonstrates masculine strength by executing a deserter of the Night's Watch despite the validity of his excuse—that he was fleeing a threat to his own life.[27] In contrast, his wife, Catelyn Stark, chooses to show mercy to Jaime Lannister, setting him free from imprisonment.[28] The hypocrisy embedded within this contrast is highlighted by Cersei's action and rejection of modern gender roles. She takes practical steps by removing all obstacles to her pursuit of power and cements her status as an antiheroine because she refuses to conform. Far from being a villain because she murders her enemies, Cersei is an antiheroine because she plans and executes an attack that demonstrates strength, determination, and the ability to outwit those who incorrectly believe that they are superior to her. She proves that they are not.

Much of Cersei's behavior in "The Winds of Winter" mirrors that of Tywin, embracing the Machiavellian qualities that she observes in his behaviors throughout the course of her life and harnesses to mete out punishment on those who she believes have wronged her. One such example of this is the revenge she takes on Septa Unella, a nun dedicated to Faith Militant who oversees Cersei's imprisonment and punishment. Although the Septa's physical torture and subsequent demise is only hinted at, she is tortured mentally by Cersei in revenge for her part in the queen's imprisonment and walk of atonement. Reinforcing the notion that Cersei emerged from her punishment stronger, the decision to single out the Septa for special attention when strategically eliminating her enemies is a demonstration of personal power. Cersei deliberately redirects the cruelty Septa enforced during her imprisonment and harnesses the same dramatic performative tendencies that were evident in season 1's clash with Ned Stark. She uses them to claim empowerment and reject the degradation that the whole experience was designed to induce. Strapped to a table in a dark cell, Septa Unella is unconscious until Cersei pours wine over her face and demands her attention:

> Confess. Confess. Confess. Confess it felt good beating me, starving me, frightening me, humiliating me. You didn't do it because you cared about my atonement. You did it because it felt good. I understand. I do things because they feel good. I drink because it feels good. I killed my husband because it felt good to be rid of him. I fuck my brother because it feels good to feel him inside me. I lie about fucking my brother because it feels good to keep our sons safe from hateful hypocrites. I killed your High Sparrow . . . because it felt good to watch [him] burn.[29]

Revealing that Septa Unella was right about her all along and she is guilty of everything the High Sparrow accused her of, Cersei's confession is a narrative device that provides the audience with an insight into her motivations. She admits to her immorality, her need for personal gratification and reckless behavior but celebrates her femininity, her agency, her *choice*. Further, her absolute rejection of shame is indicative of her determination to employ Tywin's lessons to preserve the Lannister legacy. As is evidenced by his determination to free Jaime from Robb Stark, Tywin is focused on outcomes and resolutions, refusing to wallow or succumb to the shame of having his son captured by his enemy. Cersei refuses to succumb to the shame of her walk of atonement, instead taking a more proactive approach. Her monologue is indicative of her taking ownership of her actions and her personal flaws, but it also an implement of torture that echoes Roose Bolton's message that "[t]he Lannisters send their regards"[30] as he murders Robb Stark, the son of Ned Stark and enemy of Tywin as King of the North, in "The Rains of Castamere" (3.09). Although Cersei previously wanted to withhold the truth to protect her son and preserve the integrity of his claim to the Iron Throne, the disregard for self-preservation offers an insight into the shift in power dynamics. Septa Unella no longer holds a position of power and is fully aware that she is about to die, just like Robb.

Cersei shares Tywin's need to taunt and have the last word. Whereas Bolton delivers that for Tywin, Cersei's sadistic pleasure is derived from her personal delivery of the bad news: "You're not going to die today. You're not going to die for quite a while. Ser Gregor . . . Your gods have forsaken you. This is your god now."[31] The scene is a performance, using the threat of violence to inspire a level of terror that has a potency amplified by Cersei's calmness and control. It also subverts traditional televisual and cinematic images of typically masculine torture and rape, neither of which are shown but are strongly hinted at here. Elizabeth Goldberg identifies a consistent feminization of the victim and hypermasculinization of the perpetrator in cultural representations of torture and sexual violence, but that largely depends on the patriarchal conception that women are the weaker sex.[32] Neither Septa Unella nor Cersei are coded in line with established representations. Cersei's attire is feminine despite the torture she sanctions, whereas Unella's aesthetic appearance is devoid of gender coding as a consequence of the plain habit she wears to denote membership of the Faith Militant. However, Cersei's zombified knight, Ser Gregor Clegane, provides an overt threat lurking in the shadows, so an instrument of the patriarchy is still present and is indicative of Cersei's continuing use of violence against women instead of empowering them. His presence is also an indication that Cersei cannot be truly powerful without a masculine figure to perpetrate that violence on her orders.

The whole episode can be read as an homage to Tywin, mirroring his revenge on the Starks at the Red Wedding in "The Rains of Castamere," during which extreme violence is used to secure power and sustain patriarchal norms. Cersei therefore reinforces the patriarchy via a similar action, although the application is different to an extent. Cersei's initial presence, however, deviates from Tywin's approach. Whereas he deliberately distances himself from the execution of his plans, Cersei takes ownership of them. She plays an active role in controlling her own destiny, accepting the mantle of antiheroine and manifesting the trope as a difficult, complex, morally flawed and cynical, unlikeable antiheroine woman. The moral expectations that viewers place on Cersei are often unrealistic, but her need for revenge over the villainous Septa adheres to the principles of human nature. It is impossible not to root for her and applaud her because she fulfills her desire to get justice from the woman who bullied and tortured her at her lowest point. As awful as Cersei's actions are when taken in isolation, the contextual background of the scene itself justifies them and provides the viewer with a sense of satisfaction that the antiheroine ultimately prevails.

Tywin has no need to claim responsibility for Robb Stark's murder or for the massacre of the Targaryen children because his reputation and power are already established. Further, maintaining distance allows for plausible deniability should the need arise. Cersei cannot afford to be distant from her power plays because she needs them to boost her reputation as a capable leader who is to be feared despite her gender. The parallels drawn between Cersei and Tywin here indicate that she does use the lessons of the patriarchy to win the game of thrones but the underpinnings of hegemonic masculine control of the Iron Throne remain. This problematic repositioning of power through modified gender performances serves as an example of Shiloh Carroll's claim that female disruption of gender roles is conducted through "wielding male power rather than finding power in femininity."[33] Further, Evans asserts that there is a clear acceptance of masculine power structures on the part of Cersei, facilitating an accumulation of power.[34] All three points made here are valid, but there is an acceptance that Cersei must perform masculinity to become queen, which problematizes her feminine identity. The symbolism of a woman in a seat of power is problematic because it undermines the validity of the patriarchy and the gender roles that are so deeply embedded in masculine norms and expectations. Cersei's status as queen is therefore significant regardless of the methods she uses to achieve her goal of ruling the Seven Kingdoms and signals the hypocrisy of her male predecessors in applying double standards to her. Although it is not possible to divorce Cersei's power from the methods she used to achieve it and her performance of gender, the fact remains that a strong woman, an antiheroine, is able to achieve something that the patriarchy had long sought to prevent.

Interestingly, although viewers and academics like Tania Evans have made much of Cersei's adoption of female masculinity to emulate the men in her life, little has been made of the fact that many of the traits she learns and perfects by watching Tywin are associated specifically with negative stereotypes of women. Manipulation, deviousness, malevolence and artifice are all traits associated with Cersei; Tywin also exhibits them all and yet is not emasculated. He is celebrated by his powerful male peers, although not by viewers, thus further illustrating the disjunction and double standards associated with gendered representation. Conversely, Cersei's characterization as an antiheroine occurs because she engages in behaviors that she learned from a powerful and successful proponent of the patriarchy and she is vilified for them, particularly after she becomes queen and engages in acts that secure her power base. An example of this is the capture and execution of Missandei, Daenerys's advisor and handmaiden following a successful attack on the Targaryen ships in the fourth episode of the final season, "The Last of the Starks."[35] The show is careful to emphasize that Missandei is a peaceful person, thus her violent beheading on Cersei's order is underpinned by a sense of horror. The viewer is encouraged to see the act as brutal and unnecessary but Missandei is ultimately loyal to Cersei's enemy and her death is indicative of that. Cersei is an antiheroine because she highlights this hypocrisy of modern gender roles and expectations, despite her actions rendering her thoroughly unlikeable. She demonstrates that the masculine/feminine binary is still imposed by the patriarchy to disempower women, but it does not disempower her. Instead, she uses this hypocrisy to challenge the validity of the Westerosi patriarchy.

CONCLUSION

Cersei Lannister epitomizes the twenty-first-century antiheroine. The complexity and length of the series allows her character arc to develop over time, illustrating her progress in working toward her goals and aim until they come to fruition. The narrative takes her from a subjugated woman who is forced to conform to the feminine role expected of her to an antagonist who bucks that role and subverts expectations. Cersei's determination, struggle against her own socially imposed role, and manipulative and devious approach to getting what she wants converge to position her as an antiheroine committed to her own moral standards regardless of the expectations of dominant gendered constraints. Although her father demonstrates a similar moral character, she does not wholly model herself on him—she is not a female Tywin, rather a woman who negotiates the gendered boundaries to assert a particular agenda as expression of her own agency and selfhood. By embracing the constraints of hegemonic patriarchy—the hierarchy of power it maintains—Cersei simultaneously undermines and upholds such stratifications while challenging the constraints of hegemonic patriarchy in regard to the assumed limitations of women. She strives to harness hierarchy and the structures of hegemonic patriarchy to gain power and status that would normatively be beyond her reach. She succeeds.

NOTES

1. Margaret Tally, *The Rise of the Antiheroine in TV's Third Golden Age* (Newcastle-Upon-Tyne: Cambridge Scholars Publishing, 2016), 1.

2. Tally, *The Rise of the Antiheroine*, 1–8.

3. Valerie Frankel, *Women in "Game of Thrones": Power, Conformity and Resistance* (Jefferson, NC: McFarland, 2014), 39.

4. *Game of Thrones*, "You Win or You Die," directed by Daniel Minahan, May 29, 2011.

5. Jacqueline Furby and Claire Hines, *Fantasy* (London: Routledge, 2012), 122.

6. Yvonne Tasker and Lindsay Steenberg, "Women Warriors from Chivalry to Vengeance," in *Women of Ice and Fire*, ed. Anne Gjelsvik and Rikke Schubert (London: Bloomsbury, 2016), 177; Tania Evans, "Vile, Scheming, Evil Bitches? The Monstrous Feminine Meets Hegemonic Masculine Violence in A Song of Ice and Fire and *Game of Thrones*," *Aeternum* 5, no. 1 (2018): 18.

7. Lindsey Mantoan, "Raven: Cersei Lannister, First of Her Name," in *Vying for the Iron Throne: Essays on Power, Gender, Death and Performance in HBO's "Game of Thrones,"* ed. Lindsey Mantoan and Sara Brady (Jefferson, NC: McFarland, 2018), 93.

8. Diana Marques, "Power and the Denial of Femininity in *Game of Thrones*," *Canadian Review of American Studies* 49, no. 1 (2019): 47

9. Caroline Spector, "Power and Feminism in Westeros," in *Beyond the Wall: Exploring George R. R. Martin's A Song of Ice and Fire*, ed. James Lowder (Dallas: Smart Pop, 2012), 182.

10. Elizabeth Beaton, "Female Machiavellians in Westeros," in *Women of Ice and Fire*, ed. Anne Gjelsvik and Rikke Schubert (London: Bloomsbury, 2016), 200.

11. *Game of Thrones*, "You Win or You Die," directed by Daniel Minahan, May 29, 2011.

12. Gerald Poscheschnik, *"Game of Thrones*—A Psychoanalytic Interpretation Including Some Remarks on the Psychosocial Function of Modern TV Series." *The International Journal of Psychoanalysis* 99, no. 4 (2018): 1004.

13. *Game of Thrones*, "Blackwater," directed by Neil Marshall, May 27, 2012.

14. Marilyn Francus, *Monstrous Motherhood: Eighteenth Century Culture and the Ideology of Domesticity* (Baltimore: Johns Hopkins University Press, 2013), 8.

15. C. Patel, "Expelling a Monstrous Matriarchy: Casting Cersei Lannister as Abject in A Song of Ice and Fire," *Journal of European Popular Culture* 5, no. 2 (2014), 135.

16. Patel, "Expelling a Monstrous Matriarchy," 138.

17. *Game of Thrones*, "And Now His Watch Is Ended," April 21, 2013.

18. *Game of Thrones*, "And Now His Watch Is Ended," April 21, 2013.

19. William Clapton and Laura Shepherd, "Lessons from Westeros: Gender and Power in *Game of Thrones*," *Politics* 37, no. 1 (2017): 14.

20. *Game of Thrones*, "Mother's Mercy," directed by David Nutter, June 14, 2015.

21. Jessica Needham, "Visual Misogyny: An Analysis of Female Sexual Objectification in *Game of Thrones*," *Femspec* 17 (2017): 14.

22. Evans, "Vile, Scheming, Evil Bitches?" 24.

23. Beaton, "Female Machiavellians," 199.

24. *Game of Thrones*, "Winds of Winter," directed by Miguel Sapochnik, June 26, 2016.

25. *Game of Thrones*, "Hardhome," directed by Miguel Sapochnik, May 31, 2015.

26. Ross Murray, "The Feminine Mystique: Feminism, Sexuality, Motherhood," *Journal of Graphic Novels and Comics* 2, no. 1 (2011): 61.

27. *Game of Thrones*, "Winter Is Coming," directed by Timothy van Patten, April 17, 2011.
28. *Game of Thrones*, "A Man Without Honor," directed by David Nutter, May 13, 2012.
29. *Game of Thrones*, "Winds of Winter," directed by Miguel Sapochnik, June 26, 2016.
30. *Game of Thrones*, "The Rains of Castamere," directed by David Nutter, June 2, 2013.
31. *Game of Thrones*, "Winds of Winter," directed by Miguel Sapochnik, June 26, 2016.
32. Elizabeth Goldberg, *Beyond Terror: Gender, Narrative, Human Rights* (New Brunswick, NJ: Rutgers University Press, 2007), 122.
33. Shiloh Carroll, "'You Ought to Be in Skirts and Me in Mail': Gender and History in George R. R. Martin's A Song of Ice and Fire," in *George R. R. Martin's A Song of Ice and Fire and the Medieval Literary Tradition*, ed. Bartlomiej Blaszkiewicz (Warsaw: Wydawnictwa Uniwersytetu Warszawskiego, 2015), 247.
34. Evans, "Vile, Scheming, Evil Bitches?," 18.
35. *Game of Thrones*, "The Last of the Starks," directed by David Nutter, May 5, 2019.

BIBLIOGRAPHY

Beaton, Elizabeth. "Female Machiavellians in Westeros." In *Women of Ice and Fire*, edited by Anne Gjelsvik & Rikke Schubert, 193–218. London: Bloomsbury, 2016.
Carroll, Shiloh. "'You Ought to Be in Skirts and Me in Mail': Gender and History in George R. R. Martin's A Song of Ice and Fire." In *George R. R. Martin's A Song of Ice and Fire and the Medieval Literary Tradition*, edited by Bartlomiej Blaszkiewicz, 247–259. Warsaw: Wydawnictwa Uniwersytetu Warszawskiego, 2015.
Clapton, William and Laura Shepherd. "Lessons from Westeros: Gender and Power in *Game of Thrones*." *Politics* 37, no. 1 (2017): 5–18.
Evans, Tania. "Vile, Scheming, Evil Bitches? The Monstrous Feminine Meets Hegemonic Masculine Violence in A Song of Ice and Fire and *Game of Thrones*." *Aeternum* 5, no. 1 (2018): 14–27.
Francus, Marilyn. *Monstrous Motherhood: Eighteenth Century Culture and the Ideology of Domesticity.* Baltimore: Johns Hopkins University Press, 2013.
Frankel, Valerie. *Women in "Game of Thrones": Power, Conformity and Resistance.* Jefferson, NC: McFarland, 2014.
Furby, Jacqueline and Claire Hines. *Fantasy.* London: Routledge, 2012.
Game of Thrones. "A Man Without Honor." Directed by David Nutter, May 13, 2012.
———. "And Now His Watch Is Ended." Directed by Alex Graves, April 21, 2013.
———. "Blackwater." Neil Marshall, May 27, 2012.
———. "Hardhome." Directed by Miguel Sapochnik, May 31, 2015.
———. "Mother's Mercy." Directed by David Nutter, June 14, 2015.
———. "The Last of the Starks." Directed by David Nutter, May 5, 2019.
———. "The Rains of Castamere." Directed by David Nutter, June 2, 2013.
———. "Winds of Winter." Directed by Miguel Sapochnik, June 26, 2016.
———. "Winter Is Coming." Directed by Timothy van Patten, April 17, 2011.
———. "You Win or You Die." Directed by Daniel Minahan, May 29, 2011.
Goldberg, Elizabeth. *Beyond Terror: Gender, Narrative, Human Rights.* New Brunswick, NJ: Rutgers University Press, 2007.
Mantoan, Lindsey. "Raven: Cersei Lannister, First of Her Name." In *Vying for the Iron Throne: Essays on Power, Gender, Death and Performance in HBO's "Game of Thrones,"* edited by Lindsey Mantoan and Sara Brady, 90–94. Jefferson, NC: McFarland, 2018.
Marques, Diana. "Power and the Denial of Femininity in *Game of Thrones*." *Canadian Review of American Studies* 49, no. 1 (2019): 46–65.
Murray, Ross. "The Feminine Mystique: Feminism, Sexuality, Motherhood." *Journal of Graphic Novels and Comics* 2, no. 1 (2011): 55–66.
Needham, Jessica. "Visual Misogyny: An Analysis of Female Sexual Objectification in *Game of Thrones*." *Femspec* 17 (2017): 3–19.
Patel, C. "Expelling a Monstrous Matriarchy: Casting Cersei Lannister as Abject in A Song of Ice and Fire." *Journal of European Popular Culture* 5, no. 2 (2014): 135–147.

Poscheschnik, Gerald. "*Game of Thrones*—A Psychoanalytic Interpretation Including Some Remarks on the Psychosocial Function of Modern TV Series." *The International Journal of Psychoanalysis* 99, no. 4 (2018): 1004–1016.

Spector, Carolina. "Power and Feminism in Westeros." In *Beyond the Wall: Exploring George R. R. Martin's A Song of Ice and Fire*, edited by James Lowder, 169–188. Dallas: Smart Pop, 2012.

Tally, Margaret. *The Rise of the Antiheroine in TV's Third Golden Age.* Newcastle-Upon-Tyne: Cambridge Scholars Publishing, 2016.

Tasker, Yvonne and Lindsay Steenberg. "Women Warriors from Chivalry to Vengeance." In *Women of Ice and Fire*, edited by Anne Gjelsvik and Rikke Schubert, 171–192. London: Bloomsbury, 2016.

Chapter Seven

Killing Eve and the Necessity of the Female Villain du Jour

Kathleen J. Waites

Although hailed as a new kind of female villain, the character of Villanelle actually hearkens back to an earlier big-screen original, Nikita, of Luc Besson's *La Femme Nikita* (1990) who—before she finds love—is a sociopathic drug addict, thief, and murderer. Fashioned from the fiction of male e-series writer and novelist Luke Jennings in *Codename: Villanelle*, and then re-fashioned for BBC America's *Killing Eve* (*KE*) by writer Phoebe Waller-Bridge,[1] Villanelle shares a similar lack of social conscience and rootedness with her big-screen cousin. Nikita is compelled to be an assassin to avoid imprisonment, suggesting ties between members of the establishment and illegal covert operators; by contrast, Villanelle, having been released from prison for committing violent crimes, is a groomed assassin who acts on the orders of "The Twelve" through her Russian male handler Konstantin. Whereas Nikita is motivated by fear, Villanelle is motivated by profit and the thrill of the job. In the BBC America adaptation of *Codename Villanelle*, Villanelle is an unapologetic killer who exists in her own orbit while "gaming" the men who control her. She employs the masquerade of femininity when it is convenient and useful, while eschewing its constraints. Like Nikita, and later, Lisbeth Salander of David Fincher's *The Girl with the Dragon Tattoo* (2011), *KE*'s Villanelle/Oksana is an antiheroine who somehow inspires us to champion her in spite of her wickedness. The question is why, especially since Villanelle stands apart from her screen forbearers in one crucial way: without a man's love to feminize her (Nikita in *La Femme Nikita*) or a social justice cause (combating sexual violence against women) to redeem her (Lisbeth in *The Girl with the Dragon Tattoo*), she remains untethered to morality or social conventions, and in this she is the quintessential dangerous woman. And yet, as *The Atlantic*'s Hannah Giorgis notes, Villanelle "is nearly impossible to not root for," in spite of being "cocky, playful, and ostentatious" and failing to conform to "the entertainment industry's perpetually moving goalpost of female characterization, likability."[2]

Instead of love, a social cause, or likeability, *KE*'s Villanelle has MI5's Eve Polastri, her determined investigator. Villanelle, ironically, functions as Eve's doppelganger. The homoerotic dance between them aside, in Villanelle, Eve meets her alter ego, as signified in the recurring mirror tropes sprinkled throughout the show's first season. *Buzzfeed*'s Kate Aurthur asserts that: "Eve Polastri's transformation—awakened by Villanelle—is the central subject of *Killing Eve*."[3] Through the use of mirrors and parallel editing, *Villanelle* not only reveals the protagonists' mutual fascination with one another, it also links the identity of a stylish psychopathic killer who goes it alone, with that of a brilliant but frumpy married British Intelligence officer oddly obsessed with female assassins. But far from being a modernized and sexier version of the Madonna/whore dichotomy that pits women against one another only to keep the "Other" in her allotted patriarchal space and Lacan's Symbolic Order intact, *Killing Eve* maps out new terrain, both building on and taking a sharp turn away from Jennings's spy-novel. Jen Chaney of *The Vulture* highlights the ways in which *Killing Eve* gives *Codename Villanelle* and the "male-dominated genre . . . a feminine vocabulary."[4] In so doing, *Killing Eve* explores a cultural space for female identity that straddles the line between either/or as it reclaims "Eve" from patriarchal mythology. As well, the show demonstrates that Eve's desire for knowledge is actually the source of her power, and that her identity—far from being derived from Adam—is a refracted one most clearly viewed through the lens of *another* woman, rather than *the* "Other" woman. Neither virgin nor whore and both virgin and whore, in Waller-Bridge's imaginative and darkly humorous rendering, both Eve and Villanelle are instead complicated and relatable human beings. Ultimately, BBC America's *Killing Eve* upsets the applecart of the male-dominated spy thriller genre, deconstructing the virgin/whore duality that has defined women for millennia, and exposing it as a ruse and product of a self-serving patriarchal discourse.

Investigator Eve and assassin Villanelle drive the narrative action in Luke Jennings's spy thriller, *Codename Villanelle.* However, unlike the TV show that opens with Eve arriving late for an MI5 meeting (S1, E1),[5] hinting at her social ineptness, Jennings's novel opens with a secretive meeting of "The Twelve" at the Palazzo Falconieri, in which members conclude that Salvatore Greco must be assassinated, not because he is a Sicilian mob boss and head of a ruthless cartel but because he has begun killing "members of the establishment."[6] Unlike the TV show that keeps them in the shadowy background while Villanelle and Eve populate the foreground, in the novel "The Twelve"—from whom Villanelle ultimately receives her directives—take center stage. Identified as criminal power brokers,[7] "The Twelve" operate under the cloak of conventionality. After the opening scene of their deliberations in Jennings's novel, the scene shifts to Paris where we are introduced to Villanelle,[8] formerly "Oxana Verontsova" who was plucked out of a Russian prison for murdering three members of the notorious Brothers' Circle, a criminal organization responsible for her father's death.[9] In and out of an orphanage following her mother's death and implicated in numerous other incidents of violence, including the castration of her French teacher's rapist, Oksana was eventually diagnosed with a "sociopathic personality disorder" and sent home to her "battle-instructor" father who trained her for combat.[10] This background, combined with her exceptional intelligence and language skills, made Oksana an attractive commodity and useful tool for a shadowy Russian-based group working for "The Twelve." Villanelle appreciates the fact that, whoever they are, "They had recognized her talent . . . and taken her from the lowest place in the world to the highest, where she belonged. A predator, an instrument of evolution, one of that elite to whom no moral law applied."[11] In both the novel and television version, Villanelle's ambitions define her and are the source of her power; however, Villanelle is portrayed as ultra-feminine in the novel, while in the TV version Villanelle's femininity is little more than a masquerade and tool to be employed at will.

For instance, having presented herself as the lovely Sylviane Morel and joined Salvatore Greco in his Palermo opera box, Jennings's Villanelle first seduces and then stabs the target's eye with a weaponized hair clip, paralyzing Greco before shooting him and then his two bodyguards.[12] While *Killing Eve*'s Villanelle employs the same method to subdue her Mafioso target, she assassinates Cesare Greco solely with the paralyzing stab to the eye without having to seduce him first. Moreover, she does so not in a public place, but rather, in the intimacy of Greco's Tuscany bedroom during a family celebration. Afterwards, the masquerading intruder escapes his home unscathed and alone by passing herself off as just another of the female guests (S1, E1).[13] Unlike Jennings's dolled-up Villanelle, *Killing Eve*'s casually dressed Villanelle stalks her prey from a distance, enjoying her lunch alongside her motorbike before scaling an iron rainspout to the second floor of his home in her motorcycle boots. Shortly before being killed by Villanelle, Greco—under the mistaken impression that the mysterious woman in his bedroom is a "gift" to him—observes that the matronly dress she is wearing is similar to his wife's. Indeed, *KE*'s Villanelle has traded her jean shorts for his wife's blue dress to blend into the family party, the irony being that Villanelle—in the guise of Greco's wife—effectively eliminates not only the crime boss, but also the "husband" and patriarchal authority figure of the household. In this way, *Killing Eve* slyly critiques the corrupt patriarchal power structure that produced the femme fatale in the first place, thereby setting the stage for the feminist sensibility in the Waller-Bridge adaptation of Jennings's novel.

Notably, Luke Jennings fashions a more classic femme fatale in his Villanelle, one more prone to rely on a man to achieve her illicit goals. In the novel's Greco assassination, for instance, after killing Greco and his bodyguards, Jennings's Villanelle is confronted by the mob boss's vengeful relative and rival, Leoluca Messina. Villanelle and Leoluca square-off outside the opera booth, guns raised, but instead of attempting to kill Villanelle or turn her over to authorities (or worse), Messina warns Villanelle that if she wants "to get out of here, put that gun away and follow me."[14] Unlike *KE*'s Villanelle, a loner who follows Konstantin's advice to trust no one (S1, E2),[15] Villanelle's "instinct" in *Codename Villanelle* convinces her "to obey" Leoluca,[16] thus displaying a traditional and much-maligned form of "feminine knowing." Messina then leads her backstage, and safely away from the scene of the crime and onto *his* motorcycle, after which Leoluca and Villanelle "glide into the night"[17] and part ways, but only after enjoying "brief and savage sex."[18] In addition to having accepted assistance to complete her mission from a man whom her "instinct" tells her to trust, Jennings's Villanelle is also portrayed as sexually insatiable. Her "kill" scenes are often prefaced with or followed by a sexual escapade, or a desire for one, as depicted in the Paris scene where we first meet her and in which, while contemplating having sex with an attractive Parisian couple, Villanelle's plans are disrupted by a call from Konstantin that summons her to duty.[19]

Killing Eve's Villanelle is similarly promiscuous. She engages in sexual encounters with her unfortunate "boyfriend" Sebastian whom she inadvertently kills (S1, E2),[20] a ménage à trois that abruptly ends when Konstantin walks in on it (S1, E1),[21] and a fling with an older woman whom she insists on calling Eve, following her vicious assassination of a Chinese colonel during his sex-fetish session (S1, E3).[22] However, *KE*'s sexual exploits are not drawn out, nor are they as frequent as they are in Jennings's novel. Instead, Waller-Bridge's *Killing Eve* focuses more on the homoerotic interplay between Villanelle and Eve. Another difference between the Villanelles is that, in the aftermath of her assassinations, *KE*'s quirkier Villanelle decompresses and "luxuriates in her Paris flat" (Giorgis) while listening to classical music, displaying actions that tend to humanize her. For instance, after taking note of the lovely Lilliani Rizzari bedspread in Greco's bedroom shortly before eliminating him, Villanelle is depicted in the subsequent scene, not having wild sex but basking in her Paris flat on the Lilliani Rizzari bedspread she, presumably, had just purchased (S1, E1).[23]

In yet another variance, in *KE* Villanelle's origins and true identity emerge only after Eve, alarmed by a second assassination on her watch, pursues her original suspicions about a female assassin. Ascertaining that another man could not have gotten close enough to eliminate the well-guarded target, an Eastern European politician–sex trafficker, Eve uses reasoning to deduce that the assassin must have been female (S1, E1).[24] Notably, too, we come to know Villanelle more intimately not through the eyes of an objective, third-person point of view as we do in the novel, but rather, through the probing eyes of another equally idiosyncratic woman.

Indeed, Eve's insistent desire and curiosity for "knowledge," specifically about who this female assassin is and what drives her (S1, E2),[25] propels Eve's both investigation and the narrative itself. Eve's keen mind and accumulated knowledge about female assassins also garner the attention of the head of MI6's Russian desk—Carolyn Martens, a powerful British Intelligence agent—catapulting Eve to MI6 and a supervisory role in an "unofficial official" mission to locate and stop Villanelle (S1, E2).[26] Moreover, whereas Frank fired Eve for her inquisitiveness and intrepid, unapproved interrogation of the female witness to the politician's assassination (S1, E2),[27] Carolyn rewards Eve's curiosity, cleverness, and unquenchable thirst to know—that is, to know and explore the forbidden world/fruit/psyche of the highly competent female assassin. In this way, *KE*'s Eve Polastri alludes to the biblical Eve, setting up the avant-garde identity-dance between Eve and Villanelle, or between Eve and "Eve."

The female authored adaptation deviates from Luke Jennings's *Codename Villanelle* in other crucial ways as well that reinforces its feminist sensibility. In *Codename Villanelle*, the head of MI6's Russian desk is Richard Edwards, a man that lacks Carolyn's droll wit, her complexity, and her hands-on involvement and participation in Eve's mission. For instance, in a feeble attempt to make small talk, Eve asks Carolyn if she is married: "Yes," Carolyn replies drily, "a few times," prompting Eve to raise her eyebrows (S1, E2).[28] This occurs at a time when Eve is resisting the tug of domesticity from Niko, who remains uncommonly supportive of Eve's quirks and demanding career. In another instance, while in Russia to interrogate Nadia, Villanelle's erstwhile lover and failed accomplice in a shared mission to kill Frank, Eve is also stunned to discover Carolyn primping for, and flirting with Russian contacts, Vladimir and Konstantin (S1, E5).[29] As well, Carolyn shamelessly sleeps with Villanelle's handler Konstantin (S1, E5),[30] even as Carolyn and Eve continue to pursue Villanelle and "The Twelve" via Nadia. In spite of her double dealings and sexual indiscretions, as well as the panache with which she exercises them, Carolyn's authority, power, and respectability remain intact. In yet another way then, unlike *Codename: Villanelle* and its tired sexist conventions, *Killing Eve* portrays a decidedly female-centered world minus the sexist tropes. In the article "*Killing Eve* Strayed from the Book: That Was a Smart Move," Stephanie Pomfrett highlights this point when she notes how Jennings's "Le Carre-like world . . . is the realm of old boys' networks (Eve's boss is not a world-class female spy as in the show but a patrician, privately educated man) with very few women anywhere. Eve and Villanelle work in environments dominated by men and are subjected to the male gaze—not just of the men they interact with but of their creator. We are frequently told of their attractiveness and reminded men find Villanelle's breasts too small."[31] By contrast, the only allusion to Villanelle's "small breasts" in *KE* occurs in the context of Eve's interrogation of the *female* witness to the politician's assassination who describes the killer as a "small-breasted psycho" (S1, E1).[32] In a scene that is handled with deft humor, Eve directs her assistant Elena to cross-check this detail against a database of photos of known female assassins, ultimately deducing that since the others are either large-breasted or dead, the Russian's assassination must be the work of a new, bold, and smart assassin (S1, E1).[33] The fact that it is women, not men, commenting on other women's breasts, and that the situation is neither competitive—women comparing themselves with other women—nor sexual in nature, also serves as a sly put-down of sexist tropes that abound in many popular culture texts. In addition, this scene displays Eve's determination and expertise as an investigator, and as the equal of her formidable opponent, placing Eve and Villanelle on common ground.

Another significant variation from Jennings's text is in the portrayal of Eve's husband Niko. In *Killing Eve*, the only time Niko becomes engaged in Eve's work is when he assists her by translating her interrogation of the politician's Polish girlfriend in which she describes the small-breasted assassin. *Killing Eve*'s Eve is portrayed as highly independent and self-sufficient with respect to her work. In *Codename Villanelle*, by contrast, Niko plays a much more active and decisive role in Eve's sleuthing. For instance, in *CV* it is not Eve but Niko who identifies the hairclip as the weapon used to immobilize the Italian mobster, and who concludes, as a result, that his assassin must have been a woman.[34] In another scene in the novel, Eve suspects MI5 Dennis Cradle of being a Russian mole—akin to the character Frank in *KE*—and she and her male assistants, Lance and Billy, break into his home. Failing to crack the password to his computer, Eve calls in Niko. A math whiz and "pretty damn good hacker," Niko brings two of his "smart" cohorts along with him, and once again, it is Niko's powers of observation, not Eve's, that lead to the detection of the crucial password.[35] Jennings's Eve then, depends on her husband—not to hold down the domestic fort in her absence, as he does in *Killing Eve*—but to succeed in her investigation.

While Jennings's Eve similarly prioritizes her work in *CV*, causing problems in her relationship with Niko, the novel treats both Eve and Villanelle more as plot functions than as dynamic human beings. Tellingly, too, the novel disregards the chemistry between the two women, casting them more as types—the artful femme fatale/Villanelle versus the good, though flawed Eve/Madonna. *Bustle*'s Emily Dixon reports that, in creating an authentic Villanelle for the show, the female collaborators consulted with psychiatrist Dr. Mark Firestone, who noted how "clichéd" Jennings's Villanelle is, since it draws on "literature on female psychopaths" which sees "them more as a manipulative cat's paw-like figure that . . . manipulate dumb men to do their dirty work, or the typical femme fatale."[36]

This split in female identity stems from Western mythology, specifically the Adam and Eve story in the book of Genesis, resulting in a damning view of woman/Eve/the femme fatale in the cultural imagination. Accordingly, Eve succumbs to Satan, eats the apple from the tree of the knowledge of good and evil, and tempts Adam to do the same; as a result, she is condemned to suffer in childbirth and be ruled over by Adam, while he will toil the "cursed ground" to survive, no longer to be immortal (Genesis 3:1–19).[37] In Western society, this cultural myth serves as both source and justification for women's subordinate place within patriarchal society, one that is later reinforced and certified by Freud's Oedipal theory of the psycho-sexual development of the male versus the female.[38] More importantly, combined with the insistence on women's purity and passivity in the Judeo-Christian tradition, whose prototype is the handmaid Mary,[39] the differentiation of the female from the male confirms female identity as a binary. Woman, therefore, is cast as either the Eve/femme fatale figure that is associated with evil, sexuality, and corruptibility, or as the Madonna/"good" woman figure linked to passivity, purity, and goodness. As philosopher and theologian Mary Daly argues, the Adam and Eve "myth has projected a malignant image . . . of the nature of women that is still deeply embedded in the modern psyche."[40] Moreover, this requisite split in consciousness is reflected in the "wretched caste" of the "'good' women"—represented in the "impossible ideal" of Mary—and the "'bad' women, who have been scapegoats for male sexual guilt."[41] Mary Daly explains that since no woman can live up to the Mary ideal, all women are necessarily thrown into "Eve" and "women's low caste status,"[42] and punished accordingly. In a sense then, *Killing Eve* takes up Daly's notion by recognizing the common ground in patriarchal discourse that is shared by Eve and Villanelle. However, it also deconstructs the good woman–bad woman trope by collapsing the categories, offering a fresh take on female identity and the virgin–whore paradigm.

In *Killing Eve*, Eve and Villanelle encounter one another for the first time in front of a mirror in a women's restroom at the hospital where Eve intends to interrogate the assassinated politician's girlfriend (S1, E3).[43] This scene introduces the mirror trope by which the female protagonists recognize themselves in one another. While Eve glances in the mirror and arranges her hair, Villanelle emerges from a stall. Impersonating a nurse to carry out her next kill, Villanelle pauses, apparently taken by the sight of Eve who has loosened her long, unruly hair before tying it back up. It is through the mirror that Eve first notices Villanelle, who conceals her own long hair in a bun. The camera subsequently pulls back for a medium-long shot showing both women through separate mirrors eying and acknowledging one another. In this way, the shot engages with what Laura Mulvey refers to as the "determining male gaze";[44] here, however, both are females and the look is one of recognition and not of domination. As Villanelle exits the restroom, she encourages Eve to "wear it down," highlighting her attraction to Eve as well as the importance of women's hair, not only as a marker of their shared femininity but also of their power *as* women. In an argument directed toward the courts' need to consider the cultural significance of hair in its rulings, Deborah Pergament explores the cultural meanings associated with hair which "serves as an important symbol of sexuality" in the Western tradition.[45] Paraphrasing scholar Sandor Ferenczi, Pergament further notes: "Psychoanalytic examinations of the meaning of hair in Western mythology and folk literature demonstrate that long-haired women often symbolize women as phallic monsters, (i.e., as the Medusa)."[46] In "The Laugh of the Medusa," French feminist theorist Hélène Cixous famously reclaimed the much-maligned Medusa myth from Lacan's symbolic order and the phallocentric tradition for female writers:[47] "It is by writing, from and toward women, and by taking up the challenge of speech which has been governed by the phallus, that women will confirm women in a place other than that which is reserved in and by the symbolic, that is, in a place other than silence."[48]

In its own whimsical way, *Killing Eve*, which challenges phallocentric discourse, is responding to Cixous's directive by creating an alternative space for authentic—i.e., non-male defined—female speech and identity. Moreover, while cultural meanings associated with women's hair may vary, in patriarchal societies they denote female differentiation from, and therefore subordination to, men. Within this female-centric discourse, however, the "hair" that marks and binds Villanelle and Eve together takes on a more renegade gendered meaning. Indeed, the Medusa association that one may infer from the playful hair comment and which is made in a decidedly female space, the women's bathroom, may well have been intentional. According to *Buzzfeed*'s Kate Aurthur, Waller-Bridge specifically requested the classically trained actress Fiona Shaw to play the role of Carolyn. Waller-Bridge reportedly told the actress that she had seen Medea when she "was thirteen," suggesting that the chief adaptor of the series and head writer of season 1 is keenly aware of how women are defined as "other" in Western mythology.[49]

Bernadette J. Brooten also reminds us of the role that is played by biblical traditions in shaping cultural attitudes toward female differentiation and "gender polarity," as expressed in Paul's Letters to the Romans (Rom 1:18–32) and in 1 Corinthians 11:2–16 (72). In 1 Corinthians 11:2–16: "Paul requires strict gender differentiation with respect to hairstyle and headdress" as the man is "the head of the woman" and "femaleness and maleness are not to be blurred by women cutting their hair short or men wearing it long."[50] Brooten goes on to explain that "For the man, the fear is that by looking like a woman a man loses his masculinity and can sink to the level of a woman."[51] Both Freud's Oedipal theory, and Lacan's theory of the Symbolic extending from it, legitimize this traditional sex differentiation and imbalance[52] that are visibly signified in women's long hair and permeate Western mythology, as well as popular culture as Mary Daly ably argued. While the Villanelle and Eve created by Jennings in his spy novel stray somewhat from the traditional script, both women ultimately fall in line with gender stereotypes, whereas in Waller-Bridge's TV adaptation, both female protagonists—in spite of the differences between them—go off the gender-script rails. Through the mechanism of mirrors and screens, they exercise the "look" which is historically aligned with the masculine subject, or power position,[53] and explore their identity through the lens of "another," rather than both being relegated, ironically, to Eve, or *the* "Other" woman, hence, the title, *The Killing of Eve*.

A clever combination of parallel editing and mirrors achieves this rather avant-garde representation of female identity. For instance, after learning from Konstantin that special MI6 agent Eve Polastri has been assigned to track her down, Villanelle is depicted relaxing in her bed as she conducts a search on her computer to locate and identify the agent.[54] The camera then cuts to Eve who, having just forsaken an evening with Niko to return to her office, simultaneously deduces that the assassination of the politician's girlfriend in the hospital must have been someone on staff, likely a nurse. Mimicking Villanelle's actions, she, too, begins a search on her computer, as she scrolls through photos of staff nurses, but to no avail. When the camera cuts back to Villanelle, who has been more successful in locating Eve in an online group photo at Niko's Bridge Club, we see a shock of recognition register on her face and in her action of tossing her laptop on her bed. Eve Polastri, she realizes, is the same woman whose hair Villanelle commented on in the hospital bathroom just before she killed the witness-girlfriend. In the episode's final series of frames, the camera cuts back to Eve who, failing to identify any likely suspects on her computer screen, pulls her hair upward in another sly hair-gesture, turns to coworker Bill, and in her own aha moment says, "I think I've met her," as she realizes that the "nurse" she encountered in the bathroom was the likely assassin.[55]

This cross-cutting mutual discovery scene triggers the protagonists' fascination and active obsession with one another that persists throughout the show. Within the paradigm of a conventional investigator/killer plot structure, however, it invites the viewer to consider something more elemental concerning identity, as epitomized in episode 3.[56] Upon arriving in Berlin to investigate the scene of yet another Villanelle murder—this one of a Chinese colonel at a sex-fetish facility—Eve has her suitcase stolen by Villanelle, who has staked out the crime scene in order to observe Eve in action. Deprived of her wardrobe, Eve finds it necessary to shop for a suitable dress for her dinner-meeting with a Chinese contact concerning the assassination. While Eve tries on an evening dress in the store's dressing room, Villanelle, wearing a baseball cap and jeans, lurks among the clothing racks just outside. Through a deep-focus long-shot, we see Eve surveying herself in the full-length dressing room mirror as Villanelle watches. This shot both engages with and deconstructs the function of the female image as "to-be-looked-at-ness" in service of the gaze, as outlined in Laura Mulvey's psychoanalytic reexamination of the "look" in narrative cinema that may be applied here: "The place of the 'look' defines cinema in the possibility of varying it and exposing it."[57]

Clearly, by deliberately appropriating and muddying the male gaze, *Killing Eve* does both. While Eve is in the foreground of the deep-focus shot, Villanelle remains in the background, aligning the two characters and suggesting that both are engaged in the "look" and that the one is to be seen and identified in relation to the other. In subsequent frames, Eve, not entirely satisfied with how the dress hangs on her body, returns to the changing room and, in a humorous twist, Villanelle surreptitiously hangs a belt outside the door. After Eve comes out and discovers the accessory she assumes was supplied by the shop assistant, she returns to the changing room to try it on with the dress. The camera then cuts back to a long shot of Villanelle, who surveys Eve as she exits the dressing room wearing the belt. After Eve moves out of the frame, the camera cuts to an over-the-shoulder subjective camera shot from Villanelle's perspective. Although Eve reenters the frame, and stands before the mirror to assess her body, we see her *only* through the mirror and from Villanelle's point of view. In this way, Eve has dissolved, symbolically "killing" off Adam's—patriarchy's—Eve as well as Freud's deeply wounded feminine identity.[58] Although Villanelle remains on the other side of the "law" from Eve, as we have seen, the British Intelligence Agency is not necessarily aligned with the righteous or virtuous, but rather with power brokers jockeying for control, whose motives are suspect. In other words, *Killing Eve* is not a simple matter of good guys versus bad guys or good woman versus bad woman, because reality is more complicated than that. Indeed, in the amusing scene in which Villanelle breaks into Eve's apartment and asks to be served dinner, Eve tells her she knows that Villanelle is a "psychopath" working on behalf of a hidden group ("The Twelve"), but Villanelle disabuses her of the notion that they are on opposite sides of the equation when she quips: "If you go high enough, I think you'd probably find that we are working for the same people."[59] Certainly Carolyn's behind-the-scenes affair with Villanelle's handler Konstantin and double-dealings with Russian intelligence—and possibly "The Twelve"—demonstrates that she is literally and figuratively in bed with the enemy and supports the insight that Villanelle registers here.

Although Eve continues her crusade to track down and capture Villanelle, whose assassinations are mounting, it is problematized by her knotty relationship with Villanelle and what it reveals to her about herself. For instance, after Eve manages to rescue Frank, who is on the run from Villanelle, Eve eyes Villanelle through her rear-view mirror, stopping her car in the roadway over the objections of Frank and coworker Elena.[60] A series of shots that underscore the women's connection and reciprocal exercise of the gaze follows. In an eye-level, over-the shoulder long shot from Villanelle's perspective, Eve stands on the roadway facing Villanelle, which is succeeded by a matching eye-level shot from Eve's perspective of a clearly shocked Villanelle. Both figures freeze, failing to complete their respective missions, in order to engage with their shared "look" of recognition at the other, as seen in subsequent frames. These are comprised of a series of medium shot-reverse-shots, with Eve inexplicably raising one hand and placing the other over her heart, as though greeting her adversary in peace. Villanelle, smiling in response, places the gun to her own throat before aiming it at Eve and purposely missing and sparing her. The impact of this scene on Eve's psyche and sense of identity is visibly reinforced shortly thereafter. Having delivered Frank to the safe house for protection, a discombobulated Eve decides to return home on her own by bus. Once she is seated on the bench inside the glass enclosed bus stop, we see a close-up of her blurred face reflected in a glass panel with a crack running through it. This shot highlights the split in Eve's psyche. The camera then pulls back on a dumbfounded Eve who, tracing and pressing on the crack with her forefinger, smashes the glass and startles herself into recognition as she comes to identify herself, or a part of herself, in/through Villanelle.

The mirror trope also reappears in a climactic scene in the final episode of season 1, confirming this shift in Eve's consciousness. The scene occurs when Villanelle returns to her Paris apartment bedroom to find Eve, who has tracked her down and trashed Villanelle's Paris apartment. "I think about you all the time,"[61] Eve says, indicating that she has lost "everything" (i.e., husband Niko, two jobs, and her friend and colleague, Frank) because of Villanelle, and wants to know "everything" about Villanelle. Then she slumps down onto Villanelle's bed, highlighting the fact that she wants to burrow even further into Villanelle's consciousness. A longshot of Villanelle sitting on the bed through her three-way dresser-mirror reflects the fact that Eve's identity, at least in this moment, is no longer one-half of the binary. Nor is Villanelle's, as she surrenders her gun and makes herself vulnerable to Eve, who stabs her and then instantly regrets what she has done.

Eve's pursuit of Villanelle, and indeed, Villanelle herself in a very real sense, are red herrings since what Eve is really pursuing is an authentic self-identity. Toward this end, the female villain du jour serves as a necessary device by which the binary collapses, and Eve recognizes that she is more intimately related with Villanelle than she is with the corrupt male system that manipulates both of them. Eve's identity-struggle, and the dance between her and Villanelle, continues in season 2, ending in the ironic mirroring of Villanelle shooting Eve after Eve rejects her offer to go away with her. Has the renegade part of Eve died, and will she be redeemed and brought back into the symbolic order? Only season 3 will tell.

NOTES

1. Kate Aurthur, "How *Killing Eve* Became the Perfect Show for These Wild Times," *BuzzFeedNews*, April 4, 2019. Accessed https://www.buzzfeednews.com/article/kateaurthur/killing-eve-season-2-sandra-oh-jodie-comer-bbc-america on July 30, 2019.

2. Giorgis, Hannah, "*Killing Eve* and the Riddle If Why Women Kill," *The Atlantic*, May 28, 2018. Accessed https://www.buzzfeednews.com/article/kateaurthur/killing-eve-season-2-sandra-oh-jodie-comer-bbc-america on July 31, 2019.

3. Aurthur, "How *Killing Eve* Became the Perfect Show for These Wild Times."

4. Jen Chaney, "*Killing Eve* Season Two Maintains Its Sick, Distinctively Female Sense of Humor," *The Vulture*, April 5, 2019. Accessed https://www.vulture.com/2019/04/killing-eve-season-2-review.html on May 17, 2019.

5. *Killing Eve*, "Nice Face," directed by Harry Bradbeer. Air date April 8, 2018.

6. Luke Jennings, *Codename: Villanelle* (New York: Mulholland Books, Little, Brown and Company, 2017), 5.

7. Jennings, *Codename Villanelle*, 3.

8. Jennings, *Codename Villanelle*, 6–8.

9. Jennings, *Codename Villanelle*, 11–12.

10. Jennings, *Codename Villanelle*, 11, 13.

11. Jennings, *Codename Villanelle*, 32.

12. Jennings, *Codename Villanelle*, 35–37.

13. *Killing Eve*, "Nice Face."

14. Jennings, *Codename Villanelle*, 38.

15. *Killing Eve*, "I'll Deal with Him Later," directed by Harry Bradbeer. Air date April 15, 2018.

16. Jennings, *Codename: Villanelle*, 38.

17. Jennings, *Codename: Villanelle*, 39.

18. Jennings, *Codename: Villanelle*, 40.

19. Jennings, *Codename: Villanelle*, 6–8.

20. *Killing Eve*, "I'll Deal with Him Later."

21. *Killing Eve*, "Nice Face."

22. *Killing Eve*, "Don't I Know You," directed by Jon East. Air date April 22, 2018.

23. *Killing Eve*, "Nice Face."

24. *Killing Eve*, "Nice Face."

25. *Killing Eve*, "Don't I Know You"

26. *Killing Eve*, "I'll Deal with Him Later."

27. *Killing Eve*, "I'll Deal with Him Later."

28. *Killing Eve*, "I'll Deal with Him Later."

29. *Killing Eve*, "I Have a Thing about Bathrooms," directed by Jon East. Air date May 6, 2018.

30. *Killing Eve*, "I Have a Thing about Bathrooms."

31. Stephanie Pomfrett, "*Killing Eve* Strayed from the Book: That Was a Smart Move," *Washington Post*, March 5, 2019. Accessed https://www.washingtonpost.com/entertainment/books/killing-eve-strayed-from-the-book-its-based-on-it-was-a-smart-move/2019/03/04/e2abad82-3eae-11e9-9361-301ffb5bd5e6_story.html?utm_term=.9f1bad5284fa on July 19, 2019.

32. *Killing Eve*, "Nice Face."

33. *Killing Eve*, "Nice Face."

34. Jennings, *Codename: Villanelle*, 61–62.

35. Jennings, *Codename: Villanelle*, 205–13.

36. Emily Dixon, "The Psychiatrist Who Worked On *Killing Eve* With Phoebe Waller-Bridge Explained How They Wrote Villanelle," *Bustle*, June 9, 2019. Accessed https://www.bustle.com/p/the-psychiatrist-who-worked-on-killing-eve-with-phoebe-waller-bridge-explained-how-they-wrote-villanelle-17988979 on July 18, 2019.

37. "Adam and Eve." *Encyclopedia Britannica*, Accessed https://www.britannica.com/biography/Adam-and-Eve-biblical-literary-figures on August 15 2019.

38. Patricia Harrington, "Mary and Femininity: A Psychological Critique," *Journal of Religion and Health*, Vol. 23, No. 3 (Fall, 1984): 205. Accessed https://www.jstor.org/stable/27505783?seq=1#page_scan_tab_contents on September 1, 2019.

39. Harrington, "Mary and Femininity," 205–8.

40. Mary Daly, "Exorcising Evil from Eve: The Fall into Freedom," *Beyond God the Father toward a Philosophy of Women's Liberation* (Boston: Beacon Press, 1973), 45.

41. Daly, "Exorcising Evil from Eve," 61.

42. Daly, "Exorcising Evil from Eve," 62.

43. *Killing Eve*, "I'll Deal with Him Later."

44. Laura Mulvey, "Visual Pleasure and Narrative Cinema," *Feminist Film Theory: A Reader*, ed. Sue Thornham (New York: New York University Press, 1999), 62.

45. Deborah Pergament, "It's Not Just Hair: Historical and Cultural Considerations for an Emerging Technology, *Chicago-Kent Law. Rev.*, Vol. 75, No. 41 (1999), 41–59. Accessed https://scholarship.kentlaw.iit.edu/cklawreview/vol75/iss1/4 on September 2, 2019.

46. Pergament, "It's Not Just Hair," 45.

47. Hélène Cixous, "The Laugh of the Medusa," trans. Keith Cohen and Paula Cohen, *Signs*, Vol. 1, No. 4 (summer, 1976), 884. Accessed https://edisciplinas.usp.br/pluginfile.php/66416/mod_resource/content/1/cixous-the-laugh-of-the-medusa.pdf on September 5, 2019.

48. Cixous, "The Laugh of the Medusa," 881.

49. Aurthur, "How *Killing Eve* Became the Perfect Show for These Wild Times."

50. Bernadette J. Brooten, "Paul's Views on the Nature of Women and Female Homoeroticism," *Immaculate and Powerful: The Female in Sacred Image and Social Reality*, ed. Clarissa W. Atkinson, Constance H. Buchanan, and Margaret R. Miles (Boston: Beacon Press, 1987, 78. Accessed http://people.brandeis.edu/~brooten/Articles/Pauls_Views_on_the_Nature_of_Women_and_Female_Homoeroticism.pdf on September 6, 2019.

51. Brooten, "Paul's Views on the Nature of Women and Female Homoeroticism," 76–77.

52. E. Ann Kaplan, *Women and Film: Both Sides of the Camera* (New York: Routledge Press, 1996), 26–27.

53. Mulvey, "Visual Pleasure and Narrative Cinema," 62–63.

54. *Killing Eve*, "I'll Deal with Him Later."

55. *Killing Eve*, "I'll Deal with Him Later."

56. *Killing Eve*, "Don't I Know You."

57. Mulvey, "Visual Pleasure and Narrative Cinema," 68.

58. Harrington, "Mary and Femininity," 205–6.

59. *Killing Eve*, "I Have a Thing about Bathrooms."

60. *Killing Eve*, "I Have a Thing about Bathrooms."

61. *Killing Eve*, "God, I'm Tired," Phoebe Waller-Bridge and Luke Jennings, writers. May 27, 2019. Accessed https://www.imdb.com/title/tt7081320/?ref_=ttep_ep8 on September 5, 2019.

BIBLIOGRAPHY

"Adam and Eve." In *Encyclopedia Britannica*. Last updated by editors of *Encyclopedia Britannica*, last updated December 27, 2019. https://www.britannica.com/biography/Adam-and-Eve-biblical-literary-figures.

Aurthur, Kate. "How *Killing Eve* became the Perfect Show for These Wild Times." *Buzzfeed*, April 4, 2019. https://www.buzzfeednews.com/article/kateaurthur/killing-eve-season-2-sandra-oh-jodie-comer-bbc-america.

Brooten, Bernadette J. "Paul's Views on the Nature of Women and Female Homoeroticism." In *Immaculate and Powerful: The Female in Sacred Image and Social Reality*, edited by Clarissa W. Atkinson, Constance H. Buchanan, and Margaret R. Miles, 61–87. Boston: Beacon Press, 1987.

Chaney, Jen. "*Killing Eve* Season Two Maintains Its Sick, Distinctively Female Sense of Humor." *The Vulture*, April 5, 2019. https://www.vulture.com/2019/04/killing-eve-season-2-review.html.

Cixous, Hélène. Translated by Keith Cohen and Paula Cohen, "The Laugh of the Medusa." *Signs* 1, no. 4 (Summer, 1976): 875–93. https://edisciplinas.usp.br/pluginfile.php/66416/mod_resource/content/1/cixous-the-laugh-of-the-medusa.pdf.

Daly, Mary. *Beyond God the Father toward a Philosophy of Women's Liberation*. Boston: Beacon Press, 1973.

Dixon, Emily. "The Psychiatrist Who Worked On *Killing Eve* with Phoebe Waller-Bridge Explained How They Wrote Villanelle." *Bustle*, June, 9, 2019. https://www.bustle.com/p/the-psychiatrist-who-worked-on-killing-eve-with-phoebe-waller-bridge-explained-how-they-wrote-villanelle-17988979.

Giorgios, Hannah. "*Killing Eve* and the Riddle If Why Women Kill." *The Atlantic*, May 28, 2018. https://www.buzzfeednews.com/article/kateaurthur/killing-eve-season-2-sandra-oh-jodie-comer-bbc-america.

Harrington, Patricia. "Mary and Femininity: A Psychological Critique." *Journal of Religion and Health* 23, no. 3 (Fall, 1984): 204–17. https://www.jstor.org/stable/27505783?seq=1#page_scan_tab_contents.

Jennings, Luke. *Codename Villanelle*. New York: Mulholland Books, Little, Brown and Company, 2017.

Kaplan, E. Ann. *Women and Film: Both Sides of the Camera*. New York: Routledge Press, 1996.

Killing Eve. "Don't I Know You." Directed by Jon East. Air date April 22, 2018.

⸻. "I Have a Thing about Bathrooms." Directed by Jon East. Air date May 6, 2018.

⸻. "I'll Deal with Him Later." Directed by Harry Bradbeer. Air date April 15, 2018.

⸻. "Nice Face." Directed by Harry Bradbeer. Air date April 8, 2018.

Mulvey, Laura. "Visual Pleasure and Narrative Cinema." *Feminist Film Theory: A Reader*, edited by Sue Thornham, 58–69. New York: New York University Press, 1999.

Pergament, Deborah. "It's Not Just Hair: Historical and Cultural Considerations for an Emerging Technology." In *Chicago-Kent Law. Rev.*, Vol. 75, No. 41 (1999). 41–59. Cited from Sandor Ferenczi, "On the Symbolism of the Head of the Medusa," in 2 Selected Papers 360 (1952); Sigmund Freud, "Medusa's Head," in 5 Collected Papers: 105–6. Edited by James Strachey, 1959. https://scholarship.kentlaw.iit.edu/cklawreview/vol75/iss1/4.

Pomfrett, Stephanie. "*Killing Eve* Strayed from the Book: That Was a Smart Move." *Washington Post*, March 5, 2019. https://www.washingtonpost.com/entertainment/books/killing-eve-strayed-from-the-book-its-based-on-it-was-a-smart-move/2019/03/04/e2abad82-3eae-11e9-9361-301ffb5bd5e6_story.html?utm_term=.9f1bad5284fa.

Part III

Crazy is a Sexist Word

Chapter Eight

Rewriting the Psycho Bitch

*Exploring the Psychological Complexity of the
Antiheroine in Contemporary Domestic Noir Fiction*

Liz Evans

Domestic noir is a subgenre of psychological suspense fiction, originally identified by British author Julia Crouch in 2013 as a means of marketing her own novels.[1] With an emphasis on the hidden traumas of everyday life and family networks, the category represents home as a threatening place full of secrets, lies, and betrayals, where intimate relationships rest on an essential unknowability of the Other.[2] Premised on what Crouch describes as a "broadly feminist view that the domestic sphere is a challenging and some-times dangerous prospect for its inhabitants,"[3] contemporary novels such as Erin Kelly's *He Said She Said*, Joanna Briscoe's *Sleep With Me*, and Rebecca Whitney's *The Liar's Chair* foreground unpredictable plotlines and unbid-dable female protagonists, continuing the twentieth-century tradition of so-called marriage thrillers and dark fiction in the vein of Patricia Highsmith's *Deep Water* and Daphne du Maurier's *Rebecca*.

Unsurprisingly, domestic noir has proved to be a winning formula with a predominantly female readership,[4] and this is reflected in the genre's strong commercial currency. *Gone Girl*, by Gillian Flynn, and *The Girl on The Train* by Paula Hawkins, have each sold over fifteen million copies worldwide and been successfully adapted for the screen, Lee Moriarty's best-selling *Big Little Lies* was made into an award-winning HBO minis-eries with a star-studded cast and production team; and Liv Constantine's *The Last Mrs. Parrish* is currently being dramatized for Amazon TV. Moreover, authors like Erin Kelly, Lisa Jewell, and Julia Crouch all continue to publish best-selling titles on a regular basis, offering proof of the genre's ongoing popularity.

Attempting to explore and explain the phenomenal success of domestic noir, some of the genre's authors have considered current cultural and political concerns as well as narrative devices. For Crouch, writing about the home is "a feminist act" and stories of women inhabiting unsafe homes hold social and historical value for readers who appreciate a genre that "puts female experience at the centre of the narrative, rather than just allowing it to support or decorate or provide the springboard for the main, male story."[5] Rebecca Whitney claims the appeal lies with stories where "women aren't so much the victim as the victor,"[6] and Paula Hawkins cites the compelling attraction of negative emotions, saying, "I think we're all fascinated by the dark secrets that lie at the heart of ostensibly happy relationships."[7]

But, overwhelmingly, the popularity of domestic noir has become linked with the rise of the flawed antiheroine, an atypical woman, a bad, daring, aggressive, autonomous character whose ability to hook readers owes nothing to being nice. Reflecting on the popularity of such characters, British publishing editor, Sophie Orme says, "I think a real shift has occurred from the traditional woman in peril book . . . to this new, more rounded portrayal of the central female character . . . we don't necessarily have to like the female protagonist to sympathise with her plight and be gripped by her story."[8] Liberated from the constraints of good behavior, the antiheroine has the capacity to forge powerful new archetypal images of femininity, where compliance is questioned, inquisitiveness is rewarded, and female sexuality is healthily integrated, rather than presented as shameful or dangerous.

Brimming with bold resources such as resilience, duplicity, and unpredictability, damaged but fully cognisant characters like Nora in Flynn Berry's *Under the Harrow*, Kate in Sarah Vaughan's *Anatomy of A Scandal*, and Bridget in Christobel Kent's *What We Did* take charge of the narrative, confronting and challenging varying combinations of powerful, dangerous men and patriarchal institutions as they seek justice and liberation both for themselves and other women. Determined to track down her sister's killer, Nora challenges the jurisdiction of the police force when she embarks on her own independent murder inquiry, forcing herself to reappraise her childhood memories in the process; criminal barrister Kate transgresses the ethics of her profession and risks becoming re-traumatized when she knowingly prosecutes her college rapist; and Bridget denounces the law when she conquers her long-buried fear and confronts her childhood sex abuser in order to defend her child. Widening the focus of domestic noir beyond the usual subject matter of troubled heterosexual relationships, these narratives feature disobedient, self-directed, aggressive, and psychologically complex women who orbit well beyond a male partner. Responding to threatening situations and dangerous individuals with courage and curiosity, these imperfect, emotionally scarred women seek resolution and vengeance by refusing to comply with established societal structures and recognized moral codes, thereby fulfilling the criteria of the antiheroine.

However, despite the appearance of protagonists like Nora, Kate, and Bridget, there is a concerning undertone running throughout domestic noir that simultaneously manages to diminish the significance of newly emerging representations of female anger, grief, and trauma, by upholding traditional interpretations of familiar noir tropes, in particular the femme fatale and the victim, both of whom continue to be depicted as not only unlikable and unreliable, but also psychologically unbalanced—if not fully psychopathological.

This chapter looks at the ways in which contemporary domestic noir fiction frames the female psyche, and how this impacts the effectiveness, as well as the definition of the antiheroine, beginning with a consideration of Amy Dunne in *Gone Girl* and Rachel Watson of *The Girl on the Train*, both of whom are afflicted and restricted by complex trauma and psychopathology. A comparative analysis of the psychologically complex, angry, and unappealing, but essentially stable characters of Nina Bremner in *Her* and Frances Thorpe in *Alys Always*, shows how socially difficult, unlikeable women are better placed to transcend the limits set by tragedy when their anger and aggression are not contextualized within a form of madness. Given the relationship between psychopathology, autonomy, and responsibility, the antiheroine relies on her sanity for self-agency, without which her troubled and troublesome character is eminently disempowered.

GIRL GONE MAD: AMY DUNNE

Gone Girl is the story of a dysfunctional marriage between Amy and Nick Dunne and the complicated powerplay that ensues when Amy decides to punish Nick for being unfaithful by framing him for her murder. In her erudite analysis of the novel, Eva Burke sets the debate over Amy Dunne's feminist status—trailblazing icon or offensive function of misogyny?—against what she claims are the novel's more important questions concerning the "social obligation of female likeability."[9] Gillian Flynn has addressed this issue in all three of her books, placing dark-hearted characters center stage in *Sharp Objects*, *Dark Places* and, of course, *Gone Girl*, in conscious reaction to "this idea that women are innately good, innately nurturing."[10] Since the commercial success of *Gone Girl*, in particular, domestic noir has generated no end of duplicitous narrators and transgressive protagonists, so, perhaps it is more pertinent to interrogate what happens to female likeability when psychopathology enters the agenda, and badness is collapsed into madness.

Despite saying she isn't interested in writing "psycho bitches," because "the psycho bitch is just crazy, she has no motive and so she's a dismissible person because of her psycho bitchiness,"[11] with Amy Dunne, Flynn has created a psychopathic character who embodies the age old struggle with the "dangerous, disruptive desirability of the Other,"[12] as symbolized by the patriarchally determined archetypal images of Eve, Lilith, Medea, Medusa and Pandora. These mythical femmes fatales represent an "outlawed form of female divinity, potency, genius, sexual agency, independence, vengeance and death power,"[13] yet their stories situate them as victims of their own making, casting them as women whose desirability is bound up with deviancy. They are punished for being psychologically and sexually dangerous, socially inappropriate, and culturally threatening, and are ultimately disempowered by being framed as hysterical, self-destructive, and, to varying degrees, insane. At its best, contemporary domestic noir offers an alternative space for characters such as these, where negative emotions are integrated and explored and the "angry woman emerges triumphant on the strength of her own cunning intelligence and determination,"[14] but when this anger emanates from a woman who is not just raging, but raving, the potency is altered, and the reclaimed power of female fury is once more divorced from reason, and rendered ineffective.

Celebrated for being a "far less compromising" version of the femme fatale, "who refuses to pander to male expectations"[15] Amy Dunne appears to be powerfully autonomous as she engineers her own fate, together with that of her husband Nick. In fact, Amy is a narcissist whose marriage is characterized by codependency, and the elaborately staged and exhaustively planned disappearance around which her story hinges, is ultimately an attempt to restore the sense of self-validation only Nick can provide. "Until Nick, I'd never really felt like a person because I was always a product,"[16] she says, referring to the emotional legacy of her dysfunctional, demanding parents. But with Nick, Amy is still a product, having attracted him by deliberately fashioning herself into what she perceives to be the standard idealized male fantasy, a sexually compliant persona she occasionally enjoys, but essentially disrespects, and refers to as Cool Girl.

Cool Girl is one of the many personas with which Amy expresses herself throughout the novel. Others include Amazing Amy, Diary Amy, and, eventually, after devising her own disappearance, Dead Amy. These false selves enable Amy to adapt according to what she believes other people want from her in order to generate the feedback she needs to feel validated in the world. In this way, she preserves a sense of shared identity with others that makes her feel safe, but in the process she forfeits the emergence of her individuality, moving, as "from Cool Girl to Gone Girl, from one archetypal embodiment, the acquiescent female to another: the victimised or missing woman. However, she is no closer to living an authentic existence (and arguably no more inclined towards one, having benefited from her manipulation of these archetypes)."[17] Dead Amy and her surrounding circumstances evolve as a punitive reaction to Nick's infidelity, which shoves Amy into the circumstantially prescribed role of victim, a situation of separation that amounts to a form of annihilation. Unable to experience herself beyond the way Nick feels about her, perpetually stuck in a kind of hell where "her own sense of being in herself is supplanted by a sense of being appreciated (*or otherwise*) as herself by another,"[18] Amy settles on the active absence that is Dead Amy in a bid to regain her manipulative hold on her husband. By attempting to put herself back in charge, Amy avoids the emotional death of abandonment, but because Nick is her only means of resurrection, she remains affectively disorientated within the world until his broadcast pleas to have her safely returned home provide her with the U-turn back to the familiar hell of marriage.

At the novel's conclusion, a heavily pregnant Amy appears to have settled back into her Amazing Amy persona, priding herself on being part of the "world's best, brightest nuclear family," but the marriage is a sham, and Amy, like so many ill-fated femmes fatales before her, has played directly "into the hands of the system she set out to dismantle."[19] As Nick strokes her hair on the final pages, Amy asks "Why are you so wonderful to me?"[20] but instead of telling her he loves her he says the worst thing he could possibly say to a narcissist; "Because I feel sorry for you. Because every morning you have to wake up and be you."[21] Identifying the emptiness that lies beneath the personas, at the core of her identity, Nick becomes "finally a match for Amy"[22] but in accepting that she is "my forever antagonist,"[23] he also consigns himself to the codependency of their mutually destructive relationship, begging the question who holds the power. Neither partner is free, fulfilled or even particularly changed, other than to become more aware of each other's dysfunction. As a comment on marriage, Flynn's novel is disturbingly compelling, but in terms of the antiheroine, Amy Dunne is a perplexing candidate.

British journalist Rhiannon Lucy Coslett applauds Amy for not being "a female stereotype, but an unhinged, complex, flawed villain," asking, "what could be more feminist than that?" and declaring that "perhaps true equality is admitting that women can be evil arseholes too."[24] Yet, without further examination and critical analysis of what it means to be "evil arseholes" and "flawed villains," the transgression of literary tropes, in itself, does not automatically amount to feminist engagement. Flynn herself offers a little more illumination, calling for more literary representations of women who are "pragmatically evil, bad and selfish" as opposed to "dismissably bad— trampy, vampy, bitchy types"[25] but the distinction between these two types of characters is blurred. Surely the real feminist issue here lies in the assumptions and value judgments which form the very fabric of such a dichotomy, as well as the problematic claim that tramps, vamps and bitches—however we might imagine them—are considered as being necessarily disposable within a storyline.

Flynn says she wants more discussion of female violence, more acknowledgment of women's dark side, more "good, potent female villains,"[26] but in Amy she has given us a character who is continually reacting, deferring, and manipulating others into affirming her sense of self, and constantly projecting the murderous rage she cannot bear to confront onto those others. Bad and selfish she may be, but Amy's psychopathology restricts the avenues of her resistance and diminishes the potency of her villainy, leaving her autonomy undermined and her antiheroine potential squandered.

GIRL ON A TRAIN TO NOWHERE: RACHEL WATSON

In her exploration of domestic noir's defining features, Emma V. Miller identifies the genre's "active turn"[27] away from traditional crime fiction's typical roles for female protagonists. Dead girls are comparatively absent in the novels, she notes, as are female police officers and pathologists, both of whom operate within the respective patriarchal establishments of law and medicine. The central character of domestic noir, says Miller, "is an individual, in her own space, whether that be her commute, her gym, her home or some other setting; it is the place of her choosing, and she plays a crucial role in shaping and directing the narrative."[28] However, when the heroine is portrayed as unstable, her self-agency is immediately compromised, and her choices are not so clear. As a narcissist in need of constant, excessive admiration, Amy Dunne exclusively orients herself according to others, and, while the details are markedly different, the same can be argued of *The Girl on the Train*'s Rachel Watson.

Rachel is a depressed, divorced, amnesiac thirty-two-year-old alcoholic who spends most of her time obsessing over other people's lives, acting out her psychological fantasies and projections, and desperately seeking validation from the world. Still infatuated with her ex-husband Tom, who is now married to Anna with a baby, Rachel painfully travels past her former marital home on her daily commute to work, becoming obsessed with Scott and Megan, Tom and Anna's new neighbors, who she spies through the train window. When Megan disappears in a flurry of news headlines, Rachel, believing she has witnessed a key event in what escalates into a murder investigation, lurches into a complex and dangerous situation that eventually implicates Tom, and brings her into confrontation with Anna with devastating consequences.

As the title of her story suggests, Rachel is a perpetual passenger, catching the train every day, travelling between her flat and her workplace. This journey, says Miller, is where Rachel "remains at her strongest and most comfortable . . . something she recognises herself when, following her job loss, she continues with the commute, saying: 'It's a relief to be back on the 8.04. . . . I'd rather be here, looking out at the houses beside the track, than almost anywhere else.'"[29] It's true that static situations are not safe for Rachel. She's been attacked in her marital home, sacked from the office, her flatmate wants her gone, and the shared, transitory spaces of the pub, the library, and the park do not offer privacy or sustained sanctuary. Yet, while the train keeps her in motion, all it does is transport her within a network of misery, running up and down a line of potentially dangerous locations, including her old house and her current home, delivering her to threatening situations where she continually feels endangered by either Tom, Scott, or her own paranoia, as she numbs herself with alcohol concealed in a designer water bottle. "There's no one there . . . the flat is empty," she reflects on arriving home one evening, "but that doesn't stop me checking every room, under my bed . . . in the wardrobes and the closet in the kitchen that couldn't conceal a child." Hawkins says of her novel; "Over the course of the book, the women come out of it better, and are the ones we see change and try to at least fight against their demons."[30] But it's difficult to know who she is referring to. At the end of the story, Megan is dead, Anna is left drenched in her dead husband's blood, and Rachel is still on a train, headed for new horizons perhaps, but still struggling with the same internal landscapes of addictive impulses, panic attacks, and low self-worth; still fleeing from herself.

Described by author Jean Hanff Korelitz as "your basic hot mess"[31] and by feminist academic Jacqueline Rose as a "self-pitying drunk,"[32] Rachel represents the perfect victim. Summing herself up with the words; "I lost and I drank and I drank and I lost,"[33] she has internalized the abuse meted out by her ex-husband Tom, and blames herself and her inability to get pregnant for everything that's gone wrong in her life, while her extreme yearning for a baby borders on the pathological. "I would have cut off a limb if it meant I could I have had a child"[34] she says, referring to her precarious psychological condition while undergoing IVF treatment during her marriage to Tom, while later, she snatches Tom and Anna's infant girl from their home, in an almost somnambulistic state; "I don't know what I thought I was doing. I wasn't going to hurt her."[35] Consumed by self-loathing and self-pity, motivated by shame and failure, Rachel, like Amy, has a severely compromised sense of self-agency, and makes her choices according to her damaged state of mind. "I have to make amends for being insufficient" she bemoans,[36] elsewhere summing up her life as; "messy, shabby, small. Unenviable."[37] In her mind, she transcends the role of "girl on the train" by fantasizing and obsessing about a couple she has never met as they become the center of a murder investigation, while in the real world, she continually fails to take responsibility for herself. She embarks on a course of therapy only because she discovers the therapist is involved with the couple, thereby sabotaging any effective outcome for herself from the beginning of treatment, and even after participating in the gruesome murder of her ex-husband—an act which has been perceived by some writers as doing away with the problem—her precarious psychological state prevails.

Some of Rachel's anxiety is symptomatic of the complex trauma and learned helplessness associated with domestic violence, but her self-destructive addictive behaviour, her difficulties with boundaries, her jealousy and resentment of other women, and her victim mentality suggest a strong possibility of borderline personality disorder. Defined by their "propensity for vicious interpersonal cycles and their high levels of affect dysregulation and impulsivity," sufferers of borderline personality disorder struggle to differentiate their mental states from those of other people.[38] Rachel, unable to curb her spontaneous, transgressive, risky behaviors, such as the compulsive lying and addictive drinking, the baby-snatching, attempting a personal relationship with Scott under false pretences, and seeking treatment from Megan's therapist in order to find out if he killed Megan, thus appears to be a likely candidate. This repositions her from flawed antiheroine into someone quite psychologically broken, and therefore less empowered.

Fractured female psychology is a key feature of domestic noir, and journalist Koa Beck has a point when she says; "There's a certain appeal, as a reader, in being kept guessing or intentionally deceived by a character's tenuous relationship with reality."[39] But while there is value in exposing "how women are vulnerable to fear, anxiety, envy and anger in ways that men are not,"[40] and good reason for offering subjective perspectives from women who "aren't simply victims—they are sometimes perpetrators too. They are flawed, damaged, sometimes beaten by events, sometimes victorious,"[41] the collapse of complex mental and emotional states into oversimplified depictions of madness is clearly problematic. Persistently simple patterns of negative female psychology not only impoverish representations of female experience of domestic life and complex family systems, they fuel assumptions about the proximity of women to emotional breakdown. "She's let herself spin out of control, but many of us walk a bit close to that line without crossing it," says Hawkins, as if Rachel's experience was not so unusual for divorcees, or the unemployed. "You could imagine if something dramatic happened like a failed marriage or lost job then we might."[42] However, Rachel represents an extreme, as most of us would not stalk a couple we'd spied through a window, employ the services of a therapist we suspected of murder, or jam a corkscrew into the neck of our ex-husband.

Exploring the appeal of the "Girl" novels, journalist Eva Wiseman identifies the promise of domestic noir as "the promise of darkness and mystery—small scary stories in domestic settings, where the girl is a 'girl' not because she's weak, but because she is on the verge of changing into something else. She's not simply a victim, or a wife. She will be asking questions of her place in the world."[43] Unfortunately, the presence of psychopathology undermines this promise by rendering the girl mad, which means any questions she asks are determined by the damage in her mind. Instead of transforming into something powerful, these girls, says feminist academic Jacqueline Rose, specifying the ones in *Gone Girl* and *The Girl on The Train*, feed a patriarchal system that "thrives by encouraging women to feel contempt for themselves," where their gullibility and self-punishment shores up plots that, like mainstream crime fiction, rely on a failure to read the world, except this failure "is gendered: it belongs to the women, even if the veil finally falls just in time." Without directly addressing the issue of psychopathology, Rose questions the lack of female autonomy and authority in both novels, asking, "What do these women want?" as she wonders how main female characters can amount to nothing more than "insights into hopelessness," in stories where; "Not one of them turns out to have been responsible for her fate."[44] Of course, it doesn't have to be like this.

GIRLS GONE BAD: NINA BREMNER AND FRANCES THORPE

Without the restrictions and taint of psychopathology, antiheroines like Kate in *Anatomy of a Scandal*, Brigid in *What We Did*, and Nora in *Under The Harrow* have the freedom to behave badly and make awkward demands while exercising their rights. This propels them beyond the limits of patriarchy's prescribed literary zones, into newly delineated regions of their own making where they consciously and aggressively deceive, challenge, and dodge their opponents. These women are complicated, clever, independent, and, most importantly, responsible for themselves. They haven't tumbled into madness or become embroiled in bloody violence but remain uncomfortably relatable. As author Jill Alexander Essbaum says, "You may not like her, but you can't look away because you recognize a little sliver of yourself in her."[45]

Operating on this disquieting premise are two of domestic noir's most resourceful, least likeable antiheroines; Nina Bremner of *Her*, and Frances Thorpe of *Alys Always*, both by British author Harriet Lane. In an interview with Mindy Rice Witherow, Lane describes her novels as turning unnervingly on "the sharp edge of everyday interactions, the little subtle wickednesses we inflict on each other."[46] In her interview with *Elle*, Lane explains; "You can use these apparently benign interactions in fiction and create the same dynamic that you'd find in a detective or horror novel."[47] Both Nina and Frances outsmart the traditional "Girl in the Thriller" tropes with their ambiguous, suspicious, unethical, deceptive, calculating, ambitious, and obsessive behavior, but instead of psychopathology, these women, like their creator says, are afflicted by everyday emotional horrors; the harrowing accumulations of envy and resentment, bitterness and misdirected blame, psychological projections and preoccupations with other women, and fantasies about their unlived lives. Each of them harbor fixations that have profound repercussions, but without becoming consumed or delusional, both women manage to retain self-agency, designing their own destinies without deferring to anyone else.

In *Her*, protagonist Nina has spent a lifetime feeling hurt and angry with Emma, a girl she knew briefly as a teenager, during a summer holiday that proved critical for her family. When the novel begins, Nina spies Emma, now pregnant and with a toddler son, on a street in her north London neighborhood, and, after processing the shock of seeing her again, sets about befriending her in order to try and understand the past events that shaped her life. Emma has no recollection of Nina, and while this fuels Nina's grief and resentment it also enables her to gain Emma's trust as she explores the layers of memory and misunderstanding that lie at the root of her bitterness and envy. Yet while she effectively feels victimized by Emma, unlike Rachel, Nina doesn't identify as a victim, and this leaves her free to exercise self-agency as she seeks the answers to her questions about Emma's role in the breakdown of her parents' marriage. Whether she gets them or not is another matter because the novel is more focused on process than outcome, and this, plus the nuanced, relatable characterization of both Nina and Emma—who is not as blameless as she initially appears—lends the story a psychological sophistication not present in Rachel's story. From the moment she gains access to Emma by stealing her wallet, Nina is manipulative, cunning, and deceptive, offering to babysit so she can pry, hosting dinner parties and even a holiday in France purely to find opportunities to undermine and unsettle the woman she blames for her parents' divorce. But Nina is also vulnerable, having witnessed her father flirt and go "moony"[48] over Emma all those years ago, when he described Emma as pretty and clever, suggesting to his horrified daughter that she "take a leaf out of her book."[49] Hurt and angry that Emma fails to recall this past, pivotal summer, even though, as Nina admits "Nothing *happened*. No one did anything exactly. No one said anything. It was just the last straw,"[50] Nina continues to harbor a confusion of envy and unresolved father issues making her flawed complex character less a picture of psychopathology, and more a sophisticated portrayal of the power of projection which influences the making of meaning, albeit to her detriment.

In contrast to Nina, Frances in *Alys Always* represents the antithesis of success. She is similarly driven by personal resentments, however. She too spies the perfect chance to try and rectify her situation, although for Frances this is a matter of transcending her mundane existence rather than seeking revenge. Quietly clever, but lonely, deeply unsatisfied, uncharismatic, and unfulfilled, Frances has spent a lifetime feeling overlooked and unacknowledged. "I was the good girl, biddable, compliant" she says, scornfully, realizing her amenability got her nowhere. "I did what I was told, I kept my nose clean, I was no trouble to anyone."[51] This all changes when Frances witnesses the aftermath of a fatal car accident on her way back from a visit to her parents. As the situation unfolds, in the days following the incident, she deduces the identity of the victim and spies a way to turn the tragedy to her advantage, deploying her intuition and acute powers of observation to unsettling effect as she sets about involving herself with the dead woman's husband and adult children. Morphing from a silently seething wallflower into an extremely calculated opportunist, Frances inveigles her way into a privileged lifestyle and, due to her newfound connections with the bereaved family, an enviable promotion at work.

Journalist Becca Rothfeld describes Amy Dunne as "the most evolved manifestation of the femme fatale yet,"[52] but Frances is far more deserving of this accolade. Unlike Amy, Frances strategically and successfully manipulates the man in her sights, Laurence Kyte, in order to gain a better life for herself, rather than counter-productively maintaining a wretched situation at all costs for the sake of retribution. Where Amy assumes omnipotence and speaks of "undoing" and "reassembling"[53] her husband, Frances understands the risks inherent to her chillingly subtle plan. Initially she defers to Laurence, "like someone shining a pocket mirror at the sun, I show him his own legend," but occasionally her complex emotions afford her a semblance of empathy, as well as a kind of horrified respect. Used to being regarded as "the same funny old Frances" by her family, she revels in her new, elevated status, although when she genuinely begins to fall in love, her vulnerabilities are activated; "Am I falling or flying? I can't be sure. I worry that this will work against me. I worry that I will lose my advantage, the clarity of my perspective. But I find I can't do much about it. I have to trust him."[54]

Most importantly for a contemporary version of the femme fatale, Frances's sexuality is never foregrounded. On the contrary, she is decidedly lacking in sexual powers of attraction or any tricks and techniques of seduction, instead relying on her wits, her intellect, her nerve, and her guile to incrementally creep toward her goal, foregrounding questions of ethics as she tests the flexibility of her own conscience. Her refusal to flinch confronts the moral high ground in us all, making her, like Nina, both compelling and uncomfortably relatable.

Both of Lane's antiheroines "aggressively refuse the roles they are dealt in life."[55] Embodying the daily dangers of ordinary existence, and the disturbing undercurrents that run beneath the persona, they are damaged goods, bruised and battered by the human business of childhood, adolescence, and imperfect family systems, behaving in morally questionable, yet never unfeasible ways. In this respect, Lane's books consciously take their own active turn, away from thriller territory, and further into the deep psychological terrain of domestic noir. As Nina herself observes, echoing Lane's own perspective, while talking fiction with Emma's husband Ben, most plot twists are "nothing like life, which—it seems to me—turns less on shocks or theatrics than on the small quiet moments, misunderstandings or disappointments, the things that it's easy to overlook."[56]

At its best, domestic noir foregrounds the psychological intricacies, strengths, and vulnerabilities of its characters beyond the framework of psychopathology. Focusing on the hidden side of intimate human relationships, the genre has the potential to explore how women can navigate complex emotional trauma by developing the internal resources to refuse victim status, resist sexual stereotypes, and integrate aggressive impulses, all without forfeiting mental stability. But, given the alignment between the historical development of reason with concepts of masculinity, this still represents a risky departure. As Sue Austin says; "By being located in the realm of that which is radically Other to coherent, rational, moral agency, women's aggressive energies have become entwined with experiences of madness, death and terror,"[57] and texts like *Gone Girl* and *The Girl on the Train* continue to support this principle. However, by rejecting characterization that aligns badness with madness and by relying on narratives that focus more on emotional rather than physical violence, through novels like *Her* and *Alys Always*, domestic noir can offer a positive play-space for antiheroines; psychologically complex, morally disreputable women, who flourish within powerfully subversive roles that integrate anger, aggression, and questionable behavior. In this way, new archetypal images of women can safely begin to emerge, and old ones are able to evolve.

NOTES

1. Julia Crouch, "Foreword: Notes from a Genre Bender," *Domestic Noir: The New Face of 21st Century Fiction*, edited by Laura and Henry Sutton Joyc (London: Palgrave MacMillan, 2018), vii.

2. Here, I refer to Jacques Lacan's complex definition of the Other as both "the Other as another subject" and "the Other as symbolic order," which mediates the relationship with the subject. Thus, the Object is a locus occupied by the subject, who thereby embodies the Other for another subject.

3. Crouch, "Genre Bender," http://juliacrouch.co.uk/blog/genre-bender. 25/08/2013.

4. Anita Singh, "Crime Pays: Thrillers and Detective Novels Now Outsell All Other Fiction," *The Telegraph*, 11/04/2018.

5. Crouch, "Foreword: Notes from a Genre Bender," viii.

6. Rebecca Whitney, "Are Women Hardwired to Love Thrillers?" *The Telegraph*, 2015. https://www.telegraph.co.uk/women/womens-life/11440540/Thrillers-and-crime-novels-Are-women-hardwired-to-love-them.html.

7. Rebecca Whitney, "Domestic Noir Is Bigger than Ever," *The Independent*, 2015. https://www.independent.co.uk/arts-entertainment/books/features/domestic-noir-is-bigger-than-ever-top-ten-releases-for-2015-9975488.html.

8. Rebecca Whitney, "Domestic Noir Is Bigger than Ever."

9. Eva Burke, "From Cool Girl to Dead Girl: *Gone Girl* and the Allure of Female Victim-hood," *Domestic Noir: The New Face of 21st Century Crime Fiction*, edited by Laura and Henry Sutton Joyce (London: Palgrave Macmillan, 2018), 81.

10. Oliver Burkeman, "Gillian Flynn on Her Bestseller Gone Girl and Accusations of Misogyny," *The Guardian*, 02/05/2013, 4. https://www.theguardian.com/books/2013/may/01/gillian-flynn-bestseller-gone-girl-misogyny.

11. Oliver Burkeman, "Gillian Flynn on Her Bestseller *Gone Girl* and Accusations of Misogyny," 4.

12. Sue Austin, *Women's Aggressive Fantasies: A Post-Jungian Exploration of Self-Hatred, Love and Agency* (London: Routledge, 2005), 45.

13. Jane Caputi, *Goddesses and Monsters: Women, Myth, Power and Popular Culture* (London: Popular Press, 2004), 328.

14. Susan Hopkins, "Bad Romance," *Overland*, 2016. https://overland.org.au/2016/05/bad-romance/.

15. Becca Rothfeld, "*Gone Girl*'s Feminist Update of the Old-Fashioned Femme Fatale," *The New Republic*, 2014. https://newrepublic.com/article/119743/gone-girl-has-offered-feminism-new-hero.

16. Gillian Flynn, *Gone Girl* (London: Weidenfeld & Nicolson, 2012), 211.

17. Burke, "From Cool Girl to Dead Girl," 74.

18. John Berger, *Ways of Seeing* (London: Penguin, 1972), 46.

19. Becca Rothfeld, "*Gone Girl*'s Feminist Update of the Old-Fashioned Femme Fatale."

20. Flynn, *Gone Girl*, 394.

21. Flynn, *Gone Girl*, 395.

22. Flynn, *Gone Girl*, 392.

23. Flynn, *Gone Girl*, 393.

24. Rhiannon Lucy Coslett, "Female Villains and False Accusations: A Feminist Defence of *Gone Girl*," *The New Statesman*, 2014. https://www.newstatesman.com/culture/2014/10/female-villains-and-false-accusations-feminist-defence-gone-girl.

25. Coslett, "Female Villains and False Accusations: A Feminist Defence of *Gone Girl*."

26. Coslett, "Female Villains and False Accusations: A Feminist Defence of *Gone Girl*."

27. Emma Miller, "'How Much Do You Want to Pay for This Beauty?' Domestic Noir and the Active Turn in Feminist Crime Fiction," *Domestic Noir: The New Face of 21st Century Crime Fiction*, edited by Laura and Henry Sutton Joyce (London: Palgrave Macmillan, 2018), 90.

28. Miller, "'How Much Do You Want to Pay for This Beauty?' Domestic Noir and the Active Turn in Feminist Crime Fiction," 90.

29. Miller, "'How Much Do You Want to Pay for This Beauty?' Domestic Noir and the Active Turn in Feminist Crime Fiction," 99–100.

30. India Sturgis, "Paula Hawkins: '*The Girl on the Train* Was My Last Throw of the Dice,'" *The Telegraph*, Books article in Culture section, 2016. https://www.telegraph.co.uk/books/authors/paula-hawkins-the-girl-on-the-train-was-my-last-throw-of-the-dic/.

31. Jean Hanff Korelitz. "*The Girl on the Train* by Paula Hawkins." *New York Times*, 2015, https://www.nytimes.com/2015/02/01/books/review/the-girl-on-the-train-by-paula-hawkins.html.

32. Jacqueline Rose, "Corkscrew in the Neck," *London Review of Books*, vol. 37, no. 17, 2015, 25–26.

33. Paula Hawkins, *The Girl on the Train*. Black Swan edition (London: Doubleday, 2013), 112.

34. Hawkins, *The Girl on the Train*, 254.

35. Hawkins, *The Girl on the Train*, 43.

36. Hawkins, *The Girl on the Train*, 199.

37. Hawkins, *The Girl on the Train*, 264.

38. Jean Knox, *Self-Agency in Psychotherapy: Attachment, Autonomy and Intimacy* (London: W. W. Norton & Company, 2011). *Interpersonal Neurobiology*, Allan N Schore, 16.

39. Koa Beck, "Female Characters Don't Have to Be Likeable," *The Atlantic*, 2015, https://www.theatlantic.com/entertainment/archive/2015/12/in-praise-of-fictions-unlikable-women-in-2015/421698/.

40. Hopkins, "Bad Romance."
41. Crouch, "Foreword: Notes from a Genre Bender," viii.
42. Susanna Rustin, "Paula Hawkins: The Woman Behind *The Girl on the Train*," *The Guardian*, Interview, 29/04/2013, Books. https://www.theguardian.com/books/2016/apr/29/paula-hawkins-woman-behind-the-girl-on-the-train-interview.
43. Eva Wiseman, "The Woman on the Train with a Book with 'Girl' in the Title . . ." *The Guardian*, Life and Style, 08/01/2017. https://www.theguardian.com/lifeandstyle/2017/jan/08/the-woman-on-the-train-with-a-book-with-girl-in-the-title.
44. Rose, "Corkscrew in the Neck."
45. Sarah Hughes, "The *Gone Girl* Effect Sparks Years of Flawed Women Behaving Badly," *The Observer*, feature, 03/01/2014, 2015, Books. https://www.theguardian.com/books/2015/jan/03/gone-girl-effecthttps://www.theguardian.com/books/2015/jan/03/gone-girl-effect.
46. Mandy Rice Withrow, "An Interview with Author, Harriet Lane," *The Discarded Image*, 2013. https://www.discardedimage.com/?p=3936.
47. "5 Minutes with Harriet Lane," *Elle UK*, 2014. https://www.elle.com/uk/life-and-culture/culture/articles/a22381/interview-harriet-lane-book-club-live-event-hoxton-her-novel/.
48. Harriet Lane, *Her* (Weidenfeld & Nicolson, 2014), 212.
49. Lane, *Her*, 211.
50. Lane, *Her*, 207.
51. Harriet Lane, *Alys Always* (Weidenfeld & Nicholson, 2012).
52. Rothfeld, "*Gone Girl*'s Feminist Update of the Old-Fashioned Femme Fatale."
53. Flynn, *Gone Girl*, 394.
54. Lane, *Alys Always*, 162.
55. Hopkins, "Bad Romance."
56. Lane, *Her*, 200–201.
57. Austin, *Women's Aggressive Fantasies: A Post-Jungian Exploration of Self-Hatred, Love and Agency*, 94.

BIBLIOGRAPHY

"5 Minutes with Harriet Lane." *Elle UK*, 2014. https://www.elle.com/uk/life-and-culture/culture/articles/a22381/interview-harriet-lane-book-club-live-event-hoxton-her-novel/.
Austin, Sue. *Women's Aggressive Fantasies: A Post-Jungian Exploration of Self-Hatred, Love and Agency*. London: Routledge, 2005.
Beck, Koa. "Female Characters Don't Have to Be Likeable." *The Atlantic*, 2015. https://www.theatlantic.com/entertainment/archive/2015/12/in-praise-of-fictions-unlikable-women-in-2015/421698/.
Berger, John. *Ways of Seeing*. London: Penguin, 1972.
Burke, Eva. "From Cool Girl to Dead Girl: Gone Girl and the Allure of Female Victimhood." *Domestic Noir: The New Face of 21st Century Crime Fiction*, 71–86, edited by Laura and Henry Sutton Joyce. London: Palgrave Macmillan, 2018.
Burkeman, Oliver. "Gillian Flynn on Her Bestseller Gone Girl and Accusations of Misogyny." *The Guardian*, 02/05/2013, 4. https://www.theguardian.com/books/2013/may/01/gillian-flynn-bestseller-gone-girl-misogyny.
Caputi, Jane. *Goddesses and Monsters: Women, Myth, Power and Popular Culture*. Madison: Popular Press, 2004.
Coslett, Rhiannon Lucy. "Female Villains and False Accusations: A Feminist Defence of *Gone Girl*." *The New Statesman*, 2014. https://www.newstatesman.com/culture/2014/10/female-villains-and-false-accusations-feminist-defence-gone-girl.
Crouch, Julia. "Foreword: Notes from a Genre Bender." *Domestic Noir: The New Face of 21st Century Fiction*, v–viii, edited by Laura and Henry Sutton Joyce. London: Palgrave Mac-Millan, 2018.
Flynn, Gillian. *Gone Girl*. London: Weidenfeld & Nicolson, 2012.
Hawkins, Paula. *The Girl on the Train*, Black Swan edition. London: Doubleday, 2013.

Hopkins, Susan. "Bad Romance." *Overland*, 2016. https://overland.org.au/2016/05/bad-romance/.

Hughes, Sarah. "The *Gone Girl* Effect Sparks Years of Flawed Women Behaving Badly." *The Observer*, feature, 03/01/2014, 2015, Books. https://www.theguardian.com/books/2015/jan/03/gone-girl-effect.

Joyce, Laura and Henry Sutton. *Domestic Noir: The Changing Face of 21st Century Crime Fiction.* London: Palgrave MacMillan, 2018. *Crime Files*, Clive Bloom.

Knox, Jean. *Self-Agency in Psychotherapy: Attachment, Autonomy and Intimacy.* London: W. W. Norton & Company, 2011. *Interpersonal Neurobiology*, Allan N. Schore.

Korelitz, Jean Hanff. "*The Girl on the Train* by Paula Hawkins." *New York Times*, 2015. https://www.nytimes.com/2015/02/01/books/review/the-girl-on-the-train-by-paula-hawkins.html.

Lane, Harriet. *Alys Always.* London: Weidenfeld & Nicholson, 2012.

———. *Her.* London: Weidenfeld & Nicolson, 2014.

Miller, Emma. "'How Much Do You Want to Pay for This Beauty?': Domestic Noir and the Active Turn in Feminist Crime Fiction." *Domestic Noir: The New Face of 21st Century Crime Fiction*, edited by Laura and Henry Sutton Joyce. London: Palgrave Macmillan, 2018.

Rose, Jacqueline. "Corkscrew in the Neck." *London Review of Books*, vol. 37, no. 17 (2015): 25–26. http://search.ebscohost.com/login.aspx?direct=true&db=azh&AN=109426245&site=ehost-live.

Rothfeld, Becca. "*Gone Girl*'s Feminist Update of the Old-Fashioned Femme Fatale." *The New Republic*, 2014. https://newrepublic.com/article/119743/gone-girl-has-offered-feminism-new-hero.

Rustin, Susanna. "Paula Hawkins: The Woman Behind the *Girl on the Train*." *The Guardian* Interview, 29/04/2013, Books. https://www.theguardian.com/books/2016/apr/29/paula-hawkins-woman-behind-the-girl-on-the-train-interview.

Singh, Anita. "Crime Pays: Thrillers and Detective Novels Now Outsell All Other Fiction." *The Telegraph*, 11/04/2018.

Sturgis, India. "Paula Hawkins: '*The Girl on the Train* Was My Last Throw of the Dice.'" *The Telegraph*, Books article in Culture section, 2016. https://www.telegraph.co.uk/books/authors/paula-hawkins-the-girl-on-the-train-was-my-last-throw-of-the-dic/.

Whitney, Rebecca. "Are Women Hardwired to Love Thrillers?" *The Telegraph* 2015. https://www.telegraph.co.uk/women/womens-life/11440540/Thrillers-and-crime-novels-Are-women-hardwired-to-love-them.html.

———. "Domestic Noir Is Bigger than Ever." *The Independent*, 2015. https://www.independent.co.uk/arts-entertainment/books/features/domestic-noir-is-bigger-than-ever-top-ten-releases-for-2015-9975488.html.

Wiseman, Eva. "The Woman on the Train with a Book with 'Girl' in the Title . . ." *The Guardian*, Life and Style, 08/01/2017. https://www.theguardian.com/lifeandstyle/2017/jan/08/the-woman-on-the-train-with-a-book-with-girl-in-the-title.

Withrow, Mandy Rice. "An Interview with Author, Harriet Lane." *The Discarded Image*, 2013. https://www.discardedimage.com/?p=3936.

Chapter Nine

"Maybe She's Not Such a Heinous Bitch After All"

Representations of the Antiheroine in
Crazy Ex-Girlfriend

Stephanie Salerno

THE CRAZY EX-GIRLFRIEND

The CW's *Crazy Ex-Girlfriend* (*CEG*), created by Rachel Bloom and Aline Brosh McKenna, is a unique vehicle through which to analyze contemporary representations of the antiheroine. A musical dramedy with 157 original songs, *CEG* tells the story of Rebecca Bunch (Rachel Bloom), a Jewish New York City lawyer from a broken home, who chases happiness (defined as romantic love) in West Covina, California. Rebecca is an emotionally raw, socially conscious, and passionate intellectual who is open to love even if it hurts her. Her childhood trauma limits her ability to break patterns of bad behavior, and she is plagued by undiagnosed Borderline Personality Disorder for most of her life. As a result, Rebecca is stigmatized as unstable, impulsive, and "crazy." Yet, despite her selfishness and moral failings, Rebecca is the quintessential antiheroine: dismissive, manipulative, and "capable of doing bad things for good reasons," making her a resoundingly unlikeable character.[1] With the underlying motive of finding joy, Rebecca integrates into the West Covina community, brazenly shaking things up. Rebecca dismantles the cultural falsehoods that toxic beliefs and patriarchal systems uphold through immoral, gauche, and self-centered acts. An intense feminist, she is often selfish and apathetic to others' struggles, going as far as engaging in criminal behavior at times in order to make herself look good or get what she wants. She is driven to meddle in her friends' relationships, pointing out the false joy that comes from settling for and accepting normative scripts. Over the course of the show's four seasons, Rebecca learns to articulate her emotional needs, eventually learning to care for herself as much as she cares for her friends. As a representation of an antiheroine, Rebecca may be understood as a stimulus for change who embodies the feminist killjoy trope to model and embrace self-love, community, and integrity amidst a disingenuous, toxic culture.

Airing its last episode in April 2019, *CEG* has enjoyed some scholarly attention to date, much of which focuses on its depictions of postfeminism and non-normative representation,[2] as well as how musical theater styles provide a unique narrative structure.[3] Building upon the scholarly consensus that *CEG* is a subversive musical dramedy and a critical, though not commercial, hit, I articulate in this chapter a portrait of Rebecca as an antiheroine who, by embodying the feminist killjoy Other, "disturb[s] the fragility of peace" in her quest to find happiness.[4] The series finale, "I'm in Love" (S4, E17), situates Rebecca as a volatile catalyst and a positive force of disruption in the West Covina community rather than a victim of childhood trauma and mental illness. Through narrative and performance analysis, I highlight four milestones that Rebecca achieves that epitomize how her killjoy acts (toward others and herself) destroy false or delusional perceptions of happiness for both herself and her family/friends. Throughout Rebecca's journey she learns to: (1) accept reality; (2) be vulnerable; (3) reject shame; and (4) embrace self-love. The musical parody, "Eleven O'Clock," serves as the basis for analyzing Rebecca's growth, a frame through which her milestone achievements are viewed as antiheroic acts of agency that simultaneously positively influence the West Covina community. Rebecca's milestones reflect her progression to dismantle her patriarchally influenced life and discover true love in an unexpected package.

"MEET REBECCA": ANTIHEROINE, FEMINIST KILLJOY, OTHER

Rebecca's drive to identify and nurture happiness in her life and her friends' lives suggests that there is a more honorable and meaningful goal that she is seeking to achieve and share with her community. "Deeply flawed," "edgy," and "neither uniformly good nor evil," Rebecca fits the mold of the antiheroine who eschews both conventionally feminine and masculine traits.[5] Her questionable professional ethics, erratic definition of morality, and impulse control problems lead her to neglect her own well-being or the feelings of others. Her behavior is neither good nor evil, but rooted in intentions that make those around her, including herself, happy. Rebecca is, at her core, a sex-positive, voluptuous bodied feminist antiheroine who denounces stereotypes, champions women's rights, and upholds joy over artificial success.

Margaret Tally notes that definitions of the antiheroine pale in comparison to antiheroes,[6] stating that dictionaries tend to define the antiheroine as a "female anti-hero," attaching "masculine traits such as pride, violence or seduction" to these characters.[7] This reductive practice devalues the antiheroine's individualism, agency, and personal agenda, writing off her actions as merely behaving badly.

CEG defies this norm, putting the feminist antiheroine at the center of the narrative instead of forcing her to uphold cultural standards of beauty, domesticity, and likability. In essence, the show's point is that Rebecca's journey matters, even as it is unorthodox and convoluted. To attain milestones of adulthood in her own time, Rebecca kills joy and points out hypocrisy, engaging in a type of consciousness-raising involving "becoming conscious of unhappiness but also achieving (with others) better ways of understanding unhappiness."[8] Noting that "feminist consciousness" is a "form of unhappiness," Sara Ahmed interrogates the feminist killjoy as having grown out of consciousness that resisted the paradigm of the happy housewife of the 1950s.[9] This paradigm assumes that romantic success ending in heteronormative domesticity is the ultimate female goal. *CEG* indisputably plays with this idea: Rebecca's reason for moving to West Covina is to win the affection of Josh Chan, her adolescent first love; within the confines of this delusion, achieving an adult, romantic relationship with Josh will transport her to a space of mental health and personal happiness. Throughout the series, Rebecca emotionally attaches to objects of desire (people/ideas of happiness), exemplifying what Lauren Berlant calls "cruel optimism," or the "attachment to compromised conditions of possibility whose realization is discovered either to be *im*possible, sheer fantasy, or *too* possible, and toxic."[10] The cultural pressure of feeling entitled to happiness when the object of "optimism may be . . . actively damaging to [the] subject" is an affect that demands joy even when negativity looms.[11] Rebecca's optimisms are thus affective attachments that she fixates on in order to anchor herself to what she thinks happiness looks like when she is in a state of crisis. This habit is a coping mechanism for her, "a process embedded in the ordinary that unfolds in stories about navigating what's overwhelming."[12]

Given the title of the show, it is remiss to ignore the impact Rebecca's mental illness has on her personality. A season 3 suicide attempt leads to the diagnosis of Borderline Personality Disorder, contextualizing within the narrative the nine symptoms of BPD Rebecca exhibits, including impulsive behavior, fear of abandonment, extreme mood swings, and unstable relationships.[13] Her illness exacerbates her antiheroine actions and thought processes, but she is granted leeway and "tolerance that a more traditionally villainous character would not be allowed," particularly a male antagonist.[14] The characteristics that make her difficult and unpredictable in professional and social situations stem from her feminist ideals, the parts of her personality that cannot accept patriarchal and oppressive norms that limit women to sexist stereotypes and prevent men from expressing vulnerability and non-normative masculinity. In Rebecca's case, killing joy is a distinctive quality of the antiheroine trope, an intentional counterpoint to her mental illness, which often renders her out of control. Mental illness Others Rebecca within her community, and as the severity of her condition unfurls, she learns to manage her BPD, consciously and intentionally unravelling the "crazy" stereotype and delegitimizing mental illness as an excuse for bad behavior.

Though her friends provide robust emotional support, Rebecca's battle to obtain stability is a solitary one. The inclusion of musical parody in *CEG* represents Rebecca's psychic and emotional safe space in which she process-es information and works through complex situations, including recognizing false joy; choosing to actively reject the façade of happiness; and, subse-quently, bracing herself for the pain, loneliness, rage, or uncertainty that inevitably follows. Musical parody and humor soften Rebecca's roughness, covering it with a veil of satire that simultaneously winks, nudges, and clev-erly educates the audience about feminine beauty standards, female empow-erment, and female-female competition.[15] Further, humor functions "as a safety valve," making emotionally stringent narratives more palatable to tele-vision audiences and situating musical parodies in a way that may "diminish the sting of their anti-heroine's assertiveness and aggression by presenting her Otherness as 'just a joke.'"[16] *CEG* is thus an extension of musical theater narratives in which a stigmatized Other disrupts a community (*Phantom of the Opera* and *Wicked*, for example) and, in effect, profoundly changes indi-viduals within the community. I argue that *CEG*'s narrative similarly places Rebecca, an Other, amid a hometown crowd in West Covina, where she instantaneously affects the rhythms and norms of the community.[17] As Re-becca begins to know and accept herself, becoming "alive to possibility," she makes decisions that kill her own and others' joy in favor of living honestly, finding balance, and discovering self-worth.[18]

"SHOULDN'T I HAVE EARNED A FRICKIN' EVER AFTER?" KILLING JOY AND OBJECTS OF DESIRE

Shuffling back and forth between Valentine's Day one year ago and present day, the series finale of *CEG*, "I'm in Love" (S4, E17), seeks to resolve Rebecca's love quadrangle conundrum, ultimately demonstrating how killing joy can be selfless and loving: in essence, antiheroic.[19] Mulling over a dream sequence in which three potential paths to happiness all lead to stable but unhappy futures, Rebecca's mind flits away to process her conflicted feelings via the musical parody "Eleven O'Clock." *CEG*'s nod to the classical musical theater showstopper during which a protagonist experiences a life-changing realization is an integral piece of the final episode. "Eleven O'Clock" is an ode to Rebecca's past in which she unhappily performed identities while attaching herself to objects of desire that she believed would bring her happiness. [20] The parody troubles the narrative surrounding Rebecca's attachment to optimism through the retelling of her progress since moving to West Covina. Emphasizing the past and the future, "Eleven O'Clock" has some original music and lyrics, but the middle section of the song is a pastiche of ten song fragments from previous seasons:

1. "Crazy Ex-Girlfriend Theme" (season 1 theme song)
2. "Just a Girl in Love" (season 2 theme song)
3. "You Do/You Don't Want to Be Crazy" (season 3 theme song)
4. "A Diagnosis" (S3, E6)
5. "The Darkness" (S4, E12)
6. "We'll Never Have Problems Again" (S2, E10)
7. "I'm a Good Person" (S1, E5)
8. A lyric snagged from "The End of the Movie" (S3, E4)
9. A trumpet motif of "Meet Rebecca" (season 4 theme song)
10. "Stupid Bitch" (S1, E11)

The song begins with Rebecca spacing out, retreating to her psychic sanctuary while her best friend Paula patiently waits out Rebecca's distraction. "It's Eleven O'Clock / Eleven O'Clock / And the deadline is anytime today / but I won't know by Eleven O'Clock tonight / just like I didn't know at Eleven O'Clock yesterday" Rebecca sings, serious contemplation etched across her face. The lyrics suggest that Rebecca's indecision and frustration stem from her continued attachment to the cruel optimism of romantic love. "Shouldn't I have earned a frickin' ever after?" suggests that she is aware that optimism is letting her down and failing to bring about true joy. As the turn table stage begins to rotate, the costumes Rebecca wore in the previous seasons' parodies appear, a visual reminder of the past identities she performed in her attempts to find love. Co-songwriter Jack Dolgen explained the purpose of the different styles and genres of "Eleven O'Clock":

> From the character's perspective, she really didn't have a sense of herself. She was trying on ways of who to be and how to be, and it made sense that she would genre-hop and costume-hop. And the way that [Bloom and Brosh McKenna] always imagined finishing up, it was really about coming to herself. You end exactly where you started, but fully changed. She starts out really lost, you know, and then ends basically in the beginning of her life as herself. And the songs are a way to personify that. [21]

This is a powerful contrapuntal design choice, juxtaposing different versions of Rebecca—the delusional antiheroine and optimist and the self-aware killjoy—to visually denote her emotional and mental growth, but also acknowledge her stasis. Torn between three viable choices—Josh, a symbol of uncomplicated joy from her painful youth; Nathaniel, sweet, but stifled by toxic masculinity; or Greg, a quiet complement to Rebecca's pain and dark humor—she is unable to come to a conclusion: "I've done the workbooks, taken the pills, what more can I do?" she bemoans. The parody ends in frustration, the concluding lyric suggesting that she understands that she "has to end this song" but doesn't know how. "Eleven O'Clock" emphasizes Rebecca's realization of what Ahmed notes is integral to the feminist killjoy: the awareness of "just how much there is to be unhappy about."[22] As Rebecca accepts the presence of unhappiness and grief in her life, she begins to possess a level of consciousness that recognizes loss; from that point, she is able to embrace her imperfect life, detaching from optimism and killing others' joy in the process.[23]

I'M IN LOVE?

Rebecca's urgent need to define happiness as a romantic relationship is an apt example of how optimism holds her in a pattern of obsession, disappointment, and retaliation. In each of her objects of desire, Rebecca detects promises (of love, happiness, comfort, exhilarating sex, the ability to be herself), and in pursuing these promises, her fantasies of happiness balloon. A key element in Rebecca's attachment to optimism, and her proclivity to killjoy, is misrecognition, which Berlant describes as

> The psychic process by which fantasy recalibrates what we encounter so that we can imagine that something or someone can fulfill our desire. . . . To misrecognize is . . . to project qualities onto something so that we can love, hate, and manipulate it for having those qualities—which it might or might not have.[24]

Rebecca's ability to achieve life's milestones signifies breaking the cycle of misrecognition. As she detaches from her objects of desire, she kills joy. But, in order to make a permanent break, she does not merely end relationships; she stirs up feelings of unhappiness in her partners, resulting in their own quests to change their lives. A significant mark of the feminist killjoy, Rebecca does not remove herself from the West Covina community. Rather, she is a fixture in it, a central point around which her other friends and acquaintances orbit. Her constant presence ensures that her three objects of desire—Josh Chan (Vincent Rodriquez III), Nathaniel Plimpton III (Scott Michael Foster), and Greg Serrano (Santino Fontana/Skylar Astin)[25]—cannot simply look the other way and forget Rebecca's impact, a vital mark of the antiheroine. As the optimism Rebecca carries becomes heavier and her internal identity struggles to emerge, Josh, Nathaniel, and Greg grapple with their own attachments to Rebecca and the disruption her presence has caused in their lives.

Spanning seasons 1 and 2, Rebecca and Josh's romance represents nostalgia as well as a resistance to maturity. In fixating on Josh Chan as the one person (an ideal optimism) who will bring her happiness, Rebecca romanticizes this adolescent crush, pinning her hopes and dreams on this perfect illusion. Berlant notes that fantasy "provides representations to make the subject appear intelligible," suggesting that "fantasy parses ambivalence" in a way that does not defeat the optimist.[26] In other words, delusions and diversions allow the optimist to nourish a situation that is, from a distance, clearly dysfunctional. Within the "Eleven O'Clock" medley, "West Covina" and "We'll Never Have Problems Again" address Josh and Rebecca's reliance on fantasy to perform adult relationships. Updated lyrics of these two fragments in "Eleven O'Clock" flaunt Rebecca's emotional growth. For example, the season 1 theme lyrics of "West Covina" are rewritten, shifting from "It happens to be where Josh lives / But that's not why I'm here" to "I admitted that's where Josh lived / And that's what brought me here." Additionally, the performance of the snippet differs from the season 1 approach: there is a wise and self-deprecating delivery rather than the over-bright, manic performance of season 1's "West Covina." Similarly, the spirit of the "We'll Never Have Problems Again" segment is energetic and positive, but hits on a major checkpoint along the path to maturity: "And though I knew I'd have problems again . . . I know I gotta move on to a new song but I wanna keep discoing." This lyrical update reflects focus and cognizance, abandoning the delusional disco-fantasy delivery of the season 2 parody that marked Rebecca and Josh's Facebook official relationship status. Up until Josh failed to fulfill his promise and marry her, the fantasy of Josh as her soul mate sustained Rebecca, enabling her to ignore her dissatisfaction with her professional life and utterly disregard the warning signs that indicated her mental health was further deteriorating. When the fantasy of Josh as the optimistic zenith disintegrated, Rebecca, having lost her object of desire, became unable to navigate reality.

Rebecca was not the only one living a fiction. While it appeared that Rebecca was wholly dependent on Josh, season 4 drives home the actuality that Josh used Rebecca as emotional support as well. By rejecting fantasy, Rebecca simultaneously kicked away the crutch that Josh used as he drifted aimlessly from relationship to relationship, job to job, and even homes run by maternal figures (his mother Lourdes, Hector's mother Estella, and Rebecca). Finding himself at an emotional impasse, Josh begins therapy, and this new level of introspection is a critical turning point for a man who felt called to the priesthood in order to avoid Rebecca's secrets, then abandoned the calling when it became too academically intense. Josh's newfound realism and reverence for self-improvement signals that yet another fire has gone out in his and Rebecca's relationship; his willingness to think more deeply about his emotions and relationships ages him beyond Rebecca's gilded teenaged memory. Rebecca's detachment from optimism and the dispassionate method in which she kills Josh's joy encourages him to mature into a man who has confronted his shortcomings. Rebecca forced him to fly solo, and when he did, Josh comprehended how coddled and ill-prepared he was for independence. Through the strenuous task of facing reality—the joy, the pain, and the responsibilities involved—both Rebecca's and Josh's teenage nostalgia and fairy tale fantasies faded into their memories. Significantly, they chose to embrace the memory of musical theater summer camp rather than view their failure to partner as adults as a loss. In their newfound adulthood, Rebecca and Josh form a platonic relationship that neither defines nor compromises their identities but manages to honor the path they traveled together.

Whereas Rebecca's fixation on Josh as a form of optimism is rooted in fantasy and nostalgia, Rebecca's attraction to Nathaniel is linked to comfort. Nathaniel's emotional distance permits Rebecca to avoid confronting her emotional baggage, embracing sexuality and their mutual social capital instead.[27] Wealthy, conventionally attractive, and emotionally distant, Nathaniel exudes lust and power, and his relationship with Rebecca hinges on sexual chemistry and no-strings-attached interactions. Rebecca attaches to Nathaniel during her engagement to Josh, resulting in a romantic entanglement that spans seasons 2, 3, and 4. Berlant discusses the repetition associated with cruel optimism, noting that

> The compulsion to repeat optimism, which is another definition of desire, is a condition of possibility that also risks having to survive, once again, disappointment and depression, the protracted sense that nothing will change and that no-one, especially oneself, is teachable after all.[28]

Rebecca and Nathaniel's emotional dependence shifts from being purely sexual, to an affectionate relationship, to an illicit affair, emphasizing Berlant's notion that the optimist does not learn from previous experiences.

As a disrupter in Nathaniel's life, Rebecca's impact is profound, and the effects of her presence in his life are overwhelmingly positive. The emotional turmoil he experiences when Rebecca separates from him in order to focus on her mental health leads to Nathaniel's simultaneous personal growth (portrayed in the "Fit Hot Guys Have Problems Too" parody) and regression (entering into an immediate sexual relationship with a woman from college).[29] While Nathaniel had learned to be vulnerable with Rebecca, he is unable to fully give himself over to his new relationship. Consequently, he and Rebecca carry on an affair for several months, both of them desperately hanging onto the optimism of comfort. At the end of season 3, Rebecca and Nathaniel bare their souls in the parody "Nothing Is Ever Anyone's Fault" (S3, E13) in a time of crisis; timing and Rebecca's continued struggle with BPD appear to foil their declared love. This is a significant moment in both of their lives: though Nathaniel wants Rebecca to use her mental illness as an excuse (because he loves her) for pushing Trent (Paul Welsh) off the roof of Nathaniel's home, she is compelled to take responsibility for her actions for the first time in her life (because she wants to be a better person).[30] Their mutual emotional vulnerability fractures Nathaniel and Rebecca's optimistic attachments, triggering them to turn toward what Ahmed terms the "discomfort of truth."[31] Embracing discomfort, or emotional vulnerability, smothers the damaging childhood lessons that taught them that vibrant emotions equate weakness and happiness can be bought or manipulated.

"You Do/You Don't Want to Be Crazy" and "A Diagnosis" within the "Eleven O'Clock" medley symbolize this turn toward discomfort, recalling the hardest time of Rebecca's life. Despite her troubles, Nathaniel wants her, nonetheless. This is likely because their emotional connection crystallized as a result of Rebecca's suicide attempt in the middle of season 3. In the fraught aftermath, an emotionally paralyzed Nathaniel realizes that he had been touched by mental illness as a child when his mother overdosed on sleeping pills (S3, E6). While Rebecca oscillates dramatically between craving the comfort of being "crazy" and actively avoiding resisting her impulses, Nathaniel clings to his own form of optimism, a predictable attachment to class and status which leads to feeling dissatisfied with his trophy girlfriend, living in the shadow of his father as partner of a subpar firm, and performing toxic masculinity to maintain a persona. Though the attraction to repetition is strong for both of them, Rebecca's emotional volatility fundamentally changed Nathaniel's ability to stifle his own feelings.

As Rebecca and Nathaniel turned away from optimism and actively searched for authentic forms of happiness through discomfort, both within their relationship and without, their individual feelings of self-worth and self-love took precedence. This is a major shift for Rebecca, whose self-loathing anthem, "Stupid Bitch," finds its way into "Eleven O'Clock" in a final cry for clarity, and for Nathaniel as well, who self-punishes with verbal put-downs and extreme physical challenges. Rebecca's acts of self-love and Nathaniel's new "nice" demeanor revealed that they were, in fact, incredibly compassionate, empathetic human beings. For example, when Rebecca rejects Nathaniel early on in season 4, Nathaniel realizes he cannot merely slip back into his icy, vapid demeanor and derive pleasure as he did before; his attempts to self-punish fail to make him feel better/alive.[32] Rebecca's realization that "nice" Nathaniel wasn't satisfying her deepest calling effectively kills their slowly resurrecting romance. Their mutual pro bono legal work at the county jail in season 4 is a prime example of how they both learn to derive personal fulfillment by helping those who lack privilege and power. Though they matured emotionally in tandem, their romance became unsustainable because they emotionally outgrew one another. However, similar to Josh's trajectory, Rebecca and Nathaniel's emotional growth would not have been possible had they not learned to be vulnerable together. This vulnerability includes being strong enough to decide when not being together was an act of love.

Cruel optimism creates tension between desiring an object for pleasure and attaching to a "problematic object *in advance* of its loss."[33] Rebecca's fear of love's absence upholds the vicious cycle of obsessing over men whom she has outgrown. Greg as an object of desire uniquely challenges Rebecca. With undeniable chemistry, a fierce need to one up each other, and an inability to communicate honestly, Greg tested Rebecca's perceptions and expectations of a romantic partner in seasons 1 and 2. Departing for graduate school at Emory University in Atlanta ("the Harvard of the south") early in season 2, Greg returned in *CEG*'s final season, near graduation and sober. For Rebecca, Greg's return was an opportunity to rectify past wrongs and present to him the new version of herself, proving that she too had undergone radical personal change. Eventually coming clean with him that in a BPD spiral she slept with his dad, Greg and Rebecca enter into a renewed relationship in which they seem happy. However, one major fight due to Greg's negative attitude about the amusement waterpark Raging Waters (Rebecca's version of a dream date) triggers a long-brewing BPD spiral. Attempting to protect herself from the loss of Greg and a seemingly stable, fulfilling relationship, Rebecca tries to seduce both Nathaniel and Josh in the same night, reattaching herself to former lovers, as well as her mental illness.

Nearly throwing all of her tools and hard-won knowledge about managing her BPD out the window that night leads Rebecca to name the Darkness (her "true love" who has always filled her emotional emptiness and whom she calls Tyler), something she'd never been able or willing to do. By naming the Darkness, an optimistic specter that cast a shadow over all aspects of her life for three decades, Rebecca rejects fantasy, comfort, and the crutch of avoiding treatment in favor of the easy seduction of destructive behavior. At last resisting slipping back into bad BPD habits, Rebecca breaks up with Greg in order to start medication and return to her therapy plan. Eve Kosofsky Sedgwick's theorization of shame contextualizes the struggle that Rebecca engaged in as she named the Darkness and sought out wellness, positing that shame both disrupts identity formation and establishes solidarity with other shamed subjects.[34] Rebecca immerses herself in the West Covina community because she finds kindred spirits—others who have complicated familial relationships, are dissatisfied in adulthood, or are actively hiding/avoiding adult responsibilities. Of these kindred spirits, Greg, an alcoholic, relates to Rebecca's mental health struggles more than anyone else. Her decision to put her wellness first and reject the feelings of shame associated with mental illness treatment negatively impact her relationship with Greg, stalling their advancement to a new plateau where they could both thrive professionally, romantically, and in good health. Despite the strength that they cultivate together, their mutual self-improvement transported them to a different plane, one where settling down together meant settling *for* one another.

Settling, a different form of optimism in Rebecca's life, was first teased in the Rebecca-Greg relationship in season 1.[35] Rebecca detached from the optimism of settling when she changed her patterns of behavior (naming the Darkness and rejecting the shame and stigma of mental illness treatment). Though Greg chose a similar path when he committed to sobriety, their competitive drive and toxic need to one up each other, referenced in the "I'm a Good Person" fragment in the "Eleven O'Clock" medley, fizzled out. Rebecca's forced feelings of happiness with Greg, despite their emotional growth, signals that the "cluster of desires and affects" that magnetize Rebecca to romantic love objects were not capable of actually fulfilling her emotionally.[36] Put another way, Rebecca's cruel optimism of romantic love leading to happiness is an attachment that only functions when she embraces normative expectations to "get numb with the consensual promise" an object of desire carries and "misrecognizes that promise as an achievement."[37] Though wellness/sobriety gives Rebecca and Greg more control in their lives, and settling down together would grant comfortability and predictability, marriage alone would not adequately fulfill Rebecca's desire to love herself. Thus, Rebecca meticulously kills their joy by turning away from settling: saying no to a relationship, a marriage, and a comfortable life together. Because she is able to recognize that attaching herself to Greg stifles her own creativity, Rebecca intentionally detaches herself from him, facing an unknown future with the songs in her head. Rebecca's ultimate decision to not choose any of her objects of desire in "I'm in Love" underscores Berlant's contention that obtaining the object of desire does not make pain or unhappiness disappear, an element that differentiates cruel optimism from melancholia, in which the lost object can be substituted.[38] This final and goliath anti-heroic act solidifies Rebecca as a feminist killjoy who stops at nothing to discover meaning in her life, even when that necessitates abandoning fantasies and behavioral anchors that have kept her going for most of her life.

"WELL, REBECCA, YOU'VE DONE IT NOW"

Along her multi-season journey to find happiness, Rebecca progressed from filling her time with antiheroic schemes to attract male attention, to giving up on everything, to clawing her way back to wellness. Taught by her mother Naomi at an early age to put her best face forward, Rebecca finally does

when she chooses self-love, killing all instincts toward deception and manipulation. This includes her decision to abandon law and open up her pretzel
shop, Rebetzel's Pretzels, rejecting the cutthroat performance her clients expect and finding simple joy in making and selling comfort food. Running
counter to stereotypes of women, in abandoning the suit dress and putting on
the apron, Rebecca actually makes a feminist statement: her pleasure, self-
worth, and time are more valuable than the salary of a senior law partner.
With her newfound free time and less demanding job, Rebecca is able to
explore her identity, and first discovers her knack for songwriting while
rewriting lyrics for a community theater production that features the sexist
songbook of Elliot Ellison (S4, E14).

The final musical interlude of the show, "West Covina (reprise)," focuses
on Rebecca's hidden penchant for songwriting and the sustaining force of
music in her life. Following a short scene in which her best friend Paula asks
Rebecca what she's doing when she stares off into space, Rebecca ultimately
shares her deepest secret: "When I stare off into space, I'm imagining myself
in a musical number. That's how I sometimes see big moments in my life . . .
I see myself in these songs." Still confused, Paula follows Rebecca's instruc-
tion to penetrate her secret space, a fantastic musical theater world. Rebecca
explains, "These are all the identities that I've tried to fit into. This is all the
weird and freaky and dumb and useless stuff that is my life and has led me to
nothing." Stunned, Paula counters with the final musical interlude of the
series, a reprise of a season 1 "West Covina" performance: "It's not just
some coincidence / Not random, not by chance / Who'd a thunk it / You're
remarkable / Not weird or dumb or cray / What you need / Just happens to be
here." Rebecca's decision to choose herself—her mind, her creativity, her
dreams—reflects what her BPD prevented her from seeing most of her life:
that she did, in fact, have a defined identity, one that was quirky, complex,
and, significantly, a work in progress. In choosing herself and setting boundaries with the men in her life, Rebecca rejects shame and actively embraces
self-love. In doing so, Rebecca frees herself from a lifelong pattern of emotional instability and hiding her true self from others, proving to herself that
through vulnerability and courage, her life is hers to write.

"Good finales are good finales because they bring things full circle. I love
stuff that loops back to the beginning because . . . life is chaos, and we tell
stories to make sense of that," Bloom states, speaking about the conclusion
of her show, her labor of love.[39] In the final moments of season 4, addressing
an open mic crowd, Rebecca admits that she doesn't know if what she has
written is any good, but the process of writing and telling her own story
allowed her the chance to "show the outside world what's been inside . . . all
of it, the nuances, and the gray areas." It turns out that the act of writing itself
is what makes her truly happy: "it's like I just met myself, just met Rebecca."
Without judgment, *CEG* conveys the message that everyone deserves the

opportunity to find happiness in their lives, despite past mistakes, missteps, or moral failings. For Rebecca, achieving her personal milestones (accept reality; be vulnerable; reject shame; and, embrace self-love) eradicates her lovers' corresponding optimisms: the reliability of fantasy associated with Josh; the comfort of avoiding emotional vulnerability with Nathaniel; and the stigma of mental illness with Greg; and, the fear of embracing self-love. In doing so, Josh, Nathaniel, and Greg achieve mirror milestones of their own as a result of Rebecca's antiheroic impact on their lives. Her disruption of the West Covina community eventually roused her friends and California family to seek out more than the false versions of satisfaction, happiness, and success they numbly accepted, allowing themselves their own eleventh hour reckonings. As "I'm in Love" portrays, righting past wrongs cannot change history or erase pain, but people can rewrite their stories at any time and find their own version of happiness in the process.

NOTES

1. Margaret Tally, *The Rise of the Anti-Heroine in TV's Third Golden Age* (Newcastle-Upon-Tyne: Cambridge,: Cambridge Scholars Publishing, 2016), 8.
2. See Hammerman 2017; Horn 2019.
3. See Ford and Macrossan 2019; Konkle and Burnett (forthcoming); Newman.
4. Sara Ahmed, *The Promise of Happiness* (Durham, NC: Duke University Press, 2010), 65.
5. Tally, *Rise of the Anti-Heroine*, 8.
6. See Canet 2019; Mittell 2015; and Vaage 2016.
7. Tally, *Rise of the Anti-Heroine*, 6.
8. Ahmed, *Promise of Happiness*, 87.
9. Ahmed, *Promise of Happiness*, 50–53.
10. Lauren Berlant, *Cruel Optimism* (Durham, NC: Duke University Press, 2011), 24.
11. Elizabeth Stephens, "Bad Feelings: An Affective Genealogy of Feminism," *Australian Feminist Studies* 30, no. 85 (2015): 279–280, https://doi.org/10.1080/08164649.2015.1113907.
12. Berlant, *Cruel Optimism*, 10.
13. "Borderline Personality Disorder," Mayo Clinic, accessed August 15, 2019, https://www.mayoclinic.org/diseases-conditions/borderline-personality-disorder/symptoms-causes/syc-20370237.
14. Tally, *Rise of the Anti-Heroine*, 5–6.
15. A few examples include "The Sexy Getting Ready Song" (S1, E1); "Put Yourself First" (S1, E10); "JAP Battle" (S1, E13); "Let's Generalize About Men" (S3, E2); and "JAP Battle (reprise)" (S4, E15).
16. M. Kramer, "Humour, Emotional Well-Being and the Anti-Heroine in Modern Dramedy," *Journal of Scandinavian Cinema* 9, no.1 (2019): 41. DOI: 10.1386/jsca.9.1.39_1.
17. Jessica Sternfeld, "'Pitiful Creature of Darkness': The Subhuman and the Superhuman in *The Phantom of the Opera*," in *The Oxford Handbook of Music and Disability Studies*, eds. Blake Howe et al., 795–814. New York: Oxford University Press, 2016.
18. Ahmed, *Promise of Happiness*, 78.
19. Josh, Nathaniel, and Greg each plan one perfect date in this *The Bachelor*-inspired contest. Josh plans a nostalgic camp out in the backyard of the house he and Rebecca cohabitate; Nathaniel organizes a majestic picnic strategically positioned above the Greek Theatre; and Greg plans an elaborate ride in a hot air balloon that evaporates when his car breaks down; their date is spent in a repair shop, the imperfection of it all making it perfect.

20. For example, Rebecca's response to a double break up with Greg and Josh in season 2 is to make herself over into a California blonde bombshell for the Miss Douche competition, convinced that changing her looks and personality will improve her romantic luck (S2, E4).

21. Hanh Nguyen, "*Crazy Ex-Girlfriend* Redefined Songs in Music Comedy with One Showstopping Numbers," *IndieWire*, May 15, 2019, https://www.indiewire.com/2019/05/crazy-ex-girlfriend-rachel-bloom-11-o-clock-cw-emmys-1202141234.

22. Ahmed, *Promise of Happiness*, 87.

23. Ahmed, *Promise of Happiness*, 50–53.

24. Berlant, *Cruel Optimism*, 122.

25. Greg was originally played by Santino Fontana, but scheduling conflicts prevented him from returning for the season 4 story arc. Skylar Astin replaced Fontana, and the show runners explained Greg's different appearance as the result of Rebecca's perception of the new him.

26. Berlant, *Cruel Optimism*, 122.

27. See the *Fosse* parody "Strip Away My Conscience" (S3, E2).

28. Berlant, *Cruel Optimism*, 122.

29. See "Nathaniel Gets the Message!" (S3, E9).

30. Stephanie Salerno, "'Let Us Ugly Cry': Spoofing Emotional Vulnerability in Season Three of *Crazy Ex-Girlfriend*," in *Perspectives on "Crazy Ex-Girlfriend"* (forthcoming). See "Nathaniel Is Irrelevant" (S3, E13).

31. Ahmed, *Promise of Happiness*, 79.

32. See "I Want to Be Here" (S4, E1).

33. Lauren Berlant, "Cruel Optimism," in *The Affect Theory Reader*, eds. Melissa Gregg and Gregory J. Seigworth (Durham, NC: Duke University Press, 2010), 94.

34. Eve Kosofvsky Sedgwick, *Touching Feeling: Affect, Pedagogy, Performativity* (Durham, NC: Duke University Press, 2003), 35–37.

35. See the Fred Astaire/Ginger Rogers parody "Settle for Me" (S1, E4).

36. Berlant, "Cruel Optimism," 94.

37. Berlant, *Cruel Optimism*, 28.

38. Berlant, *Cruel Optimism*, 24.

39. Nguyen, "*Crazy Ex-Girlfriend.*"

BIBLIOGRAPHY

Ahmed, Sara. *The Promise of Happiness.* Durham, NC: Duke University Press, 2010.

Berlant, Lauren. "Cruel Optimism." In *The Affect Theory Reader*, edited by Melissa Gregg and Gregory J. Seigworth, 93–117. Durham, NC: Duke University Press, 2010.

———. *Cruel Optimism.* Durham, NC: Duke University Press, 2011.

Canet, F. "More Therapy with Dr. Melfi (the character who guides viewer engagement with Tony Soprano): Relationship Arcs in Serial Antihero Narratives." *Journal of Screenwriting* 10, no. 1 (2019): 97–112. DOI: 10.1386/jocs.10.1.97_1.

Crazy Ex-Girlfriend. 2015–2019. Created by Rachel Bloom and Aline Brosh McKenna. The CW.

Ford, Jessica and Phoebe Macrossan. "The Musical Number as Feminist Intervention in *Crazy Ex-Girlfriend*." *Australian Journal of Popular Culture* 8, no. 1 (2019): 55–69. https://doi.org/10.1386/ajpc.8.1.55_1.

Hammerman, Shaina. *From Shtetl to Stardom: Jews and Hollywood.* Edited by Michael Renov and Vincent Brook. An Annual Review of the Casden Institute for the Study of the Jewish Role in American Life. Volume 14, 49–72. West Lafayette, IN: Purdue University Press, 2017.

Horn, Katrin. "'Period Sex': *Crazy Ex-Girlfriend* and the Feminist Politics of Offence." In *Media and the Politics of Offence*, edited by Anne Graefer, 127–145. Birmingham: Palgrave Macmillan, 2019.

Konkle, Amanda and Charles Burnett, eds. *Perspectives on* Crazy Ex-Girlfriend: *Quality Post-Network Television.* Forthcoming.

Kramer, M. "Humour, Emotional Well-Being and the Anti-Heroine in Modern Dramedy." *Journal of Scandinavian Cinema* 9, no. 1 (2019): 39–52. DOI: 10.1386/jsca.9.1.39_1, 41.

Mayo Clinic. "Borderline Personality Disorder." Accessed August 15, 2019. https://www.mayoclinic.org/diseases-conditions/borderline-personality-disorder/symptoms-causes/syc-20370237.

Mittell, Jason. *Complex TV: The Poetics of Contemporary Television Storytelling.* New York: New York University Press, 2015.

Newman, Michael Z. "The Rom-com/Sitcom/YouTube Musical: *Crazy Ex-Girlfriend.*" *Film Criticism* 40, no. 3 (2016): n.p. DOI:10.3998/fc.13761232.0040.311.

Nguyen, Hanh. "*Crazy Ex-Girlfriend* Redefined Songs in Music Comedy with One Showstopping Numbers." *IndieWire*, May 15, 2019. https://www.indiewire.com/2019/05/crazy-ex-girlfriend-rachel-bloom-11-o-clock-cw-emmys-1202141234.

Salerno, Stephanie. "'Let Us Ugly Cry': Spoofing Emotional Vulnerability in Season Three of *Crazy Ex-Girlfriend.*" In *Perspectives on "Crazy Ex-Girlfriend,"* eds. Amanda Konkle and Charles Burnett. Forthcoming.

Sedgwick, Eve Kosofvsky. *Touching Feeling: Affect, Pedagogy, Performativity.* Durham, NC: Duke University Press, 2003.

Stephens, Elizabeth. "Bad Feelings: An Affective Genealogy of Feminism." *Australian Feminist Studies* 30, no. 85 (2015): 279–280. https://doi.org/10.1080/08164649.2015.1113907.

Sternfeld, Jessica. "'Pitiful Creature of Darkness': The Subhuman and the Superhuman in *The Phantom of the Opera*," in *The Oxford Handbook of Music and Disability Studies*, edited by Blake Howe et. al, 795–814. New York: Oxford University Press, 2016: 795–814.

Tally, Margaret. *The Rise of the Anti-Heroine in TV's Third Golden Age.* Cambridge: Cambridge Scholars Publishing, 2016.

Vaage, Margrethe Bruun. *The Antihero in American Television.* New York: Routledge, 2016.

Chapter Ten

The Antiheroine and the Representation of PTSD

The Case of Jessica Jones

Anja Meyer

Netflix 2016 original series *Jessica Jones* features the story of an ex-superheroine working as a private investigator and dealing with mental health issues. Being abused by a sadistic villain who has used his mind-control powers on her, the series focuses on the protagonist's struggle to manage and overcome the symptoms of a mental stress disorder. Even though Jessica is gifted with superpowers like super strength and the ability to jump very high, they have no effect on the painful aftermath she is subjected to, which represents the most difficult enemy to fight. Thus, superhuman traits don't make Jessica a conventional heroine, as she doesn't care to save lives, but just wants to regain control of her life and stop hurting the people she loves. The complex characterization of the protagonist as a victim of rape, as well as a badass and assertive, sometimes to the point of rudeness, character with moral grey areas designates her as an antiheroine, a new female character that has recently taken the lead in many narratives, especially television shows.

Since the turn of the century, the emerging trend of the antiheroine has led to replacing conventional stereotypes of one-dimensional female roles, like the reliable wife or the virginal lover, with more complex characters, portrayed as dark, multifaceted, and challenging personalities. In "Antiheroines are the New Antiheroes"[1] Susi R. Holt describes these new characters as "the ones doing the killing instead of the dying; they are tortured souls, complicated, often difficult to stomach, yet they still remain the protagonists and drive the show's narratives, almost exclusively—much like the male-driven 'antihero' boom of the last few years."[2] The appearance of the antiheroine, therefore, coincides with the end of a number of series that are centered on male antiheroes,[3] like Tony Soprano of *The Sopranos*, Don Draper of *Mad Man*, or Walter White of *Breaking Bad*, who have been highly acclaimed for their flawed personalities capable of adapting and surviving to the contemporary broken world. Some examples of leading antiheroine characters, who have proven to be as morally corrupt and dangerous as their male counterparts, are *Nurse Jackie*, Carrie Mathison on *Homeland*, Claire Underwood on *House of Cards*, or Piper Chapman on *Orange Is the New Black*.

All these antiheroines are flawed characters, whose morality is often compromised by illicit decisions or violent behaviors adopted to come to justice or obtain something important. They usually manifest a dark side through a series of vices, such as alcohol and substance addiction, adultery, violent temper, and many others, often developed in response to past traumatic experiences. At first glance, antiheroines might seem dishonest and unreliable figures, but, as the storyline develops, spectators learn of their difficult past and the reasons behind certain unethical choices. What emerges, then, is the image of an ordinary human being committing more or less serious mistakes, but also struggling for right principles and personal redemption in the same way as spectators would do. As Michelle Juergen maintains, the rise of the antiheroine is a sign of "cultural progression" and "it's reflective of a desire to see not just 'strong female characters,' but *human* female characters, more fully knowable in their rawness and realness."[4]

In line with her precursors, the protagonist of *Jessica Jones* is portrayed from the beginning as a troubled character that has no fear to step over the boundaries of morality when, for instance, she commits crimes on several occasions. In the series, the notion of heroism is further dramatized by the fact that Jessica could have chosen to be a superheroine with superpowers, but openly rejects this label. Conversely, she has been the victim of a traumatizing abusive relationship, which has made her a disillusioned and vulnerable woman struggling to overcome the psychological aftermath of the past experiences. As a consequence, her inner turmoil finds expression through the use of crude language, severe alcohol addiction, and a generally violent temperament. All these elements reinforce Jessica's status as an antiheroine, who needs to recover from the experience of rape to reconstruct her own identity again and find the strength to face her past through the acknowledgment of her vulnerability.

In her analysis of the main characteristics of the antiheroine, Michelle Juergen affirms that the antiheroine is neither a systematically good or evil character but has qualities that enable her to do dangerous things or bad actions for a good cause. Jones, indeed, embodies traits traditionally regarded as masculine, like physical force, pride, and need for revenge that she often exhibits in borderline situations of danger or emergency. On the other hand, she also displays more common female traits, such as emotionality and vulnerability, revealing a precarious psychological state, as well as her desire to become a better person and protect the few people she trusts. While Jessica behaves as a badass in the outer world, she copes with the mental interferences of her inner traumatic memory on a path of personal growth and understanding. The experience of posttraumatic stress disorder, therefore, becomes the lens informing spectators of Jessica's inner darkness and the lasting effects of the trauma of rape.

ALIAS VS. JESSICA JONES

The character of Jessica Jones debuted in 2001 in the comic book series for mature readers, *Alias #1*[5] (2001–2004), created by Brian Michael Bendis and Michael Gaydos. The narrative is set within an expanded Marvel Universe (MU) where Jessica is a disillusioned ex-superhero turned private investigator who actively interacts with colleagues of the Avengers team, like Daredevil, Iron Man, Captain America, and Captain Marvel. Jessica is introduced to readers after having left her career of superheroine, while her past is revealed through a series of flashbacks. She was a superheroine called Jewel for several years, until she met a villain, the Purple Man/Zebediah Kilgrave, who subjugated her using his mind control. For eight months, Jessica committed crimes under the control of the Purple Man, until Captain Marvel finally saved her. Dispirited and traumatized by her experiences, Jessica decides to quit the superhero life to start her own business as a private investigator, running Alias Investigations. Throughout *Alias*, Jessica struggles to deal with her past and to reconnect with her family and friends, showing readers a Marvel Universe much closer to reality.[6]

In the comic books, Jessica is often directly confronted with the mainstream superheroines of the MU, such as Wonder Woman and She Hulk, who feature archetypal heroic qualities that Jessica misses, highlighting, in this way, her status of antiheroine. First of all, Jessica lacks the costumed identity typical of superheroes: she is instead presented from the beginning as a private investigator operating on her own in plain clothes. Moreover, the display of Jessica's lack of femininity in terms of physical appearance further distances her from the classical superheroine, who is usually depicted with a "voluptuous figure of thin waist and silicone breasts" highlighted by a "bathing costume's outfit."[7] While *Alias*'s superheroines follow the cultural paradigm of the hyper feminized woman, who is "smiley," seductive, strong, and always victorious, Jessica openly contrasts with them for her heavy drinking habits, the use of a crude language, and a complete aversion to societal conventions. Not only does she not care about other people's opinion, but she often displays a pessimistic attitude toward life, which reflects a damaged and turbulent soul-seeking for some inner peace. As Nicholas W. Moll explains, Jessica is further distinct from the archetypal superheroine because of the absence of a direct male counterpart. In many cases, superheroines "share their status and identity as characters with other male protagonists, relegating them to a market side-line,"[8] like in the cases of She-Hulk, Spider-Woman and Phoenix, who are all derived from their male counterparts in both costumes and powers. Jessica, instead, is introduced as an established character from the beginning and lacks any sense of membership to the group of superheroes surrounding her throughout *Alias*.

In 2015, Jessica's story was adapted for a Netflix TV series, *Jessica Jones*, followed by two other seasons in 2018 and 2019. Similar to *Alias*, *Jessica Jones* is set in the expanded Marvel Cinematic Universe (MCU), which includes superhero films and TV series produced by Marvel Studios. Like the source comic books, the TV series also follows the protagonist in her daily life struggling with the aftermath of abuses and traumatic experiences. However, the two narratives contrast in the way the Marvel Universe is depicted, producing different effects on the portrayal of the main protagonist. While *Alias* features a broad collection of superhero celebrities that the protagonist is often confronted with, *Jessica Jones* engages with a localized network of characters within which she is highly interwoven, like her childhood friend Trish Walker, her rival Kilgrave, and her lover Luke Cage. The expanded MU is only evoked through a series of references and allusions, while the storyline focuses on the protagonist's on-going drama of trauma.[9]

In the Netflix series, Jessica lost her family in a car accident and stayed in a coma for months. Later, she discovers she possesses superhuman abilities and considered the idea of pursuing a career as a superheroine, until the sociopath Kilgrave used his powers to control her mind: for a few months Jessica was subjected to his mental and physical abuses, until he apparently died in a bus accident, which freed her from his control. After such a traumatic experience, Jessica decided to run her own detective agency, Alias Investigations. The TV series starts after all these events, then recounts them through flashbacks.

From the first episode, the protagonist of *Jessica Jones* is presented as a lonely and tormented character. She usually works at night and has a strong addiction to alcohol, that she uses to combat the continuous and painful flashbacks she is subjected to. Even if physically superstrong, Jessica has given up using her powers to be a superheroine, choosing instead to take the law into her own hands. She has a personal opinion about justice and does not share the sense of common service toward humanity typical of superheroes. As a private investigator, she doesn't save lives, nor is she interested in doing that, but instead earns money from tracking unfaithful spouses and collaborating with a ruthless divorce lawyer. Even if profitable, it is not a job to be particularly proud of but gives Jessica the chance to work independently while struggling with the aftermath of her personal trauma at the hands of Kilgrave. Jessica has become a cynical woman with very low faith in humanity and, as her neighbour Malcolm notices, she uses sarcasm to distance herself from other people. Jessica's response to this criticism is simply "People do bad shit. I just avoid getting involved with them in the first place. That works for me. Most of the time."[10]

The question of Jessica's potential of being a superheroine is openly addressed in the fifth episode through a series of flashbacks dating back eighteen months, so before Kilgrave rapes her, showing an unsatisfied protagonist quitting yet another job because it is too boring and below her capacities. Her best friend Trish Walker, then, tries to convince her to become a superheroine and use her superpowers to save lives. Trish even invents the Jewel superheroine name for Jessica and creates a costume identical to the one seen in the comics: a revealing, tight-fitting off-the-shoulder suit, that Jessica strongly rejects because it is too ridiculous. Throughout the series, in fact, Jessica is always displayed in the sporty and comfortable attire of blue jeans, T-shirt, leather jacket, and boots, all of which she wears for all occasions; she dresses for her own comfort and does not need or want to show off her femininity, emphasizing even more distinctly her dissociation from the conventions of the superheroine world.

Although Jessica dismisses the idea of being a superheroine, one night she saves the life of a little girl almost hit by a taxi by stopping it with her superstrength. This is the first time Jessica does something heroic in her life and this event leads her to believe she might use her superpowers for doing something good in life. Later, in another flashback, Jessica saves a man from a group of muggers, which draws Kilgrave's attention to her abilities for the first time. From that moment, Jessica becomes Kilgrave's greatest obsession and the victim of his mind-control powers for the next six months. Further flashbacks show that Jessica's instinct to become a superheroine and do good was used against her by Kilgrave, who, attracted by her super abilities, starts controlling her mind to exploit her sexually and force her to do his dirty work, including killing an innocent woman. Once freed from him, Jessica abandons her ambition to become a superheroine, as she is too psychologically devastated by her experiences as a rape victim and accidental murderer. The awareness of having used her super strength to hurt people keeps haunting her and she is tortured by deep feelings of guilt.

In *Jessica Jones*, the notion of heroism is highly controversial, as the protagonist defines herself as a "tried and failed" heroine, evidencing the constant tension between her suppressed inclination to do good in the world and the realization that she might be dangerous to herself and others. Her thwarted attempt to be a superheroine is directly linked to the traumatic experience of rape, which has led Jessica to a terrible aftermath of psychological pain and torment during which she isolates herself, convinced she is dangerous to the people around her. Jessica Jones significantly differs from the ordinary Marvel superheroine: she refuses to become one of them, and rejects the idea of helping people with her superpowers, as they have proved to be useless, and even harmful, when she had found herself in real danger. Jessica is instead a complex and multifaceted antiheroine, who adopts violent behaviors and harmful addictions as means to control her life. After the traumatic events she has undergone, she feels hopelessly broken and strives to survive day after day. Having developed posttraumatic stress disorder, she first needs to fight the demons in her mind and work hard to regain control of her life before she can help others.

In both *Alias* and *Jessica Jones*, Jessica stands out in sharp contrast to the traditional conventions defining a superheroine. Both narratives address the issue of trauma, but while *Alias* contextualizes Jessica as one of many known superheroes and their own stories, *Jessica Jones* focuses on the complex characterization of Jones as a survivor of abuses and a narrow group of people directly interwoven with her personal drama. Having left behind the idea of heroic deeds, Jessica is the antiheroine seeking vengeance for herself and justice for her loved ones and who employs, when needed, deplorable methods. She faces, in the meantime, a difficult journey of psychological recovery. In this respect, Jessica appears in the TV series as a deeply human-ized character, whose superpowers are worthless in the long and painful process of healing she goes through, which is, indeed, her most difficult battle to face.

PTSD IN *JESSICA JONES*

The first season of the series *Jessica Jones* attempts to provide a realistic depiction of the effects of psychological and physical abuses on Jessica, who suffers from post-traumatic stress disorder (PTSD) as a result of the abuse in her past. PTSD is a psychiatric disorder occurring in people who have experi-enced or witnessed a traumatic event, like a serious accident, a natural disas-ter, war, rape, or other violent assaults, as well as verbal and emotional abuse.[11] It has been officially recognized as a distinct psychiatric disorder only since 1980 by the American Psychiatric Association, which has in-cluded the condition in the *Diagnostic and Statistical Manual of Mental Disorder*, third edition (*DSM-III*). PTSD was initially associated with the psychological damage caused by military battles. Symptoms of nervous dis-tress were often confined to the experiences of military soldiers, starting from the First World War, which caused a massive psychological devastation that physicians named "shell shock" and then the Second World War's "com-bat fatigue."

However, PTSD doesn't just affect veterans; it can develop in people of any gender, nationality, ethnicity, and age. As Judith Herman underlines: "Not until the women's liberation movement of the 1970s was it recognised that the most common post traumatic disorders are those not of men in work but the women in civilian life."[12] Despite PTSD traditionally being characterized as a male affliction, gender-sensitive researchers have demonstrated that women are more than twice as likely to develop PTSD and experience a longer duration of symptoms.[13] This is due to the fact that women and men go through different types of trauma, to which they also respond differently: while men are more predisposed to be involved in accidents, military combat, and natural disasters, women experience more incidents of sexual abuse and domestic violence, which makes them at higher risk of developing PTSD.[14] Despite the scientific evidence proving the gendered nature of PTSD diagnosis, mental health disorders still carry a stigma in our society, as do sexual assaults, causing survivors to feel ashamed and guilty. Very often women are further traumatized by being questioned about the credibility of the event, causing a deeper feeling of loneliness and rejection from a society that does not support them.[15]

In one sense, the media has contributed positively to the common understanding of PTSD as an actual disorder affecting different strata of people. However, for decades, narratives focused their attention on stories of male war veterans and the psychological consequences of war experience, reinforcing the general belief that PTSD could only affect a restricted number of individuals, and causing, at the same time, a stigmatization around all other people with PTSD. More recently, consideration has been given to women coping with PTSD caused by sexual assault and abuse: *Jessica Jones* is certainly one of the TV shows that has been able to humanize a psychological disorder and portray the shades of a difficult journey to healing.

The show is, in fact, about a woman's struggle to cope with a series of traumatic experiences, including being forced to do things under mind control, and the consequent difficult process of healing. In this way, *Jessica Jones* gives voice to a wide community of survivors having faced similar struggles, who have previously been marginalized by the cinematographic industry. As Kia Groom maintains: "while it masquerades as a show about heroes and villains, ultimately *Jessica Jones* is not a fantasy. It's the reality of existing in a patriarchal society that does everything it can to silence, dismiss, and ignore women—that strips power and agency from us at every conceivable level: domestically, romantically, politically, legally, and in the media."[16] Beyond the supernatural plot of mind control and superpowers lies the real struggle of a woman with psychological damage and her process of recovery. Jessica contextualizes the experience of an extensive number of women: the whole series thus reflects the experiences of abuse faced by many women around the world and the different ways they can and do cope with their trauma.[17]

Jessica survived various traumatic experiences since childhood: she lost her family in a tragic car accident and was in a coma for a prolonged period of time, she was then adopted by Trish's violent and abusive mother and then Jessica discovered her extraordinary physical abilities. Her trauma culminates with the psychological abuse and sexual assault at Kilgrave's hands, a sociopath that has used his powers to manipulate Jessica's mind.[18] Additionally, other women characters also survive trauma, such as Jessica's best friend Trish, was the victim of a violent mother, and Hope, another of Kilgrave's victims who, like Jessica, suffers from distress following the recent physical and psychological abuses by Kilgrave. Kilgrave has, in fact, recreated with Hope the same abusive relationship he once had with Jessica, hoping to draw Jessica's attention and eventually regain control over her. The fact that Jessica is the only one who believes Hope's story evidences the skepticism that many abused women have to face when recounting violence they have experienced. Each of these characters painfully goes through different stages of trauma, to which they respond in different ways.

NARRATIVE FLASHBACKS

Beginning from the first episode of *Jessica Jones* the technique of flashbacks is extensively adopted to let the audience discover the protagonist's past and, above all, to display her traumatic memories. Flashbacks, in this sense, are used to visually perform one of the primary diagnostic features of PTSD as described in the *Diagnostic and Statistical Manual of Mental Disorder*, fifth edition (*DSM-V*):

> The individual may experience these dissociative states that last from a few seconds to several hours or even days, during which components of the event are relived and the individual behaves as if the event were occurring at the moment. Such events occur on a continuum from brief visual or other sensory loss of awareness of present surroundings. These episodes, often referred to as "flashbacks," are typically brief but can be associated with prolonged distress and heightened arousal.[19]

Every filmic flashback is therefore specifically related to the inner, subjective world of Jessica, showing the continuous eruption of painful memories into her present. This narrative choice provides the audience with a sense of closeness and growing empathy to the main protagonist, but it also displays a mediated reality through the eyes of a slightly unreliable narrator.[20] As trauma theorist Cathy Caruth maintains: "the painful repetition of the flashback can only be understood as the absolute inability of the mind to avoid an unpleasurable event that has not been given psychic meaning in any way."[21] The sudden, pervasive return of disruptive memories is often uncontrollable and leaves both the protagonist and the audience in a state of confusion, which is itself a typical symptom of PTSD.

The first episode of *Jessica Jones* establishes trauma as an ever-present reality in the protagonist's life. In the opening scene, Jessica sits on a fire escape during a late shift of private investigation and trains her camera lens on various windows of a building across the street, until she stops on a man standing at the window and staring out, maybe at her. In that moment Jessica closes her eyes and experiences a vision of a man, later known as Kilgrave, whose voice whispers to her: "You want to do it. You know you do,"[22] causing a panic attack. She tries to calm down by repeating the street names from her childhood, a sort of mantra learned from her therapist that permits her to breathe slowly. Right after, she drinks a swig of whisky taken from a thermos. Later in the same episode, Jessica, who has presumably passed out drunk, suffers from another panic attack when a man appears close to her and aggressively licks the side of her face. Jessica gets immediately up and recites again the names of the streets in an attempt to return to reality. Even later, Jessica is driven to a restaurant by Hope, another of Kilgrave's young victims. Jessica recognizes the restaurant, triggering another flashback revealing Kilgrave as the rapist who often brought Jones to this restaurant in the period he subjugated her. Even if in the first episode the public is unaware of the protagonist's past vicissitudes, it becomes immediately clear that Jessica is tormented by the ghosts of a painful and agonizing past. Flashback scenes abruptly interrupt the linear flow of narration without explaining what has triggered them: cause-effect relations are replaced with fragmented pieces of information that the audience must link together in an attempt to find a logical meaning. Spectators are often left in a state of disorientation, being frustrated by the absence of any rational clarification: in this way, they are forced to experience the same disruptive moments of dissociation from reality faced by the protagonist herself.[23]

The audience learns of the protagonist's psychological disorder when Trisha Walker, Jessica's best friend, explicitly links the flashbacks to PTSD in a conversation with her during the first episode: "This is just your PTSD. . . . Are you still having nightmares? Flashbacks?"[24] Immediately after, she also suggests Jessica return to therapy. The explicit mention of PTSD is essential to inform spectators about a key element defining the protagonist's personality, as well as to connect the sudden eruption of flashbacks on the screen to her subjective experience of trauma. PTSD, therefore, becomes a key element and the lens for the audience to understand the recursive incursion of Jessica's past on the present storyline,[25] as well as to explain Jessica's condition as antiheroine. In the same conversation, in fact, the audience also learns of Jessica's brief past experience as superheroine, which abruptly failed once she fell under Kilgrave's control. "Tried and failed. . . . I was never the hero that you wanted me to be,"[26] says Jessica to Trisha, evidencing the frustration for not being able to control her powers to be a force for good and, instead, being forced to use them to harm others following Kilgrave's orders. Kilgrave's sabotage of Jessica's attempt to become a superheroine was painful, and the sense of guilt arising from such an experience contributed to Jessica's development of PTSD. The intrusion of trauma in Jessica's life has, therefore, subverted Jessica's potential heroism into feelings of anger, fear, and vengeance, which reflect the complex inner turmoil of an antiheroine and the constant tension between the inclination to behave well and her low capacity to control the violent reactions triggered by the painful injuries left from the past.

The ways flashbacks are presented throughout the series by intruding into the narrative not only reflect the disruptive nature of traumatic memories, but they also indicate different levels of elaboration of trauma into the protagonist's mind. Thus, there are moments in which the protagonist cannot remember certain memories, like her family's deadly car accident, and others in which she chooses not to remember. When Jessica is confronted with memories of Kilgrave in the period under his domination, filmic devices such as "discordant soundscapes, rapid zooming out, and disconcerting light effects"[27] reinforce the violent and painful nature of such remembrances, disturbing the viewer in the same way they disturb the protagonist. These flashbacks, usually featuring Kilgrave either whispering to Jessica or being inappropriately intimate with her, are introduced through sudden, intermittent lighting, shifting to purple in a foggy and dark atmosphere. The superimposition of the frames over the timeline reveals their uncontrollable nature, which neither Jessica nor the audience can escape. Spectators quickly learn that purple is the color used to indicate the eruption of Kilgrave memories in Jessica's mind, as evidenced in the flashbacks of the first episode with the purple lighting in the back of the restaurant *Il Rosso*, where Kilgrave used to bring Jessica. When she gets to the back room, Jessica sees herself having dinner with her rapist, who is only revealed from the back, in a completely purple room. For a few moments, present and past overlap and the audience is left in a state of bewilderment. In another scene, Jessica is walking along the corridor of the hotel where Kilgrave imprisoned her and, while the fire alarm is ringing, white flashes of light blink around her. As she approaches the room where she believes to find Kilgrave, the appearance of flashes of purple light anticipate the manifestation of a new traumatic memory: once inside the room, the shadow of a man suddenly appears close to Jessica whispering, "You miss me?" The man disappears in a moment, while Jessica and the audience are left terrified like they were in a horror movie.

In addition to the intrusive memories of sexual assault, which appear painfully beyond Jessica's control, other traumatic events are recalled in the form of flashbacks throughout the series. Episodes like the tragic car accident involving Jessica's family or the murder of Reva Connors keep haunting her mind. Despite their profound traumatic nature, Jessica consciously works on these memories in an attempt to understand what actually happened and to cautiously regain control of her life. The advancement of Jessica's interior journey is proven by the repeated visual sequences evoking the past incidents, which get progressively longer as the series advances to the point of providing a coherent narration of the events.[28] This is what happens, for instance, with the flashbacks related to the tragic car accident that Jessica inadvertently caused provoking the death of her parents and her brother. At the beginning of the series, some unclear glimpses recalling the tragic event are presented to the audience, but they are still too painful to be rationally interpreted by Jessica. Such flashes repetitively return to Jessica's mind, and, as the story progresses, they develop into longer clips and acquire narrative power, as they increasingly show more accurately what has happened, eventually revealing the complete tragedy, as well as the moment in which Jessica distracted her father causing the fatal accident. This process of narrative revelation symbolizes Jessica's inner journey of recovery toward the gradual acceptance of her sense of guilt. In the final episode, furthermore, the intrusion of the past through the flashback technique is subverted by Jessica herself, who decides to consciously recall the past and remember the moments of preparation for the car trip with her family in the childhood home before the accident.[29]

Another example of the way flashbacks burst into Jessica's daily life is the recurring memory of the death of Reva Connors, a woman that Jones was forced to kill under Kilgrave's control years earlier. This moment is triggered different times throughout the series to emphasise Jessica's traumatic reliving, but the most significant flashbacks occur in the third episode, when Jessica is with Luke Cage at his apartment.[30] Cage is the anonymous man staring at the window in the first episode who Jessica spies with her camera during a night shift. Over the course of the series, Jessica gets sentimentally involved with Luke. One day, while in his apartment, she opens a bathroom cabinet and finds herself unintentionally face to face with a picture of Reva, who happens to be Cage's wife. The image immediately triggers a flashback: the chronological narration of the present suddenly stops and Jessica sees, together with the audience, a short close-up of Reva falling backward in slow motion for a couple of seconds. While images of the same flashback have already emerged different times in the first episodes without any explanation, on this occasion Jessica and the audience are able to link different narrative elements in order to find a meaning for what has happened. Later, in the same episode, Jessica manages to save another victim of Kilgrave's power, policeman Simpson, from jumping off a balcony. In that moment she suddenly finds herself face-to-face with her rapist for the first time since her escape and the two look into each other's eyes, separated only by a glass window. This defining moment triggers an important extensive flashback: the audience is suddenly brought to the past watching Jessica, who, driven by Kilgrave, uses her super-strength to punch Reva to death.[31] It thus becomes clear that the prior flashes portraying Reva falling backward correspond to Jessica's perspective in the moment she attacks her and that such an action was induced by Kilgrave's mind control. The flashback, in this case, gives a clear depiction of the facts, demonstrating the possibility of the traumatic mind to gain more control over certain memories that have been gradually elaborated. Not only has Jessica come face to face with Kilgrave, her biggest source of trauma, after many years, but she is also becoming more willing to face the past and evoke what happened to her as well as how she acted.

RECOVERING FROM PTSD

During the course of the series, the development of flashbacks and the ways Jessica reacts to them show a gradual improvement of her mental health, but also confirm the arduous and intermittent process of healing for PTSD patients, who alternate moments of apparent recovery with moments of violent disruption of symptoms like depression. According to research on PTSD, taking control and confronting the past traumatic events allow patients to deal with their condition.[32] The need to gain control is, indeed, one of the main issues of the TV series, as it focuses on Jessica's progressive, and very human, handling of her traumatic experiences, rather than relying on her superhuman powers, in order to regain control of her life. Since the beginning of the series, Jessica's initial attitude of complete rejection toward her inner demons slowly evolves into the painful acknowledgment of her past, which is the starting point of the healing process for PTSD. In the first episode, Jessica wants nothing more than to escape from Kilgrave, both mentally and physically. Once she learns that her rapist is still alive, Jessica's first reaction is to plan to move far away. However, when she finds out that Kilgrave is victimizing another girl, Hope, in the same way as he did with her, Jessica decides to stay and face him rather than to escape.[33]

In the following episodes, Jessica understands that she will not be able to defeat Kilgrave on her own, but only if she accepts help from other people, like her best friend Trish. Even if she has isolated herself for a long time in an attempt to protect the few people she loves, Jessica slowly learns to open up, explaining what happened to her and seeking help. In this context, Kilgrave is not only Jessica's rapist, but he symbolically represents the physical and psychological abuses that women often experience. Seeking help and openly talking to someone trustworthy is another important step in the recovery process of PTSD and Jessica is trying to make such an effort. In the third episode, Jessica is even able to look into Kilgrave's eyes without running away, while certain flashbacks become increasingly clearer to her, as a sign that she is becoming more willing to face her past.

Despite the improvements, Jessica's healing process is difficult and characterized by many relapses. Besides the continuous appearance of disturbing flashes into Jessica's mind, she becomes violent on different occasions and gives rein to her repressed anger through her superhuman strength. Moreover, Jessica has developed a strong addiction to alcohol, consumed in high quantities throughout the series as a way to cope with symptoms of depression and intrusive memories.[34] She is frequently seen drinking different types of liquor and always brings with her a flask of whiskey that she uses as a suppressive antidote in critical moments. Jessica admits her tendency to drink alcohol for its palliative effects, which allows her to react and be operative.[35] Her dependency intensifies when she loses control of various aspects of her life, like in the central episodes of the series, when Kilgrave literally takes possession of her childhood home. The symbolic import of such an action is immense as Jessica loses control over her past that should have remained private and untouchable. Not surprisingly, in the following episode she is presented as the stereotypical alcoholic kicked out of a bar for excessive drinking and ending up on a pile of trash.[36] Jessica's alcoholism is a self-destructive behavior strongly associated with PTSD, as it provides a short-term relief to moments of serious distress, but becomes harmful and addictive in the long term.

Despite her self-destructive ways to deal with her disease, Jessica's psychological evolution progresses when, in the eighth episode, Kilgrave lures her into her childhood home and she is forced to confront a past she has always tried to repress. The audience is thus presented with a series of traumatic moments revealing Jessica's past through her eyes: the death of her family, the separation from her home and her fascination for Kilgrave. Such memories superimpose themselves in nonsequential and fragmented succession, colliding in time and space, giving spectators the idea of the recursive experience of trauma as a cyclical process. In this context, Kilgrave tells Jessica about his tragic childhood and tries to convince her that he did not rape her. Even if in a moment of extreme psychological weakness, Jessica still chooses not to trust him. At this point, she is less scared of her past and has gained more control over herself, while her choices are gradually more rational.

In the last episode, Jessica doesn't hesitate to use violence against Kilgrave and eventually kills her nemesis by snapping his neck. Even as she physically gets rid of the source of her most traumatic experiences, she cannot feel relieved, as she has not come to terms with her inner demons and still has to deal with the long-lasting effects of PTSD. In a narrative voice-over accompanying the closing scenes of the last episode, Jessica recalls the discourse on heroism just mentioned in the first episode and reflects upon the fine line distinguishing heroes from villains: "They say everyone's born a hero. But if you let it, life will push you over the line until you're the villain. Problem is, you don't always know that you've crossed that line. Maybe it's enough that the world thinks I'm a hero. Maybe, if I work long and hard maybe I can fool myself."[37] Jessica has just been released from the police after Kilgrave's death, and even if this episode could mark the start of a brilliant superheroine career, she still feels skeptical about her relationship with heroism. There is no hint of satisfaction or relief on her face, as Kilgrave's death has neither erased her PTSD, nor her sense of guilt for hurting innocent people. Jessica has to keep fighting the demons of her mind like before, while trying to focus on how to get through every day. In the concluding scenes of the series, Jessica gets back to her everyday life in her office of investigations. While she systematically deletes many voice messages of potential clients seeking her help, spectators are left with the image of an overwhelmed Jones sitting at her desk, pouring a mugful of whiskey in a cup and staring at nothing, incapable of reacting to the events around her. While the incessant and overlapping calls for help seem to recall the overwhelming incursion of trauma into her life, the final images of Jessica confirm her status as antiheroine, evidencing, in particular, the psychological isolation and inner sense of despair of those suffering from PTSD.

PTSD is inserted in the wider reflection on heroism, which frames the whole series with the initial and final considerations of Jessica, who feels that life has "pushed [her] over the line" and she still needs to work hard on herself to recover from the traumatic experience of rape. By eschewing common superheroine tropes like secret identity, costume, and self-sacrifice for the weakest, Jessica is identified as an antiheroine. The prefix "anti," however, does not imply a negation of her potential heroism, but rather another version of it. Her violent temper and ambiguous morality, in fact, are the result of a series of overwhelming situations she has undergone, that have not yet erased her inner inclination at doing something good. In the course of the series, in fact, she tries to save Hope from Kilgrave's power, and is very protective of Trisha, both of whom are fellow survivors. The fact that Jessica has superpowers, then, doesn't automatically turn her into a superheroine, but demonstrates how PTSD and other psychological disorders might affect anyone, even those individuals considered stronger and more successful in a society. Her "failed" heroism is thus related to the overwhelming effects of PTSD, but it also entails the protagonist's attempt to gradually recover despite her psychological pain. Jessica, therefore, is an antiheroine not only for her heavy drinking, crude language, and use of violence, but mostly because she struggles to and succeeds at showing her vulnerability and fallibility, she revealed her darkest sides, and still fought to improve her personal situation by learning to deal with the effects of trauma in her life. Her last words in the series suggest that she is willing to "work long and hard" to get better and become a stronger person, maybe failing again, but having at least tried.

Jessica Jones can be considered today one of the most complex treatments of PTSD affecting women in a TV series. Unlike most filmic narrations dealing with rape, the series never explicitly shows any scene of sexual assault, but only makes references to it, in order to concentrate on the terrible long-term aftermath. The fact that the show chooses to focus on what happens after rape instead of the act itself is an important step of responsible storytelling, since not only does it mirror what commonly happens in real life, but it also confers a renovated awareness of the societal perception of trauma.[38] Both Jessica and the other survivors of traumatic events, symbolically embodied in the character of Kilgrave, are given space to process their grief and, as the show itself demonstrates, the long journey to healing is made of psychological distress that each individual faces differently and with disparate results.

NOTES

1. Susi Rose Holt, "Antiheroines Are the New Antiheroes: The Killer Women of *Penny Dreadful*, *Orphan Black* and More," *Indie Wire*, June 3, 2015, https://www.indiewire.com/2015/06/antiheroines-are-the-new-antiheroes-the-killer-women-of-penny-dreadful-orphan-black-and-more-61307/.

2. Holt, "Antiheroines are the New Antiheroes."

3. Holt, "Antiheroines are the New Antiheroes," 5.

4. Holt, "Antiheroines are the New Antiheroes," 5.

5. Brian Michael Bendis and Michael Gaydos, *Alias #1–#28* (New York: MAX 2001–2004).

6. Mike Delaney, "A Brief Comic Book History of Jessica Jones," *Fandom*, March 13, 2018, https://www.fandom.com/articles/the-defenders-look-back-jessica-jones.

7. Richard Reynolds, *Superheroes: A Modern Mythology* (Jackson: University Press of Mississippi, 1992), 12–16.

8. Nicholas William Moll, "Elite and Famous. Subverting Gender in the Marvel Universe with *Jessica Jones*," in *"Jessica Jones" Scarred Superhero*, eds. Tim Rayborn and Abigail Keyes (Jefferson, NC: McFarland & Company, 2018), 31.

9. Nicholas William Moll, "Elite and Famous," 29–30.

10. *Jessica Jones*, "AKA Ladies Night," directed by S. J. Clarkson, written by Melissa Rosenberg.

11. American Psychiatric Association, available at: https://www.psychiatry.org/patients-families/ptsd/what-is-ptsd. The symptoms affecting people with PTSD are of various kinds and intensity. According to the American Psychiatric Association they can be divided into four main groups: (1) intrusive thoughts, such as repeated, involuntary memories, distressing dreams, or flashbacks of the traumatic event; (2) avoiding reminders of the traumatic event may include avoiding people, places, activities, objects and situations that bring on distressing memories; (3) negative thoughts and feelings may include on-going and distorted beliefs about oneself or others, on-going fear, horror, anger, guilt or shame; (4) arousal and reactive symptoms may include being irritable and having angry outbursts, behaving recklessly or in a self-destructive way; being easily startled, or having problems concentrating or sleeping.

12. Judith Herman, *Trauma and Recovery: The Aftermath of Violence—From Domestic Abuse to Political Terror* (New York: Basic Book, 2015), 28.

13. David F. Tolin and Edna B. Foa, "Sex Differences in Trauma and Posttraumatic Stress Disorder: A Quantitative Review of 25 Years of Research," *Psychological Bulletin* 132 (2006): 959–992.

14. Melanie Greenberg, "Why Women Have Higher Rates of PTSD than Men," *Psychology Today*, September 25, 2018, https://www.psychologytoday.com/us/blog/the-mindful-self-express/201809/why-women-have-higher-rates-ptsd-men.

15. Beverly Engel, "Why Don't Victims of Sexual Harassment Come Forward Sooner?" *Psychology Today*, November 16, 2017, https://www.psychologytoday.com/us/blog/the-compassion-chronicles/201711/why-dont-victims-sexual-harassment-come-forward-sooner.

16. Kia Groom, "So You Married a Supervillain: Watching *Jessica Jones* as a Trauma Survivor," *The Mary Sue*, December 17, 2015, https://www.themarysue.com/watching-jessica-jones-as-a-trauma-survivor/.

17. Carrie Lynn D. Reinhard and Christopher J. Olson, "Aka Marvel Does Darkness," in *"Jessica Jones" Scarred Superhero* (Jefferson, NC: McFarland & Company, 2018), eds. Tim Rayborn and Abigail Keyes, 83–104, 88.

18. Janis Breckenridge, "Sobriety Blows: Whiskey, Trauma, and Coping in Netflix's *Jessica Jones*," in *"Jessica Jones" Scarred Superhero*, eds. Tim Rayborn and Abigail Keyes (Jefferson, NC: McFarland & Company, 2018), 105–120, 105.

19. American Psychiatric Association, *Diagnostic and Statistical Manual of Mental Disorders: DSM-V-TR* (Washington, DC: American Psychiatric Association, 2013), 275.

20. Melissa Wehler, "The Haunted Hero—The Performance of Trauma in *Jessica Jones*" in *"Jessica Jones" Scarred Superhero*, eds. Tim Rayborn and Abigail Keyes (Jefferson, NC: McFarland & Company, 2018), 145–160, 150.

21. Cathy Caruth, *Unclaimed Experience: Trauma, Narrative, and History* (Baltimore: Johns Hopkins University Press, 1996), 59.

22. *Jessica Jones*, "AKA The Sandwich Saved Me," directed by S. J. Clarkson, written by Melissa Rosenberg.

23. Melissa Wehler, "The Haunted Hero," 149.

24. *Jessica Jones*, "AKA Ladies Night," directed by S. J. Clarkson, written by Melissa Rosenberg.

25. Melissa Wehler, "The Haunted Hero," 149.

26. *Jessica Jones*, "AKA Ladies Night," directed by S. J. Clarkson, written by Melissa Rosenberg.

27. Breckenridge, "Sobriety Blows," 115.

28. Breckenridge, "Sobriety Blows," 116.

29. Breckenridge, "Sobriety Blows," 116.

30. In *Alias*, the relationship of Jessica Jones and Luke Cage is introduced in the first issue, when they meet in a bar and sleep together. Luke Cage is a well-known superhero named Power Man and the first to whom Jessica confesses her past traumatic history of mind control under Kilgrave/the Purple Man. The mutual physical attraction develops into a serious relationship, which culminates with Jessica expecting a baby. The two decide to move in together and eventually get married, building a life together. Netflix's *Jessica Jones* only touches the beginning of the relationship, when the two start a physical intimate relationship after having met in the bar where Luke works as bartender. The two get even closer when they find out about each other's superpowers (Cage has unbreakable skin) and seem to start a relationship together. However, Cage is then forced to break up with Jessica when he finds out that she was involved in the murder of his wife Reva in the period under the influence of Kilgrave.

31. Wehler, "The Haunted Hero," 156.

32. Patricia A. Frazier, Heather Mortensen, and Jason Steward, "Coping Strategies as Mediators of the Relations among Perceived Control and Distress in Sexual Assault Survivors," *Journal of Counseling Psychology* 52, no. 3 (2005): 275.

33. Carrie Lynn D. Reinhard and Christopher J. Olson, "Aka Marvel Does Darkness," 91.

34. Researches have proven that survivors of sexual abuse and rape present a greater use of alcohol to manage trauma-related symptoms like intrusive memories and dissociation.

35. Breckenridge, "Sobriety Blows," 108.
36. Breckenridge, "Sobriety Blows," 114.
37. *Jessica Jones*, "AKA Ladies Night," directed by S. J. Clarkson, written by Melissa Rosenberg
38. Shauna Murphy, "Why *Jessica Jones* Chooses to Tell and Not Show When It Comes to Sexual Violence," *MTV*, September 24, 2015, http://www.mtv.com/news/2545598/jessica-jones-sexual-violence-david-tennant-interview/.

BIBLIOGRAPHY

American Psychiatric Association. *Diagnostic and Statistical Manual of Mental Disorders: DSM-V-TR.* Washington, DC: American Psychiatric Association, 2013.
Bedingfield, Will. "Why We're Destined to Sympathize with Anti-Heroes Like the Jocker." *Wired*, October 5, 2019. https://www.wired.co.uk/article/the-joker-movie-review.
Breckenridge, Janis. "Sobriety Blows. Whiskey, Trauma, and Coping in Netflix's Jessica Jones." In *Jessica Jones Scarred Superhero*, edited by Tim Rayborm and Abigail Keyes, 105–120. Jefferson, NC: Mc Farland & Company, 2018.
Brombert, Victor. *In Praise of Antiheroes. Figures and Themes in Modern European Literature 1830–1980.* Chicago/London: The University of Chicago Press, 1999.
Brunsdon, Charlotte. *Screen Tastes: Soap Opera to Satellite Dishes.* London/New York: Routledge, 2005.
Caruth, Cathy. *Unclaimed Experience: Trauma, Narrative, and History.* Baltimore: Johns Hopkins University Press, 1996.
Delaney, Mike. "A Brief Comic Book History of Jessica Jones." *Fandom*, March 13, 2018. https://www.fandom.com/articles/the-defenders-look-back-jessica-jones.
Frazier, Patricia A., Heather Mortensen, and Jason Steward. "Coping Strategies as Mediators of the Relations among Perceived Control and Distress in Sexual Assault Survivors." *Journal of Counseling Psychology* 52.3 (2005): 267–278.
Groom, Kia. "So You Married a Supervillain: Watching *Jessica Jones* as a Trauma Survivor," *The Mary Sue*, December 17, 2015. https://www.themarysue.com/watching-jessica-jones-as-a-trauma-survivor/.
Herman, Judith. *Trauma and Recovery: The Aftermath of Violence—From Domestic Abuse to Political Terror.* New York: Basic Book, 2015.
Holt, Susi Rose. "Antiheroines Are the New Antiheroes: The Killer Women of *Penny Dreadful, Orphan Black* and More," *Indie Wire*, June 3, 2015. https://www.indiewire.com/2015/06/antiheroines-are-the-new-antiheroes-the-killer-women-of-penny-dreadful-orphan-black-and-more-61307/.
Juergen, Michelle. "Why Critics Can't Handle the Female Anti-Hero." *Mic*, January 15, 2014. https://www.mic.com/articles/79047/why-critics-can-t-handle-the-female-anti-hero.
Moll, Nicholas William. "Elite and Famous. Subverting Gender in the Marvel Universe with *Jessica Jones*." In *"Jessica Jones" Scarred Superhero*, edited by Tim Rayborm and Abigail Keyes, 28–43. Jefferson, NC: Mc Farland & Company, 2018.
Murphy, Shauna. "Why *Jessica Jones* Chooses to Tell and Not Show When It Comes to Sexual Violence." *MTV*, September 24, 2015. http://www.mtv.com/news/2545598/jessica-jones-sexual-violence-david-tennant-interview/.
Packard, Cooper. "A Love-Hate Relationship: Television's Anti-Hero Archetype Reflects Society." *The De Paulia*, October 12, 2014. https://depauliaonline.com/4451/artslife/a-love-hate-relationship-televisions-anti-hero-archetype-reflects-society/.
Reinhard, Carrie Lynn D. and Christopher J. Olson. "Aka Marvel Does Darkness." In *"Jessica Jones" Scarred Superhero*, edited by Tim Rayborn and Abigail Keyes, 83, 104. Jefferson, NC: McFarland & Company, 2018.
Reynolds, Richard. *Superheroes: A Modern Mythology.* Jackson: University Press of Mississippi, 1992.

Rosenberg, Alyssa. "Why We'll Never Have a Female Tony Soprano." *Slate*, June 27, 2013. https://slate.com/human-interest/2013/06/james-gandolfini-and-the-male-anti-hero-why-well-never-have-a-female-tony-soprano.html.

Spivey, Knowlton. "Anti-Heroism in the Continuum of Good and Evil." In *The Psychology of Superheroes: An Unauthorized Exploration*, edited by Robin S. Rosenberg, 51–63. Dallas: BenBella Books, 2008.

Tally, Margaret. *The Rise of the Anti-Heroine in TV's Third Golden Age.* Newcastle-Upon-Tyne: Cambridge Scholars Publishing, 2016.

Tolin, David F. and Edna B. Foa. "Sex Differences in Trauma and Posttraumatic Stress Disorder: A Quantitative Review of 25 Years of Research." *Psychological Bulletin* 132 (2006): 959–992.

Wehler, Melissa. "The Haunted Hero—The Performance of Trauma in *Jessica Jones*." In *"Jessica Jones" Scarred Superhero*, edited by Tim Rayborn and Abigail Keyes, 145–160. Jefferson, NC: McFarland & Company, 2018.

Chapter Eleven

"Small-Breasted Psycho"

Debunking the Female Psychopath in Killing Eve

Siobhan Lyons

In the very first episode of the sleeper hit BBC series *Killing Eve*, the eccentric antagonist Villanelle, an assassin, is initially characterized by a male character in the show simply as a "small-breasted psycho," though she herself later observes that "psychopath" is a "stupid word." According to the *DSM-V* (*Diagnostic and Statistical Manual of Mental Disorders*, fifth edition), "lack of empathy, inflated self-appraisal, and superficial charm are features that have been commonly included in traditional conceptions of psychopathy."[1] Villanelle is particularly charming, has an inflated ego, and is shown to lack empathy in most (but not all) of her murders. Psychopathy also includes "high levels of attention seeking,"[2] which also applies to Villanelle, who uses murder to purposefully and playfully attract the attention of special intelligence forces and, eventually, to attract Eve's attention alone. After brazenly killing a number of high-profile targets, Villanelle finds herself in a borderline sexual cat-and-mouse game with MI6 agent Eve Polastri, whose own behavior increasingly mirrors Villanelle's.

Villanelle's world is largely determined by masculine power, notably her older male employer whom she frequently disobeys but who also acts as an unconventional father figure to her. Villanelle never inquires into the reasons behind her assassinations, and yet she is not at all passive in carrying out her role. Villanelle craves autonomy from her employers, but also indulges in the material comforts her job affords her. Moreover, her relationships with men and women abandon any sense of gender conformity. Unlike the antiheroes we are accustomed to seeing in television (straight married men like Tony Soprano, Don Draper, and Walter White), Villanelle is a bisexual, unattached woman. And unlike Soprano and White, who express reluctance about killing women, Villanelle has no qualms at all about killing men or women, expressing indifference about both the sexual and social expectations that govern society, wherein women killing other women is seen to be unthinkable.

Like Villanelle, Eve is also initially working for a man, who she frequently disobeys, before Villanelle murders him in the third episode. Already seen as an eccentric character by her husband and colleagues (she is blunt in social circles, frequently frazzled, and admires the skills of assassins in the same way that Villanelle does), Eve's behavior throughout the first and second seasons becomes increasingly "erratic" according to her friends, family, and coworkers as she becomes ever more obsessed with Villanelle's world of unconventional antics that affront the status quo for women and society at large. Because of Villanelle's own freedom in her life, she represents, for Eve, a degree of liberation not found in conventional society, and Eve eventually finds herself torn between the excitement that her job of hunting assassins offers her and the expectations of her loving husband for her to be normal.

This chapter looks at how *Killing Eve* challenges the characterization of women and psychopaths in contemporary culture; while Eve is characterized as "normal," her own behavior mirrors the more "unstable" behavior of Villanelle, showing that just as normality is relative, the term "psychotic" is erroneously used to describe complex women. While much has been written on antiheroines in recent scholarship, this chapter looks at how ideations that separate the "sane" woman from the "insane" psychopath reveal that ideas about "good" and "bad" women are constantly evolving, with both Villanelle and Eve fitting the description of "antiheroine" despite these two women supposedly representing opposite ends of the villain/hero scale.

THE "STRONG FEMALE CHARACTER" PARADOX

Unlike a number of well-known antiheroes such as Tony Soprano and Walter White, Villanelle is under no delusions about her status as a "bad person." In the first season finale of *Killing Eve*, Villanelle has kidnapped the young daughter of her handler, Konstantin, who asks her: "Are you a bad person?" Villanelle nonchalantly nods and replies "Yep."[3] While Tony Soprano famously defended his actions and believed himself to be more or less good, Villanelle understands that she is not a good person, but nevertheless maintains that the word "psychopath" does not sufficiently capture her psychology, even if she understands that that is the way that Eve and special intelligence see her. In one episode, Villanelle chastises Eve for using the word "psychopath" to describe her, saying: "You should never tell a psychopath they are a psychopath, it upsets them," suggesting that Villanelle does, indeed, acknowledge that she is considered a psychopath by those who come into contact with her. Yet she tells Eve that psychopath is a "stupid word,"[4] while also observing that so-called good, "normal" people are more than capable of doing evil things, saying: "you can see scary people a mile away, [but] it's the good people you have to worry about."[5] Thus, while Villanelle understands that she is a "bad person," she appears to consider herself too complex and interesting a person to be lumped into the psychopath category. In other words, while she acts in ways that can be deemed psychotic (murdering without remorse, manipulating people, possessing violent tendencies), Villanelle believes that she is more than just a psychopath. Eve, too, shares this assessment, calling Villanelle (in addition to a psychopath), "exceptionally bright, determined, hard-working," and "an extraordinary person."[6]

For years, television that highlighted charming antiheroes focused uniformly on men: Tony Soprano (*The Sopranos*), Walter White (*Breaking Bad*), Don Draper (*Mad Men*), Jimmy McNulty (*The Wire*), and Jimmy McGill (*Better Call Saul*), among many others. In the last few years, however, audiences have been provided with more complex female characters. Lauren Sarner calls Cersei Lannister of *Game of Thrones* "TV's greatest female anti-hero";[7] while Amanda DiPaolo argues that *Westworld*'s Dolores Abernathy: "transforms herself from the damsel in distress to a hyper-violent character who indiscriminately kills both humans and hosts alike," becoming "a villain or an antihero at best."[8]

Killing Eve has been praised for abandoning stereotypical portrayals of women. In her analysis of the SBS series *Dead Lucky*, Aimee Knight argues: "When it comes to representing gender and culture, *Dead Lucky* has the quantity but not the quality of a contemporaneous show like BBC America's *Killing Eve*."[9] *Killing Eve*, she says, "embraces the ever-so-camp aesthetic of its forebears like *Honey West* [and] is chock-full of strong, flawed, funny, weird, difficult, multidimensional women, which explains its laudatory reception from critics and audiences alike."

Killing Eve neither relies on standard depictions of women, nor does it attempt to merely flip gender binaries, as Chris Carter did with *The X-Files*. The character Dana Scully (Gillian Anderson) was initially celebrated for her appeals to logic over emotion, known as "The Scully Effect,"[10] which influenced many women who pursued STEM careers. But Anderson, as well as a number of critics, crucially pointed out the flaws in Scully's "strong woman" demeanor. Inkoo Kang, for instance, wrote of the show's "compromised feminism," which oscillates between celebrating gender equality and reverting to stereotypical tropes:

> Sure, the premise of *The X-Files* meant that Mulder needed a skeptic to play off of. But it's impossible to ignore that the show essentially set up a (highly educated) woman to be proven wrong, week after week, year after year. In her most extreme depictions, as in "syzygy" and the unreliably narrated "Bad

Blood," she's portrayed as not only the spoilsport to Mulder's soulful quester, but a nagging scold. In many other episodes, Scully simply became a damsel for Mulder to rescue, or was denied the glimpses of the paranormal that Mulder witnessed via a blow to the head. [11]

Similarly, Anderson observed that Mulder was proven right "98 percent of the time," while the "stories center around his version of things." [12] Moreover, Inkoo notes that Scully's "depth of characterisation" was lacking, as the creators confused strength with stubbornness. Carrie Fisher observed this approach to strong female leads when discussing her most famous character, Princess Leia, saying: "The only way they knew to make the character strong was to make her angry," [13] while also noting that the way the writers made her more "feminine" was to "have her take off her clothes," [14] a feature that appeared in the very first episode of *X-Files*, when Scully disrobes down to her underwear. For all the pretence of feminist strength circulating around Scully, her role habitually reverted to female stereotypes.

Tasha Robinson calls this the "strong female character" trope, or "Trinity syndrome" from the character of the same name in *The Matrix* trilogy. Trinity syndrome relates to strong female characters who are introduced in films and television before being demoted to a subservient role for the male protagonist, calling the phrase "more a marketing term than a meaningful goal." [15] She further argues that: "Even when strong, confident female characters do manage to contribute to a male-led action story, their contributions are still more likely to be marginal, or relegated entirely to nurturer roles, or victim roles, or romantic roles." [16]

As Sophia McDougall argues, "part of the patronising promise of the Strong Female Character is that she's anomalous." [17] McDougall contends that while strong female characters are increasingly apparent in popular culture, their roles do not tend to expand beyond this view of the steely, stoic woman. While male characters, she argues, can be "solitary," "manipulative," "neurotic," "rude," "abrasive," "brilliant," "vain," "whimsical," and "genius," women are now merely offered so-called better roles under the guise of "strong" female leads, which further narrows the scope of the female character: "Nowadays the princesses all know kung fu, and yet they're still the same princesses. They're still love interests, still the one girl in a team of five boys, and they're all kind of the same. . . . Their strength lets them, briefly, dominate bystanders but never dominate the plot." [18]

In *Killing Eve*, Eve Polastri and Villanelle are not merely "strong" female characters. They are both amusing, as well as being odd, driven, fashionable, vain, mischievous, intelligent, resourceful, deceptive, secretive, macabre, and undeterred by gore. Similarly, Chitra Ramaswamy argues: "the greatest pleasure of this deeply pleasurable series is spotting all the ways in which it uproots the tired old sexist tropes of spy thrillers then repots them as feminist in-jokes, patriarchal piss-takes, tasteless murders and blooms of sapphic chemistry."[19] Indeed, both Eve and Villanelle do not embody traits that society customarily associates with women, such as being kind and nurturing. As Imogen West-Knights argues, Eve is "unprofessional, obsessive, and frequently cold. Strikingly, given that Eve is not a mother, it is never explained why she isn't, or implied that she ought to be at her age."[20] Indeed, shows like *The X-Files* and *Sex and the City* frequently "needed" to explain why some of the female characters didn't have children (Dana Scully was infertile while Carrie Bradshaw was preoccupied with her writing career), suggesting that childfree women were an anomaly that needed justification to be be wholly understood. *Killing Eve*, however, has no such expectations for its titular character. West-Knights points out that, "Villanelle uses the gendered way people perceive her to her own advantage,"[21] which includes posing as any number of female stereotypes, such as the vulnerable runaway or the sex worker in order to ensnare her prey, which, throughout the series, includes both men *and* women. *Killing Eve* therefore works to show how gender stereotypes—which have historically served patriarchal power—can actually be used to give more power to women.

THE OUTSIDER

From the very first scene of the series when we are introduced to her character, Villanelle is shown to be different. Seen eating ice cream in a dimly lit shop in Vienna, Villanelle attempts to mimic the courteous smiles of a waiter and a young girl sitting at a table nearby. At first the girl does not return the smile, as Villanelle's grin appears more unsettling than genuinely polite. Instead, the girl smiles at the waiter. Eventually, however, after studying the specific contours of their smiles, Villanelle manages to imitate this conventional expression, finally eliciting a smile from the girl in return. She then stands up, tips the waiter, and purposefully knocks over the young girl's ice cream into her lap, grinning as she walks out, much to the young girl's shock.

Villanelle's initial attempt to mimic the apparently normal expressions and banal minutiae of society immediately reveals her status as an outsider, as her behavior and view of the world utterly conflicts with the status quo. As Jackson Maher notes, Villanelle is "the kind of person who admires the carnage of a shootout for its artistic merits."[22] Indeed, Villanelle idolizes murder as a fundamental expression of being human and an impressive skill to possess, something which should be celebrated. For instance, after gleefully pushing someone in front of a bus in the episode "I Hope You Like Missionary," Villanelle sends Eve a text featuring several emojis including a truck, a face with dead eyes, a ghost and a thumbs up, signifying Villanelle's enjoyment and amusement relating to murder. And in the episode "You're

Mine," Villanelle says she is "proud" of Eve murdering someone. Villanelle clearly shows that she appreciates the ability to not just kill someone, but to kill someone well and with creativity.

The introduction of Eve Polastri also defies expectations; we first see Eve screaming in horror while in bed, before her husband desperately tries to wake her up, terrified. Once she's roused from her sleep, Eve casually explains that she just fell asleep on her arms, immediately transforming the scene from one of bewildered horror to casual comedy. Her Polish husband, Niko, calls her a "freak," before she laughs and apologizes. Like Villanelle, Eve changes the scene from one emotive setting to another, ending the scene on a bizarre note that bewilders the people around them who fail to understand the women's unconventional responses. As Luna Centifanti argues: "You can see that Eve falls along a continuum as well as Villanelle. She doesn't seem particularly nervous or concerned about danger; at times she does take risks with people's safety, as well as her own."[23] Lucy Foulkes argues that "almost all of us can identify with at least some element of psychopathy."[24] But while Eve exhibits some characteristics on the psychopathy continuum (such as risk-taking and obsession), Foulkes notes that there are traits that signify true psychopathy: "aggression, substance abuse, thrill seeking . . . lack of empathy or guilt and a willingness to manipulate others." Villanelle more clearly exhibits these traits, lacking empathy for those she kills, displaying aggression and partaking in drugs. The show asks us to acknowledge the similarities between those considered to be sane and those thought of as "insane" but still reminds us that Villanelle is a more extreme manifestation of Eve, whose own behavior is brought into line by the conventions that dictate society.

Neither Villanelle nor Eve react to events or news in ways we would ordinarily expect, and although Eve is considered "sane" in comparison to Villanelle's "psychopath," both of their behaviors tend to clash with the prevailing norms of society. In one telling scene, Villanelle undergoes a psychological evaluation. She dresses up for the occasion, appearing in an elaborate pink dress. When she is shown an image of a tortured animal, Villanelle feigns disgust and shock, before the façade disappears and she begins to laugh. Similarly, Eve herself undergoes a psych evaluation in the second season and doesn't flinch when she sees a photo of a murder victim, unlike her colleagues who immediately look away.

Eve's reactions are in stark contrast to those around her. In the very first episode, Eve is impressed with Villanelle's ability to slice a politician's femoral artery without him even noticing, prompting her to mutter "Cool." Eve's obsession with female serial killers and her admiration of murder tactics isolate her on a social level from her husband and her colleagues, who accuse her of becoming increasingly erratic.

Moreover, Eve and Villanelle both share a restless drive for excitement and a fear of boredom. Eve describes Villanelle as "easily bored," while Hugo, Eve's sex-obsessed MI6 colleague, points out that he got into their line of work for the same reasons Eve did, namely, that he "didn't want to die of boredom." This fear of the banality of everyday life pushes Eve to adopt increasingly erratic behavior, from smashing a glass panel at a bus stop, to the temptation to push a man into the path of an oncoming train. As Martha Duncan argues, the fascination with crime reflects "a desire to escape from the mundane world-as-it-is into a nobler and more meaningful time and place."[25]

For Eve, Villanelle represents an escape from her mundane life into a world where life and death become a present reality, and not just theoretical possibilities. Even as an agent, Eve does her job of hunting and profiling serial killers from a safe distance. Villanelle's case, however, allows her to delve more deeply into the underbelly of society. From then on, her job is no longer confined to just paperwork, and she is liberated from the boredom that threatened to define her job, as she crosses the threshold from law enforcement to a participant of crime. In the last episode of the first season, Eve, who finally manages to track Villanelle to her chic Paris apartment, admits:

> I think about you all the time. I think about what you're wearing and what you're doing and who you're doing it with. I think about what friends you have. I think about what you eat before you work and what shampoo you use and what happened in your family. I think about your eyes and your mouth and what you feel when you kill someone. I think about what you have for breakfast. I just want to know everything.[26]

This admission leads to Eve's first severe break with societal rules as she stabs Villanelle in the stomach, an act which at once terrifies and thrills Eve, who becomes increasingly obsessive in season 2. As Alakananda Bandyopadhyay points out, "while season 1 was mostly about establishing how different Eve and Villanelle are, season 2 was about pointing out just how similar the two are. Until the very last moment."[27] Eve not only becomes even more obsessed with Villanelle and the potentially liberating effects of eschewing social conventions and laws, but also kills someone for the first time by axe-murdering them.[28] Villanelle tells Eve: "We are the same." But although we see Eve's mental state changing to become more unhinged, to the point that she kills another human being, Eve nevertheless refuses to run away with Villanelle. Angered, Villanelle shoots Eve, leaving her for dead. Having tricked Eve into killing another human being, we see that Villanelle has in essence "created" the person Eve has become, evidenced in Villanelle telling Eve: "You're mine." Villanelle views Eve as a macabre kindred spirit, a shadowy reflection of Villanelle herself, illustrating that the show's title is less about Eve's mortality and more about how her character gradually morphs into another person. Indeed, in *Killing Eve*, what constitutes "normal" behavior is challenged as Eve, a woman on the "right" side of the law, becomes ever more entangled with Villanelle's murderous psyche.

PSYCHOPATHY AND GENDER

In the very first episode, Villanelle is branded simply as a "small-breasted psycho," reducing her to the basic constituents of her physical body, as well as being labelled with an inadequate term to crudely describe her eccentric mental state. Female psychopaths are comparatively rare in popular culture. When they are depicted on-screen, it is through fairly stereotypical tropes, possessing characteristics that are, according to many psychologists, fundamentally male. Centifanti, however, explains that it is difficult to fully comprehend how much Villanelle fulfills the standard rubric of psychopathy, because we have little understanding of the female psychopath and, consequently, we rarely see female psychopaths depicted accurately in popular culture: "The problem is, we don't know a lot about [female psychopaths] because we've used a male model of psychopathy."[29] She explains that while Villanelle exhibits psychopathic traits, many are typically male ones:

> The writer [of *Killing Eve*] hit the mark, but only if she was a man. Women with psychopathy tend to be quite manipulative, and Villanelle seems to use manipulation to have fun, rather than to get what she wants. . . . She knows that being female gets her certain privileges and having beauty disarms people. That self-awareness allows her to adapt; psychopaths are able to adapt to situations and hide in plain sight. That is definitely more stereotypical of male psychopaths: their emotions can turn on a dime, because they are not feeling them deeply.[30]

Alice Vincent argues that "as with other psychological conditions—autism and schizophrenia spring to mind—psychopathy has found itself depicted in hackneyed terms on screen."[31] She explains: "There's a funny thing with female psychopaths in pop culture: they're nearly always called 'femmes fatales.' Sharon Stone in *Basic Instinct*, Rosamund Pike in *Gone Girl* and Turner in *Body Heat*: these are heartless and violent women who men just can't resist."[32] In contrast, *Killing Eve* depicts Villanelle's mental state in more nuanced ways. As Vincent puts it, Villanelle

> is neither visibly unhinged—like Angelina Jolie's Lisa in *Girl, Interrupted*— nor a noirish seductress. She's a ruthless killer (who likes "the breathy ones") but loves fancy dress; she's sexually promiscuous but distracted by reminders of her ex-girlfriend and, while cunning, Villanelle is also undeniably endearing. . . . She's a cuddly, wide-eyed kind of psychopath with an irresistibly dry sense of humour.[33]

Others disagree completely with the assessment that Villanelle is a psychopath. As Katie Heaney argues:

> In coverage of the show, the character Villanelle is routinely described as a "psychopath," and the show employs a psychiatrist to consult on the character's presumed personality disorder. But the criteria for clinical psychopathy are very specific, and often misapplied. [34]

Villanelle does, indeed, exhibit many of the traits associated with psychopathy as outlined in the *DSM*; she manipulates those around her, from her employer to complete strangers, many of whom are taken in by Villanelle's charm. She has an emotional disconnection to the reactions of others, whether it be horror or affection. We learn that after she castrated and killed the husband of her lover, Anna, Villanelle decorated Anna's apartment with balloons and a large cake to celebrate, before a horrified Anna calls the police.

Villanelle not only has a grandiose view of herself, but she is also very much an attention-seeker. As Eve's MI6 employer, Carolyn, puts it in the first episode, Villanelle is "showing off" with her kills. In season 2, Villanelle deliberately kills someone in order to get the attention of Eve and is furious when Eve does not come to investigate. To this end, Villanelle is childish and emotionally immature in her desire to have Eve become just like her. When Eve refuses to run away with her, Villanelle reacts in the only way she can understand, by shooting her.

But as many critics have pointed out, all of these actions make Villanelle more than just a "small-breasted psycho." As Heaney argues:

> Villanelle, as viewers of the show know, does very, very bad things, with little to no visible remorse. Her apparent lack of empathy may satisfy our popular perception of psychopathy on the most basic level, but there's more to it than that. In Comer's depiction, Villanelle is not just remorseless and casually cruel, but also brilliant, charming, pragmatic, and, at times, genuinely thoughtful. [35]

Indeed, in one scene, Villanelle is preparing to kill her handler, Konstantin, on new orders after escaping prison. She allows him to choose how he wants to die, and he elects to swallow pills with whiskey. After the first few pills, Konstantin tells Villanelle: "I try to be angry at you, I try to discipline you. I try to trick you into doing what I want you to do and I fail. And I fail because I love you." [36] He also tells her: "You're so different. You're so strong," and that he loves her more than his own family, all of which visibly (and reluctantly) moves Villanelle to tears, before she resumes composure and tells him to ingest more pills, before he hits her and runs away. In another episode, Villanelle is seen sobbing in front of her mirror, afraid of losing Eve and disillusioned with herself and her life. These scenes show us that in contrast to the understanding that psychopaths cannot feel genuine emotions of grief, empathy, or sadness, Villanelle is, indeed, capable of experiencing such emotions. As Lucy Nichol argues, psychopathy specifically relates to the condition of suffering from psychosis, which, she notes, excludes Villanelle: "On the contrary. We've seen her calmly plan and carry out murders without breaking a sweat or a nail. She knows exactly what she's doing and exactly what's happening around her—that's what makes her such a precise and terrifying killer."[37]

One of the more interesting traits about Villanelle is that, throughout all of her assignments, she never questions the reasons she has been sent in the first place. In one episode, Villanelle has attacked a man in an office in Berlin late at night. The man, bloodied and terrified, scrambles away, begging for his life, telling her he is a husband and father, to no avail. When he asks her, trembling, why she is trying to kill him, she simply replies, "I have absolutely no idea." Such impassiveness can easily be interpreted as submissiveness on her part. But as her dealings with Konstantin illustrate, Villanelle does not simply do whatever these men tell her to do (Villanelle is known to disobey her orders, or to deviate from the manner in which her assignments are executed, literally). Instead, Villanelle is uninterested in the reasons behind these kills and instead appears intent on earning as much money as she can and to show just how good she is at her job.

Villanelle is, in many ways, philosophical about death. Just before she kills and castrates an informant in the fifth episode of season 1,[38] she tells the frightened man:

> Your eyes will just empty. Then your soul goes in. People think that your soul or personality, whatever, leaves the body when you die. I swear it just goes further in. It falls so far in and just becomes so small that it can't control your body anymore. It's just in there, dying forever.[39]

Villanelle's genuine love of the kill, what Friedrich Nietzsche calls the "joy of the knife," is more typical of male killers. As Heaney observes:

> Hit-people are doing a job, killing who they're requested to kill. When male psychopaths kill . . . the motive is usually psychosexual, and the victims are usually strangers. When female psychopaths kill, the motive is usually money, or attention, and the victims are people they know—and they usually kill them "expeditiously," as opposed to the drawn-out, torturous murders more typical of psychopathic male killers.[40]

In Villanelle's case, murder is both sanctioned and completely random, on the one hand focused on specific targets ordered by her employer, and on the other, complete strangers who either have something Villanelle wants or who otherwise get in her way.

Villanelle's outsider mentality allows her to perceive the greater eccentricities of society. Her inability to fully comprehend the world and its trivial minutiae on the same level as most other people manifests itself in humorous ways; when she befriends a rich addict who invites her to "sups" (supper), Villanelle remarks: "why do rich people talk like children?" When a woman comes up to her in the street and compliments her elaborate outfit, asking if she can take Villanelle's photo for her Instagram page, Villanelle scoffs at her and refuses, telling the woman to "get a real life." And when Konstantin takes Villanelle to a gallery, Villanelle loudly calls the masterpieces boring, attracting a wave of "shushes" from others. In these scenes, Villanelle is neither subtle nor tactful as she openly ridicules the behavior of the new bourgeoisie, something which makes her "bizarrely relatable," in Jodie Comer's view.[41]

Although her unconventional behavior clearly situates her as an outcast, Villanelle's observations about people and life are nevertheless astute. The frenzy with which we take to social media, the adoration for artworks of, as Villanelle puts it, "naked people and grapes," and the mannerisms of the ultra-rich are presented to us from an outsider perspective and are therefore given renewed absurdity. In the world of *Killing Eve*, Villanelle reveals the absurdities we take as normal, flipping the sane/insane binary so that our own actions and behaviors are called into question. She not only criticizes how so-called normal people act but observes that "normal is boring."

A FEMINIST ASSASSIN?

After capturing the assassin Jin, a.k.a. "The Ghost," Eve interrogates her, asking: "It's unusual, isn't it, to be a woman in your line of work?" to which Jin replies: "Not so much anymore." In *Killing Eve*, gender roles seen in previous television thrillers are upended. While women are certainly murder victims, they are also the ones doing the murdering. Villanelle has been called a "feminist assassin,"[42] as she does not discriminate when it comes to murder, killing men, women, strangers, family, and lovers.

When Villanelle first comes to the attention of MI5—where Eve is employed before being promoted to MI6—Eve is the only one who believes the killer is a woman. Eve's boss at MI5, Bill, dismisses outright the possibility that the killer is a woman, saying: "There's a difference between thinking it was a woman and wishing it was a woman." This underestimation leads to Bill's brutal murder at the hands of Villanelle in only the third episode of the series, a surprising and swift departure of what many assumed would be the main male character, a role that televisual history not only prioritizes but tends to keep alive for a longer period of time.

Killing Eve not only upends gender stereotypes, but also engages with them as a marker of agency, anchoring murder itself within the "feminine" world of fashion and beauty products. Not only does Villanelle indulge in the material comforts her job affords her, but the weapons she uses to kill people are often beauty products or fashion accessories, including a hairpin plunged into a man's eye and a perfume laced with poison which kills an asthmatic businesswoman.

The show's treatment of fashion differs from other fashion-dominant shows like *Sex and the City*; the clothes and accessories act as a novel plot device that expresses many personality traits of the characters. After Eve asks her boss, Carolyn, why she never looks tired, Carolyn admits to using an expensive face cream made from pig's placenta which "smells like arse." And while escaping the hospital after being stabbed, Villanelle steals and begrudgingly slips into a pair of hideous Crocs.

Critics of fashion routinely dismiss such acts or reactions as "frivolous" or "vain." As Ramaswamy puts it: "Double standards dictate that when a woman covets nice things on screen she is shallow and materialistic (*Sex and the City*) and when a man does the exact same thing, he is a sartorial sex god (James Bond)."[43] Yet, *Killing Eve* commends the lengths that some women take (donning ugly shoes and applying arse-smelling face cream) in order to survive challenges as disparate as an all-consuming job and a stab wound. As Joanna Whitehead puts it: "Anyone with a heart couldn't fail to be moved by Villanelle's agony at having to slide her feet into a pair of Crocs,"[44] a move, Whitehead argues, which attests to Villanelle's drive to survive. Rachel Cooke concurs: "the scene where she has to place her feet in these crimes against fashion and hygiene is priceless."[45] As Whitehead notes, "Here is a woman who meets the beauty standard, but whose lack of interest in male sexual attention in a society where women's acceptability is so often invested in their ability to conform to sexual and gender norms, is wholly refreshing."[46]

Caroline Welsh argues that Villanelle's wardrobe is more than just pieces of frivolous extravagance:

> Villanelle's outfits express a powerful voice, projecting and fleshing out a narrative all of their own. In one instance, her girlish pink gown and menacing footwear combine to articulate insolence, tenacity and psychotic incongruity; a sartorial middle finger to Konstantin, her corrupt handler.[47]

Discussing similar shows such as *The Fall* and *The Killing*, Welsh argues that:

Villanelle's sartorial stunts differ significantly from the wardrobes of Gibson and Lund. These supposed "feminist icons" remain impartial to fashion, yet materialise each episode in pressed silk shirts, "power" trousers and designer knitwear; all without any active sartorial intent. Meanwhile, Comer's Villanelle is a committed fashion fanatic. Her prolific assassinations principally satisfy her appetite for sharp tailoring, brocade gowns and of course, pink tulle. And how exactly does this differ from the knitwear and blouses of previous small-screen heroines? Well, because Villanelle's sartorial narrative is one of active agency. Like most of us each morning, she makes decisions, communicates, fantasizes and evolves all through the language of fashion, and in doing so, she champions clothing as synonymous with self-expression. [48]

Indeed, while fashion is treated as spectacle in shows such as *Sex and the City*, *Killing Eve* treats fashion as an essential element that augments the inner psychology of its characters, whether it's the ruffled look of Eve, the effortlessly chic look of her employer Carolyn, or, indeed, Villanelle's eclectic tastes from flamboyant dresses, to power suits, to dismal hospital attire. In *Killing Eve*, fashion is not merely an accessory or decoration, but an absolutely vital narrative device.

While *Killing Eve* has challenged gender assumptions about women and their roles in society, the show nevertheless reminds viewers of the unavoidable endurance of patriarchy. Like other female assassins in popular culture, most notably The Bride in Quentin Tarantino's *Kill Bill* films, Villanelle is seen to take pleasure in her work as a hired killer, and just like The Bride, she is working on the orders of a man.

In the second season in particular, Villanelle finds herself under the control of various men, two of whom she eventually murders; after she escapes from the hospital with a stab wound, she is taken in by Julian, a creepy, doll-collecting stranger in Basildon, who proceeds to keep Villanelle confined to his house. He refuses to go and get any medicine for her, playfully calling her a hypochondriac, while he also refuses to open any windows or doors. After killing him and fleeing, Villanelle is rehired by "The Twelve"—an enigmatic organization that hires assassins—and is given an abusive new handler, Raymond, who strangles her into submission. Her original handler, Konstantin, later informs her that Raymond is unconventionally paid by being allowed to murder the hired killers when they are no longer needed. And in the second season finale, Raymond does indeed attempt to murder Villanelle with an axe, before being axe-murdered to death himself by Eve. Raymond's appearance, as well as Konstantin's, reminds the viewer of the often-seamless control men continue to wield over women in both domestic and labor situations, which makes Raymon's death all the more satisfying even as it horrifies.

The other major patriarchal power in the second season is Aaron Peel, the arrogant, voyeuristic tech-billionaire who strikes up an acquaintance with

Villanelle after she is hired by MI6 to get information on Peel's business dealings, namely, his work in collecting, weaponizing, and selling personal data from around the world. While Peel and Villanelle's relationship is not sexual, it is nevertheless unsettling, as Peel monitors Villanelle from hidden cameras, and he controls everything about her, from what she eats to how she dresses. On one occasion he orders her to stop eating an orange chocolate, telling her to spit it out, and on another occasion, he orders her to remove her belt since it "doesn't go" with her outfit.

The absence of a stereotypical male trait—an obsession with and expectation of sex in return for lavish gifts—makes their rendezvous all the more disconcerting. Their particular arrangement, predicated on nothing more than an exchange of luxury items and absolute control, also makes Peel's obsession for Villanelle all the more grotesque, for he genuinely sees her as an object. This becomes evident when he tells her: "You look like a painting, so still," before he orders her to sit still and not move an inch. He also describes her as a "void" and a "shadow." It is later revealed that he not only murders most of the women who he invites into his world but films the murders as well.

Rachel Chandler argues that Villanelle and Aaron "seem to share a twisted kind of affinity toward one another," but that "it becomes apparent that their "brand" of psychopathy [doesn't] quite align, as Aaron "never gets lonely" and shows no interest in talking to or sleeping with anyone, while Villanelle does "all the time."[49] While they share a fondness for murder, their differing opinions on other people tap into broader gender perceptions. As Rachel Cooke notes, "the show's primary engine is the deep interest women tend to have in other women," while also pointing out that "most of its male characters spend their time looking, and acting, baffled."[50] Not only are Villanelle and Eve deeply interested in each other on a deeper psychological level, but, as Cooke points out, Eve's relationship with her boss, Carolyn, is also of interest: "their mutual curiosity [is] always in play even when they're absolutely furious with one another."

When Eve bursts in on Aaron and Villanelle, Aaron orders Villanelle to kill Eve, offering her everything and anything she wants in exchange. After a hesitant pause, Villanelle picks up a knife from the table and slits Aaron's throat, holding him in front of a mirror, where we see him smiling at the sight of his own murder. Villanelle drops his body to the ground and exclaims, "What a dick." The scene demonstrates a casual reversal of gender dynamics, with Villanelle reducing Aaron to his genitals in the same way that women are often criticized as "cunts."

The various unstable men that Villanelle encounters—Julian, Raymond, and Aaron—not to mention the strange men she is ordered to kill, illustrates that Villanelle's own brand of psychopathy is distinctly female in nature. Although Konstantin accuses her of being unable to express genuine love,

Villanelle has nevertheless shown that she has some emotional resonance, as seen when she breaks down in front of a mirror or when Eve rejects her, while her mentality affords her a unique understanding of the world.

CONCLUSION

Male antiheroes have dominated television for the last twenty years, a trope which, as Suzanna Walters argues, was "undermined by the appeal of errant masculinity,"[51] where viewers were asked to celebrate the wayward behaviors of wayward men from Tony Soprano to Walter White. The emergence of antiheroines, by contrast, represents a significant overhaul of typical female representation in television. As Walters argues: "The antiheroes of *Breaking Bad* and *Mad Men* easily adhere to older noir tropes that valorize a kind of strong but broken lone wolf who simply can't play by the rules, rules often signified as enforced by a nagging feminine presence." Yet shows like *Weeds* and *Orange Is the New Black*, Walters writes, pushed television into new territory: "These new antiheroines are not merely criminal outliers who are villainized and extruded from the body politic, but rather represent the development of a substantive—and new—imagery of female power." In this sense, villainy has become an opportunity for women to seize or regain power ordinarily wielded by men, giving women more nuanced roles than just "nagging wife" or "hot sidekick."

In a world that has historically diagnosed complex women with labels such as "crazy," "mad," "hysterical," "unhinged," and "unstable," *Killing Eve* excels at challenging the enduring perceptions about women and sanity that society continues to uphold. Although she's shown to be callous, odd, and at times inept at social conventions, Villanelle is nevertheless wryly observant about the eccentricities of everyday life and the persistent hypocrisies that define society. Both she and Eve are constantly asked to conform to society's expectations of behavior. For however much they may differ, Eve and Villanelle are shown to possess similar characteristics: risk taking, a lack of friends, an obsession with work, and a fear of boredom. Although it acknowledges that these women have committed brutal or questionable acts, *Killing Eve* rejects the prognosis of "psychopath" to describe women who evade characterization, suggesting that society itself is abnormal.

Both Eve and Villanelle contribute to a growing discourse on antiheroines, changing the way in which women have been depicted on television by having them engage in acts ordinarily reserved for men, including murder and torture. Although *Killing Eve* does not celebrate violence, it does highlight the divergent ways in which violence acts as a potential form of liberation for women in a world accustomed to aggressive masculinity. The kind of aggressive femininity found in *Killing Eve*, moreover, evades male-endorsed stereotypes ("crazy bitch," "psycho"), and instead depicts female aggression as a form of empowerment. The characterization of Villanelle as a "small-breasted psycho," therefore, becomes a deliberate gesture that reflects the way in which female aggression has previously been framed, and the way in which it can be used as a source of power.

NOTES

1. *Diagnostic and Statistical Manual of Mental Disorders* (Arlington, VA: American Psychiatric Association 2013), 660.

2. *DSM*, 765.

3. *Killing Eve*, "God, I'm Tired," directed by Damon Thomas. Air date May 27, 2019.

4. *Killing Eve*, "I Have a Thing about Bathrooms," directed by Jon East. Air date May 6, 2018.

5. *Killing Eve*, "Do You Know How to Dispose of a Body?" directed by Damon Thomas. Air date 7 April 2019.

6. *Killing Eve*, "I Have a Thing about Bathrooms," May 6, 2018.

7. "*Game Of Thrones* Created TV's Greatest Female Anti-Hero in Cersei Lannister," *Inverse*, March 13, 2016, https://www.inverse.com/article/14126-game-of-thrones-created-tv-s-greatest-female-anti-hero-in-cersei-lannister.

8. "If Androids Dream, Are They More than Sheep? Westworld, Robots and Legal Rights," *Dialogue: The Interdisciplinary Journal of Popular Culture and Pedagogy*, Volume 6, Issue 2 (2019): 6, journaldialogue.org/issues/v6-issue-2/if-androids-dream-are-they-more-than-sheep-robot-protagonists-and-human-rights/.

9. Aimee Knight, "Tough Chick: Bad Cops and Difficult Women in SBS's *Dead Lucky*," *Metro Magazine*, Issue 199 (Mar 2019): 52–53.

10. "The Scully Effect: I Want to Believe in STEM, 21st Century Fox," Geena Davis Institute on Gender in Media, and J. Walter Thompson Intelligence, 2018, https://seejane.org/research-informs-empowers/the-scully-effect-i-want-to-believe-in-stem/.

11. Inkoo Kang, "The Betrayal of Dana Scully: *The X-Files* Has Been Terrible to Its Lead for a Generation," *The Village Voice*, March 14, 2018, https://www.villagevoice.com/2018/03/14/the-betrayal-of-dana-scully-the-x-files-has-been-terrible-to-its-lead-for-a-generation/.

12. Kang, 2018.

13. Carol Caldwell, "Carrie Fisher: A Few Words on Princess Leia, Fame and Feminism," *Rolling Stone*, July 21, 1983.

14. Caldwell, 1983, https://www.rollingstone.com/movies/movie-news/carrie-fisher-a-few-words-on-princess-leia-fame-and-feminism-190633/.

15. Tasha Robinson, "We're Losing All Our Strong Female Characters to Trinity Syndrome," *The Dissolve*, June 16, 2014, https://thedissolve.com/features/exposition/618-were-losing-all-our-strong-female-characters-to-tr/.

16. Robinson, "We're Losing All Our Strong Female Characters."

17. Sophia McDougall, "I Hate Strong Female Characters," *New Statesman*, August 15, 2013, https://www.newstatesman.com/culture/2013/08/i-hate-strong-female-characters

18. McDougall, "I Hate Strong Female Characters."

19. Chitra Ramaswamy, "From Fridging to Nagging Husbands: How *Killing Eve* Upturns Sexist Clichés," *The Guardian*, October 12, 2018, https://www.theguardian.com/tv-and-radio/2018/oct/12/from-fridging-to-nagging-husbands-how-killing-eve-upturns-sexist-cliches.

20. Imogen West-Knights, "On *Killing Eve*," *Another Gaze: A Feminist Film Journal*, January 10, 2019, https://www.anothergaze.com/on-killing-eve/.

21. West-Knights, "On *Killing Eve*."

22. Jackson Maher, "Difficult Women: Why We Love *Killing Eve*'s Psychopath," Skip Intro, June 29, 2018. https://www.youtube.com/watch?v=boEh7PekJA8.

23. Cited in Alice Vincent, "Villanelle, Analysed: *Killing Eve* and the Truth about Female Psychopaths," *The Telegraph*, September 18, 2018, https://www.telegraph.co.uk/tv/2018/09/18/villenelle-analysed-killing-eve-truth-female-psychopaths/.

24. Lucy Foulkes, "The Psychopath in You," *The Guardian*, June 10, 2016, https://www.theguardian.com/science/head-quarters/2016/jun/10/the-psychopath-in-you-psychopathic-traits-spectrum.

25. Martha Grace Duncan, *Romantic Outlaws, Beloved Prisons: The Unconscious Meanings of Crime and Punishment* (New York and London: New York University Press, 1996), 5.

26. *Killing Eve*, "God I'm Tired," May 27, 2018.

27. Alakananda Bandyopadhyay, *"Killing Eve* Season 2 Finale Deconstructs Eve as a Psychopath while Questioning Her Feelings for Villanelle," *Media Entertainment Arts World Wide*, May 26, 2019, https://meaww.com/killing-eve-season-2-episode-8-finale-review-youre-mine-deconstructs-eve-psychopath-villanelle.

28. *Killing Eve*, "You're Mine," directed by Damon Thomas. Air date May 26, 2019.

29. *Killing Eve*, "You're Mine."

30. *Killing Eve*, "You're Mine."

31. Vincent, "Villanelle, Analysed."

32. Vincent, "Villanelle, Analysed."

33. Vincent, "Villanelle, Analysed."

34. Katie Heaney, "What Do We Know about Female Psychopaths?," *The Cut*, April 4, 2019, https://www.thecut.com/2019/04/is-killing-eves-villanelle-an-accurate-female-psychopath.html.

35. Heaney, "What Do We Know about Female Psychopaths?"

36. *Killing Eve*, "I Don't Want to Be Free," directed by Damon Thomas. Air Date 20 May 2018.

37. Lucy Nichol, *"Killing Eve's* Villanelle is not psychotic and calling her so is just as dangerous as she is," *Metro*, April 8, 2019, https://metro.co.uk/2019/04/08/killing-eves-villanelle-not-psychotic-calling-just-dangerous-9134406/.

38. *Killing Eve*, "I Have a Thing about Bathrooms."

39. *Killing Eve*, "I Have a Thing about Bathrooms."

40. Heaney, "What Do We Know about Female Psychopaths?"

41. Cited in Naomi Gordon, *"Killing Eve's* Jodie Comer Explains Why We're All Rooting for Villanelle," *Harper's Bazaar*, October 9, 2018, https://www.harpersbazaar.com/uk/culture/entertainment/a23632892/killing-eve-jodie-comer-on-playing-villanelle/.

42. Hanh Nguyen, *"Killing Eve*: BBC America's Feminist Assassin Series Just Went from Fun and Addictive to Essential Viewing," *IndieWire*, April 22, 2018, https://www.indiewire.com/2018/04/killing-eve-episode-3-dont-i-know-you-recap-spoilers-1201955859/.

43. Ramaswamy, "From Fridging to Nagging Husbands."

44. Joanna Whitehead, *"Killing Eve* Isn't Guilty of Queerbaiting—But it Is Keeping Us on Our Toes," *Independent*, June 9, 2019, https://www.independent.co.uk/voices/killing-eve-queerbaiting-villanelle-season-2-bbc-jodie-comer-a8950966.html.

45. Rachel Cooke, "In Its Portrayal of Men and Women, *Killing Eve* Echoes Life—With Added Weapons." *New Statesman*, June 11, 2019. https://www.newstatesman.com/culture/tv-radio/2019/06/its-portrayal-men-and-women-killing-eve-echoes-life-added-weapons.

46. Whitehead, *"Killing Eve* Isn't Guilty of Queerbaiting."

47. Caroline Welsh, "Autonomous Fashion: The Unlikely Heroine of *Killing Eve*," *Into the Fold*, February 22, 2019, https://www.intothefoldmag.com/2019/02/autonomous-fashion-the-unlikely-heroine-of-killing-eve/.

48. Welsh, "Autonomous Fashion: The Unlikely Heroine of *Killing Eve*."

49. Rachel Chandler, *"Killing Eve:* Season 2, Episode 7: Wide Awake," *The Simple Cinephile*, May 23, 2019, https://thesimplecinephile.com/2019/05/23/killing-eve-episode7/.

50. Cooke, "In Its Portrayal of Men and Women."

51. "Lesbian Request Approved: Sex, Power and Desire in *Orange Is the New Black*," in *Television Antiheroines: Women Behaving Badly in Crime and Prison Drama*, Milly Buonanno (ed.) (Chicago: Chicago University Press, 2017), 201.

BIBLIOGRAPHY

Caldwell, Carol. "Carrie Fisher: A Few Words on Princess Leia, Fame and Feminism." *Rolling Stone*, July 21, 1983. https://www.rollingstone.com/movies/movie-news/carrie-fisher-a-few-words-on-princess-leia-fame-and-feminism-190633/.

Chandler, Rachel. "*Killing Eve*: Season 2, Episode 7: Wide Awake." *The Simple Cinephile*, May 23, 2019. https://thesimplecinephile.com/2019/05/23/killing-eve-episode7/.

Cooke, Rachel. "In Its Portrayal of Men and Women, *Killing Eve* Echoes Life—With Added Weapons." *New Statesman*, June 11, 2019. https://www.newstatesman.com/culture/tv-radio/2019/06/its-portrayal-men-and-women-killing-eve-echoes-life-added-weapons.

DiPaolo, Amanda. "If Androids Dream, Are They More than Sheep?: Westworld, Robots and Legal Rights." *Dialogue: The Interdisciplinary Journal of Popular Culture and Pedagogy.* Volume 6, Issue 2 (2019): 1–13. journaldialogue.org/issues/v6-issue-2/if-androids-dream-are-they-more-than-sheep-robotprotagonists-and-human-rights/.

Duncan, Martha Grace. *Romantic Outlaws, Beloved Prisons: The Unconscious Meanings of Crime and Punishment.* New York and London: New York University Press, 1996.

Foulkes, Lucy. "The Psychopath in You." *The Guardian*, June 10, 2016. https://www.theguardian.com/science/head-quarters/2016/jun/10/the-psychopath-in-you-psychopathic-traits-spectrum.

Harris, Katherine and Peter Ridley. "I Never Did This When I Was a Man," *Soundings: A Journal of Politics and Culture*, Issue 71 (Spring 2019): 107–114.

Kang, Inkoo. "The Betrayal of Dana Scully: *The X-Files* Has Been Terrible to Its Lead for a Generation." *The Village Voice*, March 14, 2018. https://www.villagevoice.com/2018/03/14/the-betrayal-of-dana-scully-the-x-files-has-been-terrible-to-its-lead-for-a-generation/.

Killing Eve. "Do You Know How to Dispose of a Body?" Directed by Damon Thomas. Air date April 7, 2019.

———. "God, I'm Tired." Directed by Damon Thomas. Air date May 27, 2019.

———. "I Don't Want to be Free." Directed by Damon Thomas. Air Date May 20, 2018.

———. "I Have a Thing about Bathrooms." Directed by Jon East. Air date May 6, 2018.

———. "You're Mine." Directed by Damon Thomas. Air date May 26, 2019.

Knight, Aimee. "Tough Chick: Bad Cops and Difficult Women in SBS's *Dead Lucky*." *Metro Magazine*, Issue 199 (Mar 2019): 52–53.

Maher, Jackson. "Difficult Women: Why We Love *Killing Eve*'s Psychopath." *Skip Intro*, June 29, 2018. https://www.youtube.com/watch?v=boEh7PekJA8.

McDougall, Sophia. "I Hate Strong Female Characters." *New Statesman America*, August 15, 2013. https://www.newstatesman.com/culture/2013/08/i-hate-strong-female-characters.

Nguyen, Hanh. "*Killing Eve*: BBC America's Feminist Assassin Series Just Went from Fun and Addictive to Essential Viewing." *IndieWire*, April 22, 2018. https://www.indiewire.com/2018/04/killing-eve-episode-3-dont-i-know-you-recap-spoilers-1201955859/.

Ramaswamy, Chitra. "From Fridging to Nagging Husbands: How *Killing Eve* Upturns Sexist Clichés." *The Guardian*, October 12, 2018. https://www.theguardian.com/tv-and-radio/2018/oct/12/from-fridging-to-nagging-husbands-how-killing-eve-upturns-sexist-cliches.

Robinson, Tasha. "We're Losing All Our Strong Female Characters to Trinity Syndrome." *The Dissolve*, June 16, 2014. http://thedissolve.com/features/exposition/618-were-losing-all-our-strong-female-characters-to-tr/.

Tracy, Natasha. "Psychopathic Traits and Characteristics of a Psychopath." HealthyPlace, August 6, 2015. Retrieved on 2019, August 26. https://www.healthyplace.com/personality-disorders/psychopath/psychopathic-traits-and-characteristics-of-a-psychopath.

Vincent, Alice. "Villanelle, Analysed: *Killing Eve* and the Truth about Female Psychopaths." *The Telegraph*, June 6, 2019. https://www.telegraph.co.uk/tv/2019/06/06/villanelle-analysed-killing-eve-truth-female-psychopaths/.

Walters, Suzanne Danuta. "Lesbian Request Approved: Sex, Power and Desire in *Orange Is the New Black*." In *Television Antiheroines: Women Behaving Badly in Crime and Prison Drama*, Milly Buonanno (ed.), 199–216. Chicago: Chicago University Press, 2017.

Welsh, Caroline. "Autonomous Fashion: The Unlikely Heroine of *Killing Eve*." *Into the Fold*, February 22, 2019. https://www.intothefoldmag.com/2019/02/autonomous-fashion-the-unlikely-heroine-of-killing-eve/.

West-Knight, Imogen. "On *Killing Eve*." *Another Gaze: A Feminist Film Journal*, January 10, 2019. https://www.anothergaze.com/on-killing-eve/.

Index

About the Editors and Contributors

ABOUT THE EDITORS

Dr. **Gretchen Busl** is an associate professor and graduate program coordinator in English, Speech, and Foreign Languages at Texas Woman's University. She earned a PhD in literature with a minor in gender studies from the University of Notre Dame in 2012. Her work on narrative and gender has been published in *Modern Language Review*, *Critique: Studies in Contemporary Literature*, and *English Studies*.

Both **Melanie Haas** and **N. A. Pierce** have strong backgrounds in feminist literary criticism and rhetoric. Both editors are working toward completion of doctoral degrees in rhetoric (Haas) and English literature (Pierce). Haas, chair of the Humanities and Social Sciences Department at Southeast Arkansas College, is completing her PhD at Texas Woman's University and her dissertation will provide a feminist narratological and rhetorical examination of issues of power demonstrated in the hit television show *Scandal*. Pierce is a doctoral student at Old Dominion University and addresses feminist postcolonial speculative fictions, representations of women in popular culture and media, and Anglophone African Diasporic literatures in various contemporary and nineteenth-century texts.

ABOUT THE CONTRIBUTORS

Brenda Boudreau is a professor of English at McKendree University where she teaches American literature, film and composition. She writes on both film and television and her most recent publications were essays on *Dexter*, *Breaking Bad*, and *Stranger Things*. She has served on the Popular Culture Association board and is currently serving as vice president of awards.

Louise Coopey is a PhD researcher in film and television at the University of Birmingham. Her main research interests concern representation and the construction of identity on-screen. She has published several articles online for everyday audiences about *Game of Thrones*, focusing on the topics of damaging masculinity, monstrous motherhood, and the series' relevance in British politics. Her recent work includes a chapter on *Game of Thrones'* Epic 9s for the forthcoming *Moments in Television* collection.

Liz Evans is a British journalist and author, who has written on rock music, women's issues, psychology, lifestyle, and parenting for a wide selection of British and Australian titles. She is a qualified psychodynamic psychotherapist with an MA in Jungian studies from the University of Essex, and has published academic papers on ecofeminism, ecopsychology and Jungian theory. She is currently researching contemporary domestic noir from a feminist psychoanalytic perspective for a scholarship-funded PhD in creative writing at the University of Tasmania.

Siobhan Lyons is a writer and scholar in media and cultural studies. Her books include *Death and the Machine: Intersections of Mortality and Robotics* (2018), and *Ruin Porn and the Obsession with Decay* (2018). Her work has also been included in *Understanding Nietzsche, Understanding Modernism* (2019), *Westworld and Philosophy* (2018), *Approaching "Twin Peaks"* (2017), and *Philosophical Approaches to the Devil* (2016) among others.

Anja Meyer holds a PhD in modern languages, literatures, and cultures from the University of Verona. Her areas of research include English literature, theater studies, trauma studies, and visual studies. Her works include "Multimodal Interferences in Woody Allen's Midnight in Paris," "The Disaster Selfie: Images of Popular Virtual Trauma," and "La Rielaborazione Parodica di Riccardo III nella Drammaturgia Brechtiana," in *Richard III dal Testo alla Scena*.

Melanie Piper holds a PhD in film and television from the University of Queensland, Australia, where she now teaches in the School of Communication and Arts. Her research interests include various intersections of screen characters, docudrama and biopic, online fan discourses, celebrity, and stand-up comedy.

Lucinda Rasmussen is an associate lecturer with the University of Alberta where she teaches English literature and writing studies. She is an award-winning instructor whose research focuses on the representation and dissemination of narratives by and about contemporary twentieth- and twenty-first-century Western women in both literature and popular culture. In particular, Lucinda is interested in studying texts in which the ageing woman of postfeminism is currently being represented. Her forthcoming scholarship on Indigenous film-maker Elle-Máijá Tailfeathers's work calls attention to white supremacy and on life writing by the late Paula Gunn Allen.

Stephanie Salerno received her PhD in American culture studies from Bowling Green State University. Her writing has appeared in *The Popular Culture Studies Journal*, *The Journal of Popular Culture*, and *Performance Matters*. As a scholar of media studies, popular music, and women's studies, her research interests include musical performance and liveness, queer studies, and trauma studies.

Henriette-Juliane Seeliger is a scholar of English literature, culture, and media. She holds degrees from the University of Chester, the University of Bamberg, and the City College of New York. She teaches and publishes primarily in the fields of gender studies, postcolonial studies, and media studies and is especially interested in topics relating to adaptations, masculinity, and feminism. Her current work addresses historicizing the construction of masculinity in recent English period drama series.

Tiara Sukhan has a PhD in media studies from the University of Western Ontario where she now serves as an adjunct lecturer in the Media, Information and Technology program. Her fields of interest include women's television, radio, and television as entertainment media and international media and social change.

Kate J. Waites is a full professor of English and gender studies in Nova Southeastern University's Department of Literature and Modern Languages in the College of Arts, Humanities, and Social Sciences, and in NSU's Honors College. Cofounder of NSU's Gender Studies program and the NSU chapter of the American Association of University Women, she teaches a wide range of literature, film studies, and gender studies classes. Her scholarly work focuses on film studies and the representation of women in visual media. Her work has appeared in a variety of scholarly journals and in edited texts. Most recently, "Hollywood's Warrior Woman for the New Millennium" appeared in *Bad Girls and Transgressive Women in Contemporary Television, Fiction, and Film*, and "Feminism Reboot in *Mad Max: Fury Road* and Hulu's *The Handmaid's Tale*" was published in *Utopias and Dystopias in the Age of Trump: Images in Literature and Visual Arts*.

www.ingramcontent.com/pod-product-compliance
Lightning Source LLC
Chambersburg PA
CBHW022311280326
41932CB00010B/1060